'*Please Miss* will awe you with its swung prose, its hairpin generic turns, and its bouts of gleeful self-scrutiny ... One chapter through and you're ready to draw with Lavery, stand with her, hold with her.'

Paul Saint-Amour, Walter H. & Leonore C. Annenberg Professor in the Humanities, University of Pennsylvania

'A transition-memoir-as-fever-dream ... *Please Miss* underscores the point that literature has evolved past the need for overcooked tell-all transition memoirs by presenting us with an hallucinatory journey that's both hilarious and bizarre.'

Morgan Page, artist and activist, 2014 Lambda Literary Fellow

PRAISE FOR *Please Miss*

'A dizzying mix of theory and pastiche, metafiction and memory ... Hilarious and sexy and terrifying in its brilliance. But don't worry – Lavery is an avalanche you'll be glad to be buried under.'

Carmen Maria Machado, author of *In the Dream House*

'A polychromatic, wild and joyous gambol through a world which is like ours but blessedly twisted ... Come for the laugh-out-loud miniature windsock on page one, stay for the fascinating analysis of a discarded pig part in *Jude the Obscure*, end up profoundly moved.'

Maggie Nelson, author of *The Argonauts*

'As enthralling as an intimate all-night conversation with the brainy high femme BFF you wish you had. I wish it upon everyone.'

Melissa Febos, author of *Girlhood*

'A daring, perverse, mind-blowing, intellectual, hilarious, outrageous, inspired work of art that somehow is touchingly sincere while giving no fucks whatsoever. I read this laughing out loud, clutching my pearls, my mind exploding in wonder.'

Michelle Tea, author of *Against Memoir*

'Like opening the Hamley's selection of jack-in-the boxes and being hit in the face with a series of boxing gloves, cream pies, and cultural conundrums AND LOVING IT. Absorbing everything from clowns to Dickens as porno parody, this is a memoir like no other.'

Lauren John Joseph, author of *At Certain Points We Touch*

'Funny and warm and incredibly clever, and horny in a way that makes sex sound like the most natural thing in the world . . . it is remarkable.'

Marie Le Conte, author of *Honourable Misfits*

'Hot, sick, painfully vivid.'

Sophie Lewis, author of *Full Surrogacy Now*

'An unclassifiable pastiche of genuine beauty, a meta-memoir that takes its humor as seriously as its philosophy. Lush, louche, and utterly virtuosic.'

Jordy Rosenberg, author of *Confessions of the Fox*

'Simultaneously mythic and demystifying . . . a beautiful, personal story about hope, joy, our bodies, and the meaty stories we build from them.'

Seiriol Davies, playwright and artist, author of *How to Win Against History*

'Grace Lavery has somehow managed to blend a rich overview of trans philosophy and theory with a languid, playful sexuality and humor . . . It's a work of great seriousness that doesn't take itself seriously at all.'

Nicole Cliffe, author, columnist, editor at *The Toast*

please miss

please miss

A HEARTBREAKING WORK
OF STAGGERING PENIS

grace lavery

In 'On Truth and Lies in an Extra-Moral Sense', Nietzsche defines truth as 'a sum of human relations which have been poetically and rhetorically intensified, transferred, and embellished.' Accordingly readers should not expect any act of writing to depict the nonfictional world with anything like unmediated accuracy, and certainly not one authored by someone pretentious enough to remind them of the fact *on the copyright page*. What I mean is: certain names and identifying details have been changed.

This edition first published in the United Kingdom in 2022 by
Daunt Books Originals
83 Marylebone High Street
London W1U 4QW

1

Copyright © 2022 Grace Lavery

First published in 2022 by Seal Press, an imprint of Perseus Books, LLC, a subsidiary of Hachette Book Group, Inc. The publisher is not responsible for websites (or their content) that are not owned by the publisher.

A CIP catalogue record for this title
is available from the British Library.

ISBN 978-1-914198-04-5

Print book interior design by Trish Wilkinson
Prelim pages typeset by Marsha Swan
Printed and bound by TJ Books Limited

www.dauntbookspublishing.co.uk

For Jane Lavery, the unusual woman
who I believe gave birth to me

The rankness of bad faith supposes the availability of more direct, honest ways to express need, whereas everyone knows that the only socially credible subject is the stoic who, whatever his gender, obeys the gag rule incumbent on being a man.

—D. A. Miller, *Place for Us*

I have a vacant stare cuz I'm a robot,
I've got hollow lungs [*I bet your toes are strong!*]
With soft-skin engineered to feel girl-like,
I'll stay forever young, yeah.

—Vanessa Hudgens, "Don't Stare into the Sun,"
from *High School Musical: A Bad Lip Reading*

contents

CHAPTER ONE

JUGGALO CHICKEN DRINK

My friends, I have solved my penis problem!

Or rather, my friend D solved it for me. We were walking together around the marina next to my apartment in Berkeley, and we were talking about our genitals. Most of the time, my penis does very little but flop around enthusiastically, like a miniature windsock man at a showroom for toy cars. Once in a while, it takes a stab at stiffening, gets halfway through, and then gives up. On such occasions it feels like a coil of fetal spine. There is something disgraceful about the experience, not merely because that very image—as though I were laying my own miscarried fetus across my hand—is utterly obscene. But more, because this atrophied and broken fragment still contains something that I want, something that I want more of.

"A desire (e.g., for a dick) drowned in a bigger desire for its absence?" I asked.

"Yes, I suppose," D responded.

We tumbled into a parking lot, near to an abandoned Japanese steakhouse. D has no dick;—or rather, they have an array of them, various sizes and shapes. A wind blows across the parking lot. It is difficult to historicize. Perhaps this Japanese restaurant opened in the early 2000s, when West Berkeley was being redeveloped, and perhaps they imagined they could tempt the gentrifiers half a mile further outland for teppanyaki and a view of Sausalito? And perhaps people did not want to make the journey, but rather wanted to stay on Fourth Street, which was pretty in an entirely Northern Californian way—a few trees, and a lot of very expensive-looking boutiques selling artisanal wool products, travel books, and insipid-tasting tamales.

Or perhaps they were chased out by these turkeys. A squad of turkeys, in a tree in the parking lot. Four girl turkeys clustered around one entirely malevolent boy turkey, a pantomime turkey version of Gary Oldman's *Dracula*. A turkey resplendent in black plumage, fringed in electric blue.

As D and I passed the turkeys, I was describing my guilt at another one of these baby-spine hard-ons that had occurred that morning when, after having woken up early, I was entertaining myself by reading *Riverdale* recaps on my phone. One of the recaps recorded that Mädchen Amick's character had said something sarcastic like "shove it up your ass," or "my ass," or something with "ass" in it, and all of a sudden I'm shuffling into the bathroom, holding the unchristian waste of my masculinity in my hand. It's all very dramatic.

But where did the guilt come from? My shriveled little fellow looked, from one angle, like a phallus, or at least an instance of phallic sexual desire, which a lot of *us girls* (assuredly including me) are keen to do away with for any number of reasons. If it was accompanied by pleasure, as it was for me, it might then also intensify the fear that, after all, what they say about us is true, that we are self-deluded boys attempting to get close to women for nefarious sexual purposes. It is difficult for trans women who love women to treat our own phallic sexuality as anything other than a disgraceful giveaway.

I'm saying something obvious, I'm embarrassing myself. Let me tell you about D. They are very short and very hot. Like a short, hot dyke. Got it? They look implausibly like Selena Gomez. They have Crohn's. Like me, D is an alcoholic and drug addict, and we both like the same kinds of drugs: the ones that make one feel *very aware one is having an intense experience.* Neither of us has used drugs or alcohol in a few years, and we have different strategies for handling the fact. Mine have included prayer, and a high daily dose of synthetic estradiol; theirs have included bass fishing, and submerging every morsel of food in front of them in a lagoon of English mustard.

They have queries about their dicks, too. D likes to fuck—indeed, D has developed a sort of theology of fucking, a sense that fucking will either save the world or, at least, create a new world so beautiful that we won't mind letting the old one die. They can be both selective and cruel: they reserve lifeboats for those they happen to find hot, and screw the rest. I suppose one redeeming feature is that they find many people hot, and that there's plenty of overlap with some of my own types—yoga bitches, closeted milfs, masc bottoms.

D's pattern of speech is quick, remorseless, absolute. We met at a "community event" a few years ago, and I went up to them afterwards and made a joke about my sex change, which they (kindly) understood as deliberately gauche. Another, more visibly cheerful lesbian joined me and made a couple of more tentative jokes in D's direction, but D was focused on me—very early transition, short spiky hair, messed-up lipgloss, and a slutty denim skirt. I may as well have been wearing a button that said, "you don't have to be crazy to work here, but it helps!"

"I feel guilty because the moment of losing my dick—and I realize chemical castration is a process with more gradations than we usually allow—but anyway there was a moment, a cusp—that cusp moment was important."

"Spiritual?"

"Yes, and it confirmed something about my sex change. Subtly, through internal means. Like, a surgeon could only be shaping the outside."

The fundamental problem with the whole notion of using surgical means to effect a sex change is this: *the grass is always greener.* The desire to turn into a woman proves that you aren't one; desire and identity are antithetical principles. This, bluntly, is Hannibal Lecter logic. But it's also kind of true.

D, a non-binary woman, has installed the desire for a dick within their pussy hole. It is a remarkable solution to the problem. They explain:

"I love my dicks. I love to look down and know that it is my dick, and that it is fucking you, and that nobody ever had a bigger one or fucked you better with it."

I nod.

"But recently I have been using my strapless dick more. It starts inside me, at the root chakra, and pulls itself out of my cunt, out into the world. I feel it pushing inside me and growing out of me. When I fuck you"—and here I should add, D has never fucked me, alas—"you are inside me and outside."

My eyes dilated. Were the turkeys following me? D continued:

"The dick is mine, and it is in me. I enjoy the sense that the dick is nestled, in the pussy."

My mind flashes to Adorno, who writes about nestling.[1] He doesn't use the word "dick." It is the first time something clicks with me; the melancholic attachment to the dick that flares up in the form of guilt, moves through the phantom pussy, and nestles within.

This was the third of three big conversations about my penis problem, and the most recent. From my current perspective, I suppose my penis is hardly a problem for me at all. Years later, I have found myself able to call my penis a "clit," like we are supposed to, and it doesn't always feel embarrassing to do so. I'll probably get bottom surgery one day, years later, but it's not urgent—I already have an interiority, and I know where it is and what to do with it.

On the way home from the marina, I stop into Hole Foods to pick up a Juggalo Chicken Drink. The year was 2017, and meat-based Juggalo beverages—the beverage wing of the Insane Clown Posse—were everywhere. I'm afraid I got snagged on the marketing jingle that was ubiquitous that year, delivered in that rugged ICP style:

I do the Juggalo chicken juice rap all day, SON
Grab a cup of chicken and I'm on my way, MOM
Juice a tasty chicken I call that "fowl play," YO
Bottle up the chicken like a poultry FAYGO.

I didn't even know what "faygo" meant, but it sounded effeminate—in any case, I don't know much about Juggalo culture. I think I watched Juggalo porn once, but now I recall it, it seems so unlikely: a tiny woman spinning around on her head in front of a very fat man. Not improbable to contemplate in itself, and it feels quite hot, the sense of similarity and difference, like watching Kristin Chenoweth standing next to Allison Janney.

I like soup, in general, and I'm not above a soup-based beverage of almost any kind—I've certainly pounded the odd gazpacho like I was beating down a whiskey sour. "Juggalo" was such a good word, like "jugged hare," a hare braised in its own blood. And then there was the suggestive triptych: chicken, bone, broth.

Chicken.

Bone.

Broth.

Chicken: chick, hen, egg, hatch, girl, not a rooster, not a cock.

Bone: fuck, dick, fuck, dick.

Broth: brother, juice, medium, liquor, substrate, reagent.

A bone in a liquor; an egg fuck in a medium, a chick's dick bone reagent, not-cock-dick-substrate. I don't even know whether they still sell the Juggalo chicken drinks or not, or whether they ever did outside of California. I've moved across the country, and my tastes have changed. But then I'm old-school.

A truly insane clown posse wouldn't advertise the fact.

I got back to my apartment and kissed Danny, the famous writer who was my boyfriend at the time, and who is now my husband.

"Danny, I have solved my penis problem! Or, rather, my friend D solved it for me," except I said D's real name. Reader, you might have thought that my calling my Crohn's-afflicted mega-top friend "D" was a reference to dick, which would have been very knowing, but the letter really is the initial of their last name. (D, incidentally, believes that they are instantly recognizable from the description contained herein—I suppose there aren't too many hot, cokehead, Crohn's-afflicted, mega-top pop-leprechauns in the East Bay. Though if you imagine "Crohn's" could just refer to any autoimmune condition, I can think of twenty off the top of my head.)

"Oh, darling, I'm *so* glad," he responded, boyfriendly. "How so?"

"Well," I began. "I have been worried that the capacity for these little mini-erections I get every now and then are an existential threat to my transition. I've been worried about this because I can't deny that I enjoy them, and nor can I deny that I enjoy them in a way that feels like an echo of the way I used to enjoy having a functioning dick. So, my dick doesn't work at present but there is a fragment of trapped, uh, libido, that is stuck inside there and needs some kind of emancipation."

"I don't understand," said simple Danny. God, he was blessed.

"Well, I want to deny or repress the pleasure because I don't want to seem like a bad or fake transsexual. Nothing would be worse! Remember *The Silence of the Lambs*?"

That, he did.

"So, I don't want to be like that. But I can't deny that I *do* experience pleasure in my dick, and the way in which I experience that pleasure is both psychically and anatomically distinct! Do you see my problem?"

That, too, he did.

"I don't think it's a good idea for me to pretend not to feel pleasure? But it can be difficult to avow the kinds of pleasure that one *does* feel. When one is a 'transsexual'—," I added, making clear from my tone that "transsexual" was a word I placed in scare quotes.

At this point, I realized that my friend Sarah was also in the room, standing behind me, and she responded to my anxiety in this way:

"Grace, I'm so glad that you're already able to acknowledge this. Some trans women, it takes years. It can be so difficult. You're killing it, baby. I love you."

"I love you too, Sarah," I replied. It was true.

"Okay, you two, I've got to head out," said Sarah, and just walked out of the apartment, having delivered what I had to admit was a sprezzatura cameo.

I continued:

"So, anyway, I was speaking with D about this and of course as you know they have a complex relation to genitals in general, and they talked about the particular paradigm of wearing a strapless dildo, rooted inside them, and then using that as a phallus. Like, it is not exactly the 'lesbian phallus' in the Judith Butler sense (which is already a term placed under a certain kind of erasure) because it is a phallus whose location is important.[2] The phallus is *already inside something.*"

"Like a yolk," Danny said, looking at the half-finished Juggalo Chicken Drink I had just placed on the counter, which had a big picture of an egg on the packaging.

"Exactly! Now you're really getting it!"

Danny paused. Then:

"I like the idea of a dick in a medium. I'm not sure there's too much more to this idea than that?"

"I think it's an incredibly rich and suggestive image! A yolk in a drink of chicken: *binding the child in its own amniotic medium.* A synthetic object that accomplishes the phallic task that a mere penis is bound to fail to perform, but one that is rooted inside the body, in a manner that privileges the pussy as an active force in fucking!"

"Are you sure it's active? It sounds a little like it's just a slightly different way of thinking about vaginal passivity."

"Ugh, why do you get to be Socrates, asshole?" I huffed, impatiently.

But that was hot, so I brushed up towards him and pushed my soft bosom into his face. I ran my hand through his hair and tousled it.

"Danny, Danny, Danny, always so cynical," I mused.

I pulled him up by the hair and led him into the bedroom. I pushed him onto the bed and tore off his pastel purple t-shirt with my hands, exposing his large surgical scars. I allowed myself to look at them, to drink in the elegance of this new chest. "Plucky" is one word that I have for it.

Danny was a little annoyed at how roughly he had been handled, or was at least pretending to be annoyed. I love it when I can't tell. I let my fingers move along the ridge of his scars, across his body. He scrunched up his lips into a little moue, and I smiled back at him.

There are two ways to get Danny to open his mouth when he doesn't want to. The first is to put my fingers over his nostrils so that he has to open his mouth to breathe. The other is to ask him a direct question that he won't be able to resist answering. These tricks are useful because Danny sometimes likes to tighten up his mouth in a sexy little sulk, as though the game were to stuff one's whole fist into his oral cavity without applying any pressure.

This time I went for the nose technique. When he gasped for air, I slipped the index and middle fingers of my right hand between his lips, and onto his tongue. He smiled, defeated. I curled up my ring and pinky fingers outside of his mouth, and then tucked them in too. Finally I placed my thumb in the middle of my hand, and placed my whole fist inside his mouth. My fist was now a knot that connected us through his face, radiating up through my arm and down through his neck as though parts of the same unbroken cable. Danny's back began to arch—it is somehow a nautical maneuver, the kind that sailors might have deployed, and it began to feel as though we were on a boat.

I straddled him, smiling. His mouth gaped open on all sides, and the corners began to bend into a smile. "I love you," I said, and he burbled comically from under my fist: *mmmmmmuff-mmmmoooo*. I stroked his beautiful cheek with my left hand, delighting in the burrs of his beard, a few days out from the last shave.

Eventually I pulled my hand out of his face, and moved it down his body towards his genitals, which were profoundly aroused. I fucked him with my hand until he came; I didn't break eye contact the entire time; it was very satisfying.

As I held him in my arms afterwards, we cooed and brr-ed, until he said:

"Baby I think my real concern here isn't the point about vaginal passivity. Like, that's not a problem you're going to solve at this stage anyway, and I can already see how D's version of this is more complicated than the usual ways in which I tend to think about things. I guess my bigger worry is just that you're once again turning to memoir to try to access the truth of trans life."

"As opposed to?"

"Like, as opposed to history, or anthropology, or I don't know, what about *lyric poetry*, or maybe some kind of historical fiction? And people love sci-fi."

"Well, first, I guess I do think there's some anthropological dimension to memoir that I've been thinking about recently, and that lyric isn't a fundamentally distinct class of enunciation. And then also I just like—I mean, I'm like a George Eliot person, or whatever, the most difficult thing is just to say what something feels like; like I guess that's phenomenology—"

I had made my case less persuasively than anticipated. Danny was kind in his response:

"I just mean, *expositions of trans life as it is lived* is sort of the only genre that trans people have historically been allowed to work in."

"Well, I've not been allowed to work in it."

(That was a better argument, I thought.)

"But if you insist," I continued, "what about this: somewhere in the middle of space is the planet Gronglattflaps, and on the planet of Grongrattflaps everyone has a dick in the middle of their pussy, and that's what genitals are."

"Yes," Danny replied, sarcastically, "because that's exactly what science fiction sounds like."

"My point is that it's just an idea delivery system, I'm not really interested in genre. Except porn, I guess that's the other genre I'm interested in."

"The other genre trans people have been allowed to work in."

"There's a Sybil Lamb line about that, actually," I said, "but we don't need to go into that right now."

We lay in bed together, avoiding our agents, worrying that we had nothing left to say to each other or anyone else.

"I guess the problem is that nothing really interests me except my own thoughts," one of us said, eventually.

The following day was Monday, and I received an anonymous note in the mail. It was postmarked New York, NY, and the handwritten address read:

```
Prof. Grace Lavery
The "New Professor"
English Department
UC Berkeley
California, United States of America
```

On the back of the envelope was a doodle, the kind of doodle one leaves on the back of an envelope that happens to be in front of one when one is caught on the phone with a distressed relative. Poking out above the fold was a crude rendition of a sinister clown, black eyed and gothy—dankly reminiscent of something one might find on the packet of a poultry potation.

This wasn't the first time I'd received an odd letter at work. My first year on the faculty I had received an enveloped postmarked San Diego which contained (a) a very short essay offering a history of the Japanese navy's conduct during the First World War, (b) glossy, magazine-style photographs of American military personnel stationed in Southeast Asia, with my faculty profile picture cut out and stuck onto the background, and (c) the typescript of what seemed to have been an old racist ballad about Japan.

I had taken it to the campus cops—I wouldn't do that now—and they said, "Professor Lavery, I have some good news and some bad news. The good news is that everyone gets one of these. The bad news is that this jabroni does seem to have a few less spices than the average cut of salami—the cut-out photographs are a new development."

So anyway, I opened the envelope and inside was a note written in Courier, unmarked and unsigned, that read as follows:

```
So, I don't want to sound like a nutball here,
but it's time for a real true confession: I'm
```

frightened of a clown. I'm wary of his eccentric manner and his unusual appearance. His choices make me feel ill at ease, and the language he uses—well, I find it unnerving. No, this is not satire, friend—I really am just plain bloody chilled by a clown, and if it's all the same to you, I'd rather not see him when he comes to my town, or invite him to my house for any purpose.

I know this sounds crackers. "What, a little insane clown man, America's sweetheart?" you're probably saying. And it's true. Suddenly it seems like the clowns are everywhere, doesn't it? Like the sakura blooms at festival. Like tarragon in my Uncle Buster's imaginative twist on the mint julep. Flowers swell fat with clowns and out they burst, young and masculine and juicy. One runs a digit over the pod and inside it, and finds the merry shards that provide so many American children with genteel delight.

Yet I am afeared of his taste in music, which I find perverse; and perhaps I find it worse yet than that. I demur from his sexual habits, which he insists on broadcasting. I find his prose style off-putting, and though I am not among those who will hold him solely responsible on that point, nor will I submit myself to further questioning on the matter. I will confess that the little clown fellow of whom I speak I find to be quite thoroughly overrated on that front and many more besides. I wonder at the judgment of those who have supported his career so far. To me, it is as though he has some kind of malevolent hold over his benefactors—though of course I don't wish my own distaste to slip into outlandish and paranoid stereotype. This particular clown just isn't for me, that's all.

I see his face before me as I write, and to be perfectly candid, I find it quite unpleasant to contemplate. I understand that others may find his red nose to indicate merriment, but to me it seems crass. Many would find this clown's smile, which stretches warmly between his ears, to be welcoming and playful, but frankly, I think it verges on the sinister. His playful tufts of hair, which sprout at irregular intervals across his face and neck? Not to my taste at all, I'm afraid.

For example: does he commit crimes, this clown man? Personally, I wouldn't aver it—although, now I ponder the matter more carefully, I wonder whether perhaps he shoplifts from time to time, or texts while he's driving. In most people I would consider these small infractions to be charming, evidence of an appealing rebellious streak. But in the little clown man, I find them pettifogging and dishonest. Why should he flout rules that the rest of us are obliged to follow, which we mostly do, to the best of our ability? I wonder, even, whether it isn't further evidence of that willful cast of mind that underlies many of the qualities I find least tolerable in him—his insistent *being*, his presence, his refusal to disappear or die off, as I would that he would.

It has taken me a while to realize that I'm not made angry by him, as I initially thought. I believed that I wished to exterminate him by my own hand, to show him what it feels like, and to say, "ha, now YOU know what it feels like," so that he would know what it feels like when someone says that to you. Not nice, in short! But no, it's not anger, not at root. At its base, I am afraid of what makes a little clown man tick, of his quiddity, his characteristic essence. I shudder when I contemplate his innards. I worry, frankly, that he may have guts much like mine—indistinguishable from mine, even, perhaps, under that lovely round belly of his. What if his guts are identical to mine? The thought quite unravels me—I find myself disappearing into an echo, a hollow whisper in my own cheeks.

I am chary of a little clown man. Should I see him, I will surely repeat several merciless social maneuvers. First, in all likelihood, I shall receive him coolly in the presence of others. Others will be left in no doubt concerning the nature of our relationship. Second, I shall make dismissive eyes upon him, and tilt my hips just so, to ensure that he knows that, to my mind, he doesn't belong here. Third, I shall talk dismissively of his field of expertise without acknowledging that such is it. Fourth, when I leave his company, I shall conspicuously neglect to wish him farewell, but simply wander off carelessly, tossing my head perhaps as if to say, "look at me, I have just thwarted a clown."

Look at me, America, for I have just thwarted a clown. All shall know it. The clown was a cipher. The clown never hurt anyone. I knew what I was doing and I did it anyway. The clown was a patsy. The clown was a metaphor for the setting aside of childish things. The clown was a metaphor for sexual matters. The clown was a figure for literality. The clown was me all along. The clown was unrepresentable joy. The clown was fellowship and youth. The clown was sawdust and sweat and smiles. The clown was liquidity and paint. I loved the clown. I covet the clown. Please, clown, come back and learn how to love me; teach me how to love myself; remind me of that which I have forgotten; come back, clown, we are ready for you. I love you, and always did.

It's difficult, obviously, when one finds that one's antagonists are clearly suffering with some quite devastating mental disability. Of course, part of me wanted to mock the author of this letter—to parade it round the department, flashing it to colleagues as proof of both the *kind of pressure I'm under, as a public figure*, and also of the sheer lunacy of the anti-trans bigots who pester me. ("Clown," for whatever reason, is a common term of abuse among them.) But of course, I couldn't be sure that, having done so, my colleagues might not think either that I was inappropriately mocking someone afflicted, apparently, with a delusional psychosis, or, which was worse, that the scrambled prose of my correspondent might, in some way, reflect badly on me—as though it was my responsibility, which I sometimes fear that it is, to obtain for myself a high class of hater.

So I kept it to myself, spending the rest of the day wondering about clowns—the clowns I have known and loved—for, strangely, I have known and loved many—and those clowns whom I have ever disliked, fewer in number but more vividly kept in mind, if anything. Why, Americans, why do you think that there is something transgressive about finding clowns frightening in the first place? You're supposed to find them frightening—you're Americans. Finding clowns creepy is as intrinsic to Americanness as is finding Kermit the Frog charming, and genuflecting before your suburban Svengali, Mister Rogers. It's because you all hate pleasure and are uncomfortable with ambiguity. You think clowns don't know what you think about them? That's why they're laughing—they get it and you don't.

When I got home I thought I would torment Danny with some questions about scary clowns. Danny doesn't really think in these terms—which, I realize, are just straight-up Batman terms. "In every couple, there's a Star Wars one and a Batman one," as the saying goes, and our division is as classical as one might expect. You can't really get me too riled up about whether the Jedis are a kind of aristocracy, and you can't do anything to Danny with Batman except irritate him with the kind of casuistical nonsense that the Nolan movies especially have been incapable of avoiding.

"If you got a call from the Joker on your Batphone, and the Joker said he had put explosives on two boats, one of which was full of crimes and the other was full of normies, and you had to decide which one to blow up or else he would detonate both the boats (*toute les deux bateaux*), how would you go about choosing, for is there not more rejoicing in the kingdom of heaven for the sinner who repenteth?"

"Grace, darling, I actually just don't care, and you know that, and I don't know why we're doing this again?"

"Okay, but aren't the Joker and Batman really two sides of the same coin, when you think about it? And talking of coins, isn't Two-Face the same coin as the Joker/Batman but seen in a mirror, such that one might think one were seeing four coin sides and yet from another perspective one is seeing only one? For did Dante Gabriel Rossetti not write in his famous 'Sonnet on the Sonnet' with which he opens the *House of Life* sequence, in the octet, 'a sonnet is a moment's monument,' and then in the same sonnet's sestet claim 'a sonnet is a coin, its face reveals / the Soul, the converse, to what Power 'tis due'?[3] Like, for Rossetti, the sonnet is the conjoining of two bifurcated things, and none of them allow one to see any of the others without violating the metaphor. So, like, you can't see the sonnet's soul and the soul's allegiance at the same time? Is that why Joker/Two-Face crossovers are rare and weak, because they are two sides of different coins?"

"Yes, but I, like, *literally* don't care."

"Okay, but what is it with falling into vats of things? Obelix, too—different franchise tho. But like, the Joker, Clayface . . . I am thirty-four years old and I have never fallen into a vat of anything. I've never even seen a vat big enough for a person to fall into, I don't think? I don't know how many vats I've seen total. Maybe they had more vats in the old days, or the vats were bigger, like how we used to have bigger computers and shit. What's the biggest vat you've ever seen?"

"Are you fucking practicing your tight five on me? I mean this might work at the Comedy Store, but we can't all be Louis C.K., can we?"

Which shut me up.

A penis is not a dick; a penis is *definitively* not a dick. A dick is the thing that a penis is not; insofar as a given object is (a) a penis, it is thereto also (b) not a dick.

The day I came out at work, I spent some time trying to work out whether the "characteristic part of a barrow-pig" that hits the title character in the face in an early chapter of *Jude the Obscure* was a penis or a dick.

> In his deep concentration on these transactions of the future Jude's walk had slackened, and he was now standing quite still, looking at the ground as though the future were thrown thereon by a magic lantern. On a sudden something smacked him sharply in the ear, and he became aware that a soft cold substance had been flung at him, and had fallen at his feet.
>
> A glance told him what it was—a piece of flesh, the characteristic part of a barrow-pig, which the countrymen used for greasing their boots, as it was useless for any other purpose. Pigs were rather plentiful hereabout, being bred and fattened in large numbers in certain parts of North Wessex.[4]

"Characteristic part" is an odd phrase, since it implies a part that is more than a part, that is either indistinguishable from other parts (and therefore not exactly a part at all) or whose particular qualities determine the identity of the whole under some taxonomic scheme—and I suppose we are meant to think of the latter, that the "characteristic part of a barrow pig" is that part which qualifies the organism in question as a barrow pig, rather than anything else. And under the taxonomic scheme in question—agricultural argot—a "barrow pig," as distinct from a "gilt pig" (but also from a "stud"), is a male pig that has been castrated. So this particular "characteristic part" is especially strange, since it is only characteristic of a barrow-pig once it is no longer part of the barrow pig at all—once it has been removed.

This perhaps all sounds pedantic, but this is after all the territory one gets into once one starts euphemizing—as Hardy well knows. The language of meat is full of these kinds of subtleties, which flash between mere flesh and matter full of meaning—one wants to say "pregnant with meaning," which gives one a sense of the difficulty.

A dick is not a penis, but also a pig is not a hog; flesh is not meat. A "soft cold substance" could be a penis, but could hardly be a dick—dicks are paradigmatically hard and hot. Hardness is not the difference between a penis and a dick, or at least not in a binary way: penises can be hard, but not hard in the way a *dick* should be hard. Nobody else's penis is as hard as the dick of my dreams, and my penis was never as hard as I'd hoped. Nor is a dick, exactly, "substance," although it is substantial (in the somewhat paradoxical sense that a phantom is substantial). The signs initially point to this pig piece as a penis.

But I eventually plumped for the other option: *hog cock*. This flesh piece has two features in common with a dick that it does not share with a penis: it is *porcine*, and it is a *piggy projectile*. A dick is always piglike. The French word for snout (the most piglike bit of a pig) is *le groin*, as I learned to my disappointment in a French bistro when, having ordered a dish of pig offal entitled *La tentation de Saint-Antoine*, it transpired that Saint Anthony had apparently not been tempted by a swine's bellend, but rather by the cartilaginous slab with which he grubs for truffles. The pig grubs in the dirt, he roots in the filth with his *groin*. A dream that the softcold substances with which we are all too familiar (Hardy doesn't use a comma, so thus is the single adjective describing all that is disappointing) can hardly hope to match.

And nothing that hits one on the side of one's face was ever a penis; I *throw my dick at you*; he *throws his dick at me*; they *throw their dicks at each other*. The gif of all those frankfurters cascading into that woman's face: dicks, not penises. Porky, and thrown.

I wasn't sure that the students were especially interested in this distinction, but the difference between a material body and the body as it is fantasized into existence, formalized, and mythologized was all that was on my mind. If my claims above about the incompatibility of penis and dick are true, I think it follows (though it is verifiable on other grounds too) that the disappointingness of the penis is *itself* the definitive hinge at which the body's inability to represent itself becomes visible.

When Butler describes the foreclosure of the penis as an operative condition of the Lacanian phallus, they mean that the very negation of the penis in the name of the phallus positions the penis (material, disappointing) as the key to the disenchantment of the body. Not only is the penis not like a dick, but that not-likeness types a myriad of other ways in which the body is not like our psychic representation of it. One could think of other candidates—brain and heart, for example—but it's true that the metaphoricity of "dick"/"phallus" incorporates, as those metaphors do not, the supplementary metaphor of *materiality*.

Sex is the figure for literality, Joan Copjec says, relatedly. Though literality and materiality all too rarely coincide.

There is another possibility: the bosom. Is "the bosom" a part of the body (like a penis), or a representation of a part of the body (like a dick)? A person's response to this question correlates, I have found, with their feelings about the word "lap": some think a lap is the part of the body between the groin and the lower thighs, perhaps including the space between the legs. Others think it is a function of sitting. Likewise, some think "the bosom" is the breasts, and perhaps cleavage (space between). Others think it a function of squeezing.

Jude the Obscure wonders about this, too: at one point, Jude's first love interest (Arabella, who lobbed the hog schlong) places a cochin egg in her bosom, which she calls "an old custom," adding, "I suppose it is natural for a woman to want to bring live things into the world."[5] It's an odd moment, that neither Jude nor this reader can fully decipher. Clearly, the egg inside the breast imitates an egg in a womb. But is this a fertility ritual, designed to provoke conception by mimicking it? To that extent, and beyond, it is surely also a travesty of fertility, in which human conception is likened to the unmysterious act of implanting an egg into folds of flesh. Conception without interiority.

A bosom, a cleft: representations, folds, pleats.

Danny's seemingly willful reductiveness around the question of D's dick had annoyed me. As had his skepticism about memoir. I was drawn to memoir because I thought nobody would be able to correct me—but on this point I was exactly wrong. The first time I showed any of the autobiographical writing I've published to my mother, she just went through it all saying, "nope . . . nope . . . didn't happen . . . you're making it up . . . nope . . . where does this even come from . . ." etc., etc.

"Dispiriting" isn't the word. "We fondly hope," as the titular character's mother puts it in *Christie Malry's Own Double-Entry*, "that there is going to be a reckoning," ideally of the kind where some common authority, agreed upon by all sides, will let us know who was right and who was wrong.[6] But that kind of eschatology seems probably a little outside the scope of a transition memoir, even a transition memoir that, like all the rest, is *different from all the rest*. But a reckoning where the facts could be agreed upon—most specifically, a reckoning whereby my mother could be compelled, by the courts if necessary, to agree to the facts of my youth: this did not seem outrageous, when I started. And yet now the idea is entirely laughable.

It is a little like this: I am eleven or so years old and I am concerned about my mother's smoking. It triggers a fear of abandonment. I whine at her to quit smoking, and, after several weeks of pestering, she agrees. One night, I wake up a couple of hours after I fell asleep—bolt upright, terrified. I come downstairs to find my mother in the living room, on her own, with a lit cigarette in an ashtray balanced on her knee. When she sees me in the doorway, she places the ashtray and the lit cigarette underneath the coffee table, out of sight.

I say, "Mum, you're smoking."

She says, "no, I'm not."

I say, "I saw the cigarette in the ashtray that you just put under the table."

She says, "no, that was the television remote."

I say, "why did you put it out of sight then?"

She says, "I didn't need it any more. Because you were coming into the room, and I love you."

It didn't matter, of course—the room was full of smoke. There was no denying it as a fact, and yet in the domain of language the idea had been routed. I did not believe her, and of course she knew that, but she also knew that she'd blocked all the exits. Blocked them off with love.

Did this really happen? If you asked my mother, she would probably say no, of course not, that I am making it up, perhaps adding that I am a liar, that I am just trying to hurt her because in order to stay in this world that I have built, I have to repeatedly repudiate her, and the environment I came from. Most days she would say that, but on some days she might say, "what does it matter anyway? It was a joke, it was funny." And the thing is that she isn't really a monster—the story is monstrous, but it's one of very few I have about her which are—she's just someone with whom it is impossible to agree upon the facts. It is easy enough to agree upon the values. Her values are quite admirable, as it goes.

This all makes narrating a prehistory of something like a sex change especially difficult, because of a felt injunction that tells me I *must* find Grace in my past, that if I don't then I am living deceptively or pathologically. I am supposed to say, "I always knew," when the truth is that I didn't always know. I sometimes suspected; occasionally, I wished. I played intermittently, and sometimes I *did* know—sometimes I knew nothing else. But "I always knew" is an especially unreasonable standard by which to rank the legitimacy of various transitions, because it implies two things—(1) that it was always true; (2) that we have consistent access to truths about ourselves. Even if (1) is true—and I have my doubts, both in my own case and as a matter of political strategy—(2) is obviously nonsense. Even the knowledge of one's own desires—let's say, of one's sexual object choices—is subject to refinement, even if the rough contours remain consistent. I always knew I liked girls, for example, but what did that knowledge actually consist of until I had met some actual girls, and learned in real detail, by trial and error, exactly what it was that I liked?

My feelings about boys, while no less erotically charged, were more selectively distributed, and more nuanced. I liked them when they were posh and gay and clever, and had more complex, more vigorous, feelings about them when, as was more usually the case even at my posh boys' school, they were crude and beefy. I didn't grow up with a dad and was always profoundly grateful for the fact; still, I cannot unironically appreciate a dad. Some of that changed when I started dating—which I did chaotically and omnivorously from the get-go—my tastes shifted from elegant scarves to oaky legs and leonine manes, but it was still a minority of my interest. My first kiss with a boy, aged fifteen or so, was mesmerizing partly because of the meatiness of the boy in question. Somehow, a kid my age had more stubble than I ever reached with twenty years of testosterone "post-puberty," and I remember his bristles scraping my face, his teeth biting into me. It was passionate and messy and hot, and I wanted more than he was willing to give me, but even so I knew that the hardness I wanted from boys was less important than the softness I wanted from girls.

Somewhat to my surprise, and everyone else's disdain. It was wrong for someone so conspicuously feminine to also want to date girls. One day, I came back from the bathroom to find that some waggish schoolboy rogue had written, "I act gay to get chicks" on my pencil case. It was a fair cop, to be honest, which is one reason I'm a little wary of that criticism when it is made of others. Everyone knew—my mother, everyone at school, *everyone*—that I should have been dating boys. There was a soft, condescending attitude towards gay men that underpinned that expectation— gay men are sweet and flowery, and Jos is sweet and flowery— that felt like the exact opposite of the kind of relation I wanted with boys, and also (I was ashamed to admit) *just not really my deal*. So although I can't say, "I always knew x," I can say, "I never knew not-x," and perhaps even, "I always knew not-y."

—have you ever had the experience of realizing, mid-anecdote, that you are telling a story wrong, that you are overstating or misrepresenting something, or that there is an important detail that you are choosing to overlook? Here is the story I told people throughout my twenties: "oh yes, I had a very genderqueer youth, I wore dresses through college, and it was all very playful and experimental. I'm happy I had those experiences, but eventually I got my first job after college and the real world intervened. Then it was back to reality!" For many years, I often used to say, "oh I would probably be trans if I were younger but we didn't really have that in Birmingham in the 90s, or Oxford (!) or Brighton (!!!) in the 00s, or Philadelphia during the Obama presidency . . ." On the one hand, it was a feeling that actually transitioning was impossible—the best one could do was approximate with some kind of pastiche or subversion, and that didn't interest me, or struck me as conservative or something. Instead I got very into being professionally subversive, and outflanking anyone I could with ever-more edgy and oblique self-descriptions, all of which were hokey and easily seen through.

One day, a couple of weeks after I took my last drink, I was telling this story (you can guess to whom) and I realized I had left out a crucial detail: what was the first job? I left college in 2004, and there was only one job I wanted—I wanted to work in a pub, which had felt like the best part of my third year at Oxford, working as a barman at the King's Arms, and spending my wages each evening on the beer I would carry home afterwards. Other than that, I was sick of Oxford, its pretensions and its filigree, and I wanted to return to what I could postulate were my roots (they weren't) by taking low-paying shift work and committing to it with a zeal that I had previously given to *perhaps* Byron and *perhaps* Joyce, but that mostly I had withheld from my studies on the basis of a spurious class resentment. Not that such resentment is in general spurious, but mine was—I arrived at Oxford with a posh accent, having come from a posh school. True, I had been one of the most conspicuously oikish kids there, but I'd been there since I was eleven, and as much as I hated the poshness with which it had marked me, I also knew on some level that it had sunk to the core; had eaten and digested whatever version of me pre-existed King Edward's.

So, a sort of bogus prolishness propelled me away from London, and pubs sounded ideal to a young alcohol enthusiast, because one has an almost unfettered access to alcohol and, if one works carefully, can be drunk throughout the day. After heading to Brighton, I showed up for my first shift at the William the Fourth pub in a tidy brown dress, perhaps with some cute little hair thing in. My mother, knowing something was up with all these dresses, but having no idea how to ask me about them, said of this one, "I like you in dresses; they really accentuate the masculinity of your frame." It really was sweet, though the opposite of what I wanted to hear on both counts. The bar manager, meanwhile, an unpleasant older heterosexual, was apoplectic: "what the FUCK do you think you are wearing; get the FUCK out of here and don't come back until you are dressed like a normal person." So: I left, I put on a t-shirt and jeans, I came back, and that was that. The "real world."

When I got sober, I lost the certainty that the real world—the world of jobs, of bad men with money, the serious world—had stopped me from doing what I wanted to do. I realized that I had chosen not to continue to dress that way, or to try to work out why I wanted to dress that way. For one thing, my employment prospects had been pretty good, and if I had been at a job that had felt continuous with my college years, rather than discontinuous, I would probably have dressed continuously too. Even at the William the Fourth, I could probably have stood my ground and gotten away with it, but doing so would have entailed acknowledging that presenting in a feminine way was actually important to me, and what was very clear was that getting fucked up was just more important, infinitely more important. And so I left that awkward teen behind and turned her into a quirky backstory, until such a time as I could think to do differently.

Séafra Goldblum (*alarmist*):   I am a girl that dreamed I was a boy. But that dream is over.

Do I have a problem with this fucking Insane Clown Posse nonsense? It couldn't be less my thing—couldn't be further away from me, to be perfectly honest—yet I'm drinking a couple of these things a day. And worse, I've allowed myself to become suckered into various loyalty schemes—a "match three" iPhone game (chicken/bone/broth); stamp cards; Insta hashtagging. The latter was an accident—I just happened to have one of these drinks in my hand in one of Danny's Insta pics, and one of my students saw it, and told me that *she also loved the Juggalo Chicken Drink*, and that if you took pictures of yourself drinking it on Insta and hash tagged #JuggaloChick4Lyfe, they enter you in a draw to win a big stash of drink. She and her girlfriend had entered themselves a few times and ended up winning tickets to the Gathering of the Juggalos. Just a joke, obviously, haha—these tony NorCal lesbian youngsters were just in it for the lulz—but still, a holiday is a holiday and some of the shit that went down, my *word*.

It sounds dumb, but in late 2017 the online Juggalo Chicken Drink community got extremely excited about the idea of re-booting classic movie franchises with Juggalo themes. It's obviously not the sort of thing I'd go in for—again, to be clear, *I'm not a Juggalo*—but it was a fun conversation, and there were all kinds of cool ideas—a Juggalo James Bond ("the name's Bond . . . Juggalomes Bond"), a Juggalo remake of *Toys* in honor of the late, great Robin Williams. I guess the ICP Beverage Franchise got wind of it and decided to make it an official thing: people were supposed to send in pitches, and then the best one would win a certain quantity of JuggaloBuxx, a cryptocurrency which you can spend at the Gathering of the Juggalos, as well as a couple of other Juggalo stores they're opening.

Worth a punt, I thought. It's strange but, as I was going up for tenure (with a high degree of confidence in my chances), I couldn't stop thinking, *what happened to my creative work?* I used to be so mm . . . poetic, and it's all just gotten sucked up. Sure, a Juggalo movie is a long way from the goals I had in my teenage years, but maybe it's a starting point, maybe it could go somewhere interesting, start a few conversations.

So I settled on what felt to me the most intuitively Juggalo-friendly franchise, *Ghostbusters*, and more specifically on the most emphatically Juggalo character within that franchise, that was both capaciously jolly and primally menacing: the Stay Puft Marshmallow Man. I realized that if I wanted to get taken seriously, I would actually have to minimize the quantity of *direct* Juggalo references to as close to zero as could reasonably be established, so my goal was to import a kind of basic Juggalo vibe without actually mentioning Juggalos.

I realize that within the Busterverse, Puft is a logo, rather than a person—but what my movie presupposes is: what if he weren't? What leads a man to conduct a rampage through New

York City? One quick answer, of course, is that he was a manifestation of Gozer the Destructor, given sweet candy flesh from the mind of Raymond "Rat" Stantz. But that's too simple. Why *this* corporate logo? Why now, Ray? What made the Marshmallow Man come into your head at just that moment? What's he thinking, what does he want, this "marshmallow" man?

Okay: the year is 1961, and the place is Elk Grove Village, Illinois, a new town planned and built a decade previous by the Centex Corporation, to house its workers. Everything is perfect in this small town—perhaps a little *too* perfect, if you know what I mean. A shot lingers on a picket fence, which suddenly doesn't look like a nice fence but actually looks like a scary fence, like a **bad fence**. There arrives into this town a successful, middle-aged businessman named Alex Doumakes, who in 1954 had patented a method for producing marshmallow confectionary, and was moving out to Illinois to develop his business. Did he have a secret? You bet your ass he had a secret. He kept it in a letter, in a woman's handwriting, on the shelf. But it's candy time and the swinging candy pops are here!! Lalala, goes the bubblegum soundtrack playing all the hits of the period that you can remember. "My Baby's Got a Marshmallow Heart," by Frenchie and the Benches; "Daddy Sweeten My Tooth," by Ellie Bowdler; and "Keep Those Marshmallow Pies Away from My Man's Cheatin' Eyes" by Belle Frond and Her Generous Orchestra.

Soon we are introduced to S. Taylor Puffterberg, a recently jilted loser and passionate early-career 1950s Juggalo who takes a job at the Doumakes plant. Puffterberg's a real hard ball of cheese, just can't crack a break for nobody. He lives with his mother, played by some old bitch you recognize, and they spend their evenings playing canasta while she tells him stories of other men she fucked while his father was away at the war. They have a great vibe, you don't even find it creepy at first. Then you do. Oh *my*, then you do. Taylor, as he is known, has a sweetheart, played by Rachel McAdams, the waitress at the local diner—where she serves mostly banoffee pie, tiramisu, and other anachronistic confectionaries. Your teeth hurt when you look at her, in a cute little powder-blue apron. One time you see her sniffing glue with her boyfriend, a mean, recently graduated former high school jock named Ray Stantz, and you hate him. He's mean to her, too— Taylor sees him knocking her about in the parking lot behind the diner one night—how can men be so brutal? Yet still she keeps coming back for it. How can women be so sweet, and so stupid?

TAYLOR: you wearin' a new shiner there, Jenny?
JENNY: just leave it Taylor. [*She turns her head away from him, towards the camera.*] I'm okay.

"Lollipop, lollipop, oh lolly-lollipop, lollipop!" And then an old-timey commercial that says very rapidly, "Doumakes makes the best marshmallows, marshmallows for you, marshmallows for ya gal! Make ya marshmallow a Doumakes marshmallow, and make hers one too! Make mine Doumakes!" The poignancy is so draining you could just *die*.

You know the rest:

1. Taylor becomes the confidante of Doumakes, who involves him in a serious of increasingly nefarious schemes, culminating in his being forced at gunpoint to push someone into a vat of boiling liquid marshmallow at the plant;
2. Taylor also becomes the face of Doumakes marshmallows, where he is given the demeaning nickname "Stay Puft";
3. Taylor's mom turns mean and calls him a "freak" one night—if we shoot it right we can get Patricia Clarkson a nom for best supporting;

4. Taylor seeks revenge on Ray for attacking Jenny, so he gives him some poisoned marshmallows—which Ray then gives to Jenny!;

5. Wracked with guilt for having killed her, Taylor confronts Doumakes for having goaded him into a life of crime—or was it capitalism itself that did it??—but Doumakes just taunts him—"come on, Taylor, grow a pair! This is what you always wanted, my little sweet-toothed fairy boy!";

6. His guilt turned to rage, Taylor murders Doumakes, and jumps into the vat of liquid marshmallow himself to become . . .

THE STAY PUFT MARSHMALLOW MAN. The movie ends with him looking in the mirror, a creature of pure wobbly whiteness, holding the old-timey razor with which he just killed his mom in his right hand, and saying in a creepy, clicky voice: "Well, Stay Puft. What are you gonna do now?" as we FADE TO BLACK. Sophisticated credits—a serif font and a slow old song as we reflect on how far we have all come over the last three and a half hours, each of us a marshmallow man in our own way.

☑ *Did you know?* Alex Doumakes was a real person, he invented the marshmallow.[7]

Sometimes, trans women take Viagra, or equivalent. I only discovered this perfectly intuitive datum since moving to New York, although perhaps my sisters in California are all hopping on the 'agra, too. It is a perfectly intuitive use of a medicine: it allows one's penis to become erect, but does not require any kind of hormonal intervention—so one can have erections ("achieve erections," and bravo on your achievement, sir) without hormonal intervention, i.e., without re-introducing testosterone into one's endocrine system. Some people I've spoken to enjoy the delights a hard dick can supply when deployed by someone with an estrogenated endocrine system; others have used Viagra for work, and have more ambivalent feelings about it. I recently decided I wanted to try it, though I'm not entirely sure of my motivations. I used to enjoy the ways I had sex, and wondered whether it might be possible to put on the knowledge with the power, to use a slightly inapposite Yeats metaphor. (Yeats never wrote the perfect line for a woman deciding to resurrect her penis, sadly; "Leda and the Swan" is the closest thing we have.)

Some of the more difficult to talk about aspects of my transition have been those elements that concern my masculinity. What even is masculinity, in a trans woman? Clearly it is possible to have swagger, passion, directness, and for these elements to be deeply feminine (as I think they tend to be in me). Then there is clockiness, the behavioral, auditory, and visual cues that lead people to call me "sir," like my slightly heavy gait and my deep voice—but these aren't "masculine," exactly, at least not in the way (say) Chris Pratt is masculine. I have among my friends a handful of trans women who have achieved a chill equanimity about certain putatively masculine forms of social participation (broeyness, say); these have always been women who are years and years past their transition, and are rarely clocked. I love it in them, but I can't see it happening to me any time soon: I spent my life pre-estrogen trying to get away from men, I doubt I'll miss them at any point. Never say never, I guess. Anyway I don't think these are the only ways of thinking about masculinity in trans women; in me, at least, there is a seam of experience that feels masculine, or co-extensive with something that I used to understand as masculinity: the hosting instinct, especially the form of hosting proper to sex. Welcoming people to one's life, one's room, one's body. Not that anyone necessarily adopts a masculine position when they perform hostliness in this sense— I'm realizing it sounds like receptivity, with its complex relation to femininity, from which I think it is quite distinct in fact—but for me, hosting feels masculine in some way. I thought it would be fun to endow that side of myself with a dick.

The company that prescribes and sells generic Viagra sends you chic little packets, like silky little condom packets, dusty with lube. You tear the thing open, pop three at a time, and wait. It takes an hour, according to the instructions/directions (Viagra is both a gadget and a medication). I had been told, by various parties, to stay hydrated. You are also told to use them for the first time without any expectation of having sex, just to feel out the effect that they will have on your body—which made sense to me, so I tucked myself into Danny's body, cosy and intimate but not sexy.

I wonder whether the obvious blurriness of that distinction was, cognitively speaking, part of the reason why my experience with Viagra was so utterly, utterly terrifying? Having never taken dick pills before, I did not know whether they would produce or merely respond to a feeling of sexual arousal. That is, whether the medicine itself would construe my cosiness as a kind of sexual come-on, against the evidence of my own sensorium. I wanted to be cosy, not aroused, and I have a sharp sense of the distinction—but what if the drugs erode that sense, and push me into a sexual intimacy against my own interest? At which point I realized the horrifying truth: I had slipped myself a roofie, and for an hour I would just have to wait for the feeling to overwhelm me. I have had few more distressing hours in the course of my transition than that one. I immediately sensed that I had betrayed myself, that I had given up the thing that I cherished (my womanhood) in the pursuit of something paradigmatically abundant and low value. I felt guilty, because of my inability to share this potentially rather fun experience with other trans women, and perhaps because of the strange genital-centrism I was experiencing, and refusing (or at least failing) to push through. I had hoped for feelings of warmth, growth, and power, and instead I spent the first hour of this trip crying uncontrollably, my mind (uncharacteristically) obsessing over bottom dysphoria. I felt frightened that if I got hard, I would run into the kitchen and grab the sharpest knife from the drawer. I felt—and this can only be a disgracefully lurid image, but it is true, in the way feelings are true—as though my body was violating itself.

After the first hour, the panic began to ebb—still, I didn't get hard, and I didn't really stop sobbing. My partner was, of course, beautiful and elegant and glorious, and held me kindly and warmly. I felt guilty because I knew the idea of me sprouting a cock was kind of appealing to him—as how could it not be?—and I think he felt a little afraid that he had pressured me (which he hadn't). We lay in bed and watched the final episodes of *Bojack Horseman*, talking occasionally about addiction narratives, justice, and healing. The previous evening, he had grasped my head and told me that he had always been moved by my capacity for healing. "What choice do we have?" I had responded, in an effortlessly cool, *Rebel Without a Cause* kind of way. I am not healed, as my experience with the Viagra shows; so much seems to outlast the capacity of any mental or spiritual procedure to produce healing—the universe of suffering we move through together. It's funny in that sense that *Bojack* ends with prison, in the ruins of the show's narratives of recovery, therapy, healing, and growth. The only thing that "works," at least narratively, is metaphorical incarceration, the utter deprivation of freedom. Difficult to know, then, how to continue to relate stories, to and about ourselves, in which we have been hurt and have hurt others, since the only possible end of the stories would be something like ". . . and that's why I detransitioned; that's how I came to abandon my own principles; that's how I proved myself wrong about everything; that's how I became utterly faithless; that's how I relapsed; that's how I was taken down a peg or two; that's how I sowed the seeds of my own destruction; that's how I turned into my mother after all; that's how I became unlovable; that's how I disappeared from the scene of my own being."

For me, I suppose, the dick is a mark of trauma. This, also, is no surprise, though; if I take the metaphor of "trauma" literally, it will change the way I think about bottom surgery. No longer a transformation, but the healing of a scar. It will take a while, I'm not ready yet. But I know things now, many valuable things. I am always disappointed by the simplicity of my transition, especially when it is placed next to other women's, which always seem more glamorous and subtle to me. "I want to be a woman, of course I don't want a hard dick, for fuck's sake!" turns out to have been the message, and if that seems like genital essentialism or a cumbersome investment in "the binary," I will just have to own that. (I am always confused, by the way, at the ease with which people can assume that any trans person will object to "the binary," as though it were a real thing.) I can absolutely affirm, celebrate, and delight in my sisters who have been able to develop more subtle relationships with their dick than I apparently can at this point. And I leave open the possibility of going back for more, I have a whole drawer full of dick pills and I'll try anything twice.

But I know things now. One night recently, before the recent crisis, Danny and I and two of our friends went to see Tituss Burgess sing Sondheim at Carnegie Hall. He didn't sing

"I Know Things Now"—it was mostly deep cuts, to the great satisfaction of the two serious theater gays in the box with us—it was overwhelming. In the show's closing sequence, Tituss told us a story of growing up in Georgia and discovering *Sunday in the Park with George* on PBS.[8] "I didn't know what the fuck I was watching," he said, but then said he understood what was happening as a kind of worship and a kind of certainty. "I have heard God called by many names by now, but the first name I had for him was Stephen." A bit much I thought, British. He then sang "Sunday," and I wept again, the third time that day. Like a big girl's blouse.

After I moved to the US in 2008, my trips back to the UK were less frequent but more spectacular than I anticipated. The first time around, after an eventful year my friends had waved my wife and I a tearful farewell, only to learn that our marriage fell apart shortly after because I had decided I was bisexual, which in this case meant wanting to date a lesbian. The first time someone had told me I was bisexual, it was one of my male college fuck buddies, who was responding to a collapse of confidence after I had failed to suck a guy off efficiently in a bathroom. Anyway, the wife and I, now on course to divorce, still had the exact same friends in London as we'd always had, and we were awkwardly obliged to share meetups with old pals, trying with an obscene pantomimic vigor to appear normal. We sang a duet of "The Winner Takes It All" at a shitty karaoke bar on Mare Street; people watched, aghast, and we sort of hated each other.

The second time, I met some friends in Brighton, headed to the beach, and sploshed around naked on the shingle. I drank beer as the sun set, and then we trekked over to a real ale pub, of the kind that (since the smoking ban) smelt consistently of unconscionable flatulence. The real ale aesthetic always felt antique, and therefore implicitly mature—as cheddar matures, perhaps—an impression cemented by the pubs' names: The Friendly Gunsmith, The Frenchman's Merriment. The beers themselves were named so quirkily as to embarrass, rather than induce reverie: an overfondness for badgers, for whatever reason.

There, a few beers in, my friends and I were to rendezvous with the charismatic heterosexual man whose guidance I had allowed myself to desire for years, and who, since the first time he had met me, demanded my approval with a world-ending finality. And then things are blurry, as they get in the haze of a blackout, in and out of vision, choking out words, holding one's own. A party chunder, and a repeat rinse with the Goblin's Badger. The next morning I was shown a photograph of myself standing proudly in front of a lake of thick yellow vomit that I had hurled into a backstreet gutter. "Ooh, I look like John Travolta," I said, rather stretching the point.

In between those two events, however—the vomming and the photograph—I have flashes of stuck visual images, caught in a moment and spread over a surface. I was, in fact, on my knees in front of the heterosexual man, mouth open, throat gagging and catching, tongue switching and swirling around his midriff, where he thrust into my hungry, detachable face—a head of stiff young broccoli, which I gobbled gobbled gobbled. Why broccoli? At whose instigation? Mine, presumably, or whatever I was carrying inside my body to propel me into such a position— where the heterosexual man laughed and placed his hand on my head and fucked me with the broccoli while—and I cannot quite believe this to be true, but I do not need to believe what my body knows—other members of his entourage filmed me on what must have been a very early model, perhaps the very first model, of an iPhone. When the following morning I begged them to delete the video, I was told that they would upload it to YouTube with the caption "broccoli blow-job!!!" which I stopped searching every day only after three or so years had passed and I could convince myself that any students who did see it would no longer believe they were seeing me.

To get sober—and here, one inevitably uses vocabulary that will baffle those not in the know, some of whom (perhaps) will balk—is to use language that one has not used before, if one could put it that way; it is to absorb and internalize a method of language use that is far from intuitive, and whose counter-intuitiveness is the whole of the point. One learns that others, that all, have spoken these bizarre and off-putting words and phrases before, and then one begins to hear traces of them everywhere—a line in a Johnny Cash song, or a remark in an interview with David Bowie. One finds oneself in the company of one's heroes, the very people whom one was chasing from bar to bar, having glimpsed them early on in the evening—here they are, the best and most charming narcissists one has met, wise and knowing, possessed at last of the confident smile of someone whose stash of cocaine has proven, functionally, limitless. A Keith Richards type saying, "you can get even higher without drugs, man!" seems infuriatingly self-righteous, until one realizes he means it entirely literally—he is getting fucked up on *the absence of cocaine*, sucking oxygen from the air like smoke from a glass pipe. If one can't get even higher without drugs, after all, one is likely to continue to use drugs, since getting high is fun, and if one could be persuaded to stop doing so by an argument from moral principle, one is unlikely to find oneself with such a problem in the first place.

At some point, one opens The Book, which has been read by each who had trodden this path; The Book, which gives its name to The Program, which in turn gives its name to The Movement. This tricolon is one of the mystical signs embossed onto the structures of sobriety by the old masonic hucksters who wrote this stuff—then promptly died, got into acid, got drunk again, or somehow, miraculously, survived and remained sober, in some cases for many years. One reads the words knowing all this—and knowing much else besides—but knowing too that the claim is simply "it works. It really does." What is the "it"? The Program. What is "working"? What it does. "It," one might say, is the Program's way of saying "id," the "Es" of psychoanalysis. The thing that is you, that is the truest you that you can never know or see, but which orients and pre-exists your desires, and for which there is no negation, no "no." By the time you are reading these words (or "I" is), you are no longer in any doubt about Its existence, but you are strongly skeptical that it has any will other than to destroy you and turn you to a charred gash—*It*, as you'll recall, is another name for Pennywise the Dancing Clown.

You will read the book (which is not "It," although it contains It) slowly—ruminating and annotating in highlighter and biro, absorbing the lore, imprinting your own codex with your words, the words of the psychoanalytic "Ich." The paratexts and prefaces, antique medical discriminations, caveats and codicils—these you will be asked to absorb even before The Book begins in earnest, and it takes weeks, months—in some cases, literally years—before you finally read: "Chapter One: A Wilson's Tale." That cackhanded pun sets the tone of clumsy/folksy literacy that governs the whole "tale," a word that, while obviously taken from Shakespeare in this context, the titular Wilson imbues with a powerful new meaning—a genre of narration, "telling one's tale" quickly becomes part of the work of recovery, perhaps the most important part. The recovery tale is a tale without a moral, but with a rhythm, and that rhythm is one of the most beautiful narrative forms I have acquired. Since it has never been bettered than in "A Wilson's Tale," I shall simply transcribe the text here, with apologies to The Program for taking a liberty with their generous relinquishment of intellectual property rights:

A WILSON'S TALE

My brother, perhaps too much time has passed since the great pole-sitting fad of the mid-1920s? I had better remind you: in the cold Philadelphia January of 1924, a handsome former steeple-jack named Alvin "Shipwreck" Kelly, sat on a small chair at the top of a pole for nearly fourteen hours. All of us, the Philadelphia squadron of Young Lads, who saw him, were changed forever by the incident. Soon, we were sitting atop flagpoles of our own, erected in our own backyards. Those in the position of watcher would stand below, admiring the regal elegance of the sitter and awaiting our turn. When it was our turn to sit, we watched benevolently over our audience, drinking in every drop of time. We sat for longer and longer—a whole day, two, a week (our mothers or wives sending up provisions). Of course, sitting was preferable to watching. Soon, we couldn't bear to spend so much time on the ground—our groups splintered into smaller and smaller units, to maximize our time on the poles. Months would pass, and our circles dwindled until there were just two of us—one watcher and one sitter. My pole partner was named Jiminy Jounce. He died in the Crisis.

It was up a pole that I tasted my first droplet of the good life, aged fourteen—in the form of a thimble of malt liquor, which had been shot up the pole by my mother or wife (I forget which). Here was glory, concentrated and distilled, that sang on the tongue and coated the throat with love. I had left school a year earlier, having determined that it behooved me to acquire a trade, and thereupon to encounter a wealthy gentleman, and to follow him to my fortune. The pole-sitting fad having taken more and more of my time, I found that my plan to shine shoes worked especially well: first, because the hours were relatively flexible, and second, because it could in fact be accomplished while pole sitting, provided that a second pole was constructed nearby, only a couple of feet higher, such that my customer's shoes were level with my lap, or abdomen. Each customer having been served, I would call upon my wife (or mother) to send up a small bowl of brown mash, and a tuppence of malt. And I would suck them both up and count myself a king.

From time to time, men would come and stand under me, drawn to "the Pole-Sitting Shoe-Leather Lad," as I was known, or "piascesello" for short (adapted from the initials). My mother (I think) constructed a sign for me, in a mock-Italian hand: "Il Piascesello! Come-a see-a the-a amazing-a pole-sitting-a boy-a!," with a picture of a traditional Italian plumber, sucking his mustache. And "amazing" did not feel too strong a word. Here I was, living life. And didn't I have everything I needed? A steady stream of admirers, who would toss their heads in admiration, and a view of my neighbor's gardens. Sometimes, for my sins, I peeked a look through my neighbors' windows, and caught a glimpse of a wife's negligee, or a husband's hanging dong. When my wife had gone to bed (my mother having already done so) I dreamed of everything I would do to them if I ever came down the pole. As I grew into manhood, I found myself naturally growing competitive, and desirous of the usual appointments of a man's station. The problem was, having placed myself at the top of my pole one week— and only one week—later than a gentleman in Nebraska named

Nobby Malachi, I was unable to descend without losing forever my claim on the national, which was to say world, record. So such a station as was to be appointed to me would need to conform to my pole-sitting lifestyle. For was I not on top of the world? My wife died, and another was supplied to me under the Provisions Act, although since she had no shoes to shine, she remained on the ground while the deed was done, padré on the second pole, Oxfords plum akimbo. While there was mash and malt to winch, what did I care? These were high times indeed.

The 1929 crash, of course, smashed the pole-sitting fad in the nads, and suddenly the crowds stopped assembling, too busy throwing reams of paper out of the window to care about such an esoteric old custom. I dare say it even seemed quaint to some. Still, my wife (or mother—I stopped noticing) would ensure that no formerly august old dosser would pass Lancaster Avenue without be whooshed up the pole and polished by the no-longer-young Piascesello, and then once the codger had been permitted to descend, I was permitted in turn my mash and malt. In truth, by the time I was twenty-five, I lost track of much besides the mash and malt—each morning I would screech for it, and my wife (my mother having died, which made things a little easier to remember) would place the mash and malt on the tray, winch it up, and I would suckle. I had been there—how many years? Ten? My feet would grow grey and bloodless, and my ass, which had begun to incorporate the chair like a splint grafted into a bone, had lost all feeling. The neighbor's wife's breasts began to droop, his own dong to withdraw. Yet I dreamed only of outlasting the Malachi.

Which goal I achieved on April 1, 1939—April Fool's Day—when Malachi breathed his last, and succumbed to a pneumonia he had picked up in a late Nebraska frost. By now the glory days of pole sitting were long gone, but I reflected on the passing of my great rival—whom I had never met, but from whom I had never grown farther in fifteen years—with great poignancy. I decided to place a pall upon my legs, which draped all twenty feet to the ground. The invention of the domestic Shine-O-Matic had rendered my only salable skill quite redundant, and so I simply demanded that my wife (or mistress) engineer a couple of troughs—one each for malt and mash—and send up a couple of straws, so that I could sip at will. The thought occurred to me that surely I had lost my mind—surely, no human being has spent his entire life up a pole? Might I have been the first, truly? So I considered coming down, but then recalled the existence of another gentleman named Pungo McGarritigle in Kansas, who embarked upon his own journey a week after mine. Were I to descend, McGarritigle would win—and wouldn't his feelings, upon so doing, be as filled with bitter ruefulness as my own had been when I heard of the death of Malachi?

I still had mash and malt by the bucket, and if my wife was broken, I simply promoted the mistress—an advantage of which scheme being that it engendered the pleasant task of procuring a new mistress! Occasionally a neighborhood wag would shit in the mash, or puke in the malt, but the taste bothered me less than expected. One might imagine that a life spent on such a limited diet would induce a great sensitivity to minor changes to the slop's composition; but indeed it was not so, as the malt had long been leavened with battery acid and other astringents, which sharpened the effect but quite deadened my palate entirely. Days and nights became interchangeable—I would sleep, wake, sup, and sleep, in an untidy jumble of time—at intervals, I would perceive boots in front of me, and shine them, sometimes licking or caressing them. At other times I was quite sure that the boots were delusions caused by my unusual condition. None of my wifes or mistresses was ever able to satisfy me on this point—or, I need hardly say, on the other. I bound my straws into my mouth, one each side, to keep a steady stream and relieve the necessity of turning my head, which had become a terrible burden.

On Christmas Day 1957, when I had been up my pole for twenty three years and six months or so—ironically, perhaps, I had failed to note the exact date of my commencement—news reached me of the tragic and premature death of the only man alive whose name I still retained—Pungo McGarritigle, who had passed from the inhalation of dust. I began to feel my frame collapse inside my skin, my bones liquefy. I pictured McGarritigle as a smart, ambitious child, coming up behind me—and now to picture him dead? And therefore to know not merely that I was the last of my kind left alive, but that if anyone were, at any point in the future, to resurrect the once popular fad of pole sitting, they would have to do so counting from nothing—neither I, nor Malachi, nor McGarritigle would survive to witness them, to provide encouragement or share strategies. Perhaps this was just as well. This life had become a solitary one. Perhaps it was always to be so. Mash and malt.

I had realized, then, both that I no longer had a title to defend—and that nobody, for as long as I could possibly be alive, would ever match my pole-sitting record. I had won! Yet it was a hollow victory—and it was to be my last.

After the passing of an especially recalcitrant wife, sometime in the early sixties, I was visited by a pair of smart, already-polished Oxfords—that I would have recognized anywhere. They were the very padré that had given me in matrimony for the first time, here to share some news that was to change my life.

"Well, Wilson, you've got yourself in a pretty pickle here, haven't you?" said the shoes.

"I can't deny it, padré," I replied.

"If you're willing to hear it, I should like to spend a moment of your time outlining some very basic methods—simple but not, I am afraid to say, easy—by which your present station might be relieved. Will you hear me out?" asked the shoes, tongues flapping.

"What choice have I? Surely the Lord has never seen one so wretched as I," I replied.

"You may yet be surprised, young man," said the shoes, knowingly. He then added: "and yet, I am afraid there is one thing I must ask you before I proceed. One thing only, but it is a rule to which you must hew with iron certainty. Will you know what it is?"

"Yes, padré," I said.

"It is this: you must keep an open mind in matters spiritual. You will not be obliged to believe anything that you have not experienced, and yet you must not deny the spiritual component of such experiences as you do have. Are you willing?"

I said that I was.

They continued, "good. You see, Wilson, I was once like you—except instead of sitting at the top of a pole, I interred myself in the ground for stretches at a time. In my youth, I was quite the self-burialist! My mother—I *think* it was my mother—would open a hole in the ground, and through it she would pour the mash and malt into my own maw. Sometimes I would hear shoes stomping overhead. Often I would dream—such dreams, such dreams. Every now and then I would pull myself out of the earth, gasp for breath, assure myself that this had been the last time I would ever go into the hole, and sure enough, I would be back in the hole again within a day. I couldn't understand my own mind."

I asked the shoes what happened next.

"Next, Wilson?" they replied. "Well, on one of my trips above ground I met a man—a pastor, as it goes, who sat me down and told me his tale, much as I am doing to you now. It turned out he had been, himself, accustomed to spending long periods of time locked inside wardrobes—initially his own wardrobe, but increasingly other people's wardrobes. Of course he was followed by a mother or wife to supply him with his brown mash and malt, but otherwise he found his sport was the only relief or nourishment his mind would allow."

What happened to him, I asked the shoes.

"Well, one day, he met a man—but I suspect we must draw a line somewhere, Wilson."

I told the shoes I was in agreement. *"Va bene!"* I said, in Italian.

"It was then that this man passed on to my wardrobe-dwelling friend certain mental techniques—tricks, of the mind, if you like—which I now propose to pass on to you. Are you willing to hear them?"

I told the shoes that I was indeed. And then, up my pole, they proceeded to teach me what I have since come to think of as "The Footsteps I Follow," of such importance are they to the relief of my condition. They shall be detailed at large in the chapters that follow, but suffice it to say that they changed my life beyond recognition, and taught my body and soul relief that I had previously suspected would forever remain beyond my ken. Fear of other people and of economic insecurity has left me; sanity has been restored.

Today, my life is unrecognizable from the mash-and-malt-swilling swine of my youth and middle years. Though I am older now, my body feels spryer than ever—upon occasion, I stand up and wave to passers-by, who may happen to walk down the street. I have, finally, mixed the mash and malt into a single swill, which removes the need for a second straw altogether, and I have passed the straw (now made of the finest malleable plastic available to mankind!) through my nasal cavity and down into my throat, so that even the tasks of mastication and inhalation have been rendered unnecessary. My buttocks have, finally, seized up entirely around the worn lump of metal that used to be a "chair"—no clenching is necessary, and I am fixed in place by a metal rod that passes up through my body and binds me. Quite like my dear Christ am I even! My body wrenched inside out, hosed by a mother-woman in the summer months, and roasted slowly underneath by another woman–wife in the cold Philadelphia winters. On a clear day I can see the bend of the Schuylkill as it winds past Conshohocken. My waste is extruded by the pole itself. I will surely die soon. Others may work for utopia—for me, it is already here.

I felt like I needed to have sex with some clowns—see how that might shake things up, maybe knock a few things loose. I asked a Jugalette sex worker I'd met on the forums whether she knew any men in New York who would be prepared to enact a scary clown scene with me. I wanted four. Pennywise, Michael Shawn Crahan from Slipknot, the Man Who Laughs, and John Wayne Gacy as Pogo the Clown.

The conceit was simple: a harmless clown show in my living room. I sat on my couch, dressed in an outfit neutral as regards age and gender. T-shirt and grey sweatpants.

At first they did separate acts.

Pennywise, otherwise known as "the Dancing Clown," would of course do his dance. Specifically, the Macarena. With his cross eyes, enormous sharpened teeth, sprouts of red-hot hair, and thick spider legs stitched to his back like wings on a child's corpse, he placed his right hand out, palm down, and then his left, palm down. Then he turned over his right hand, then his left. Then he placed his hands on his shoulders, behind his head, across his torso, and then, one by one, his hips. Finally, he dipped his ass down into a groove he found just below his knee. Then he clapped, turned ninety degrees to the left, and repeated the whole thing. I nodded along to the groove and sipped on my Juggalo Chicken Drink.

Whatever one thinks of Slipknot, and I'll admit that they're not exactly my cup of char, Shawn Crahan is a virtuosic drummer. So I wanted someone in the role who could play a little drums. And he stood in front of me, rubber mask over his face with lank orange hair streaming down the sides, with a snare drum around his waist, singing "The Little Drummer Boy." His voice was low but sweet, not entirely unlike Bing Crosby's, who sang the song with another famous creep. I felt a nostalgic emotion begin to stir in the part of my anatomy the French call *le bassin*.

The Man Who Laughs stepped forwards, as though straight out of the traveling freak show in which he'd earned his bread. Surely he'd picked up a tumble or two in the meantime? Sure enough, here he comes, with a little handstand against the wall, a little cartwheel across the space. Carnival music plays in the background; it isn't frightening at all, despite the slice across his face; it is just a face, just a body. We all have bodies, even clowns.

Lastly, John Wayne Gacy—the riskiest one, for obvious reasons—and needed to be handled with most sensitivity. Gacy was a child rapist and murderer, as well as someone who was called a "sissy" by his mother. It was important not to make light of these crimes—but also important not to shy away from the business of processing the trauma they have created. We have to find new stories, even for old monsters. So I had Gacy amble around the room, laughing merrily, spraying me in the face with water from a flower, honking on a little horn, and tickling himself.

When each of the four acts was done, the first three all joined Gacy and they sang "Send in the Clowns," but the version that Krusty the Klown sings in "Krusty Gets Kancelled."

Send in those soulful and doleful
Schmaltz-by-the-bowlful clowns.

Bowlfuls of schmaltz indeed—I'd prepared one for each of them as a sticky treat.

Send in the clowns . . .

And then Danny came into the room and sang, "they're alrea-dy here."

CHAPTER TWO
FINGER LIMES

THE MISSION: to become The Martian Girl from *Mars Attacks!* Green, lovely, alien girl, and subsequently to murder the Motherfucking President of the Motherfucking United States.

✳ ✳ ✳

Think of Lisa Marie, playing the otherwise nameless Martian Girl whose appearance in Tim Burton's 1996 alien invasion disaster comedy arrests the generic montage of different characters from across America, responding in comical vignettes to the appearance of flying saucers, to deliver the movie's first—and, it turns out, final—narrative set piece, a continuous narrative that lasts from the Girl's appearance outside the Capitol Building in Washington, DC, through a sexual encounter with the

White House Press Secretary, Jerry Ross (Martin Short), to her murder of Ross, attempted assassination of the President, and death at the hands of the President's Secret Service bodyguards.[1] The Girl's arrival marks the beginning of a full-scale invasion of Earth, but she herself is sacrificed.

She is not a real Girl, though there is no other word for her. Her hyperfeminine face and figure, her ghostly, back-up singer gait, and her beehive-sized beehive blonde hair notwithstanding, underneath this flesh suit is a skinny little green goblin, possessed of the same swivel eyes and shrubby green brain as every other Martian. But to Jerry Ross, she is indistinguishable from the hot, flashy sex workers he talked to earlier in the movie—non-transsexual women costumed like drag queens—and his proposition of her follows the same sleazy, almost likable, rhythm.

Jerry, we have to assume, is what trans women sometimes call "a chaser": He believes he has found just another trans woman he can pay to fuck, but what he doesn't realize is that the transness of this woman will end his world, end his life. He has fundamentally misunderstood her transness as parodic femininity, whereas we, the viewers, know that the Girl—pure, unrestrainable femme will—is pursuing with irrepressible momentum the only goal that pure femme will ever pursue: I'm going to kill the motherfucking President of the United States of America.

She chews gum receptively and allows herself to be seduced by Jerry, following him into a limousine, into the White House, and into the secret "Kennedy Room" (decorated with a *Romeo + Juliet*–style fish tank and a large, motile circular bed, for fucking on). First, he tries to pluck the gum from her mouth, then she bites his finger off and feeds it to the fish. Finally, she bludgeons him to death with a statuette. The death of Jerry Ross was the first successful action of the trans femme revolution;

the Martian Girl's death at the hands of the American State our first infamous defeat.

So as you'll have gathered, after I had been taking *synthetic* estrogen, and suppressing my *natural* testosterone, for about six months, my dick stopped working properly, and a new seam of sensation was found just behind it, running from right at the back part of my scrotum to a couple of inches above my asshole. It required a funeral.

This was the second important conversation I'd ever had about my penis problem—the first won't come until quite a lot later (towards the end of the fourth chapter). I want to tell them in reverse order because it's how lives are really narrated—backwards, from the moment of reflection. But I also realize there's a good bit of repetition—honestly, the first will differ from the second in only a couple of situational particulars. I'm not trying to be clever—or I mean, this isn't supposed to be an especially clever device, obviously the book *in general* is an attempt to be clever— but the repetition is just part of the truth of routinized life, and the retrospection is a product of the situation in which this particular tale is being told. Please do me the honor of forgetting you've read this paragraph—it's housekeeping, really, just trying to walk the needier readers through some structural aspects of the work that they might find challenging. Stewart Lee does it, and he's very popular.

Anyway it was about six months after I'd started taking estrogen, and I was back in the clinic for another checkup. I protested to my doctor—*but doctor, I am afraid that I have lost the, ah, the conventional use of my, how should I say it*—but his response was, in retrospect, quite easy to predict.

"Miss Lavery," he started.

"—*Doctor* Lavery, thank you," I interrupted, cuntily. In my defense, this had felt like a hard-won solution to the potential problem of how to address someone in early transition.

"My apologies, *Doctor* Lavery, but you see, the medicine that you have been taking, we have decided to set you on a rather high dose."

"I see."

"Now, your body *likes* estrogen. It does. *She* does. You have achieved significant gains."

Weight gains, I thought to myself but didn't say, again just like some terrible cunt.

"I am glad you think so, Doctor."

"But you see, you must also reflect upon why you decided to take this medicine. You came to this clinic to embark upon the process of transforming your body into a woman's body. Elsewhere in your life, you have set about the still more laborious process of transforming the *story* of your body into the *story* of a woman's body."

"You say this much, Doctor, and yet you aren't wrong."

"Now, you remark that you have lost the power to produce turgidity in your *membrum virile*. And so it may very well be. But I ask you, what did you expect to happen, you dozy mare?"

"Well, now, Doctor, when you put it like that. But would you believe that when this started, nothing frightened me more than undergoing such a loss?"

"Doctor Lavery, I believe in the truth of your words. Indeed, the experience you relate is neither uncommon nor surprising."

"Ah, is it so? I got into a terrible fight with my boyfriend—well, at the time he was merely my platonic best friend—but I got into a terrible fight with him nonetheless, when we were hanging out with some trans people shortly before I started hormonal therapy. An older person who was just starting on estradiol was reflecting with the group that she (perhaps "they"? I'm not entirely sure—I think "she" is likelier, Doctor) had recently seen an attractive babe in a supermarket, and expected to feel the pang of dick blood that, for decades, she had been accustomed to feel merrily jostling its way into her glans. And yet, suppressed by spironolactone, no such blood did so merrily jostle. And I felt mournful with her, especially after a much younger tran (younger in human years, but significantly her senior *en termes de changement*) cackled, with an explosive jollity which I thought she wore quite cruelly, *well, it's chemical castration, honey, what do you expect!"*

My doctor's face wrinkled. "And you found the younger woman's remarks too acerbic?"

"Well, I felt the old dame warranted a degree of respect. My boyfriend—my best friend at the time—disagreed, saying that perhaps the younger woman's response had been a little sharp elbowed, but after all it was no more than these boomers deserved, with their access to cheap loans and something about housing that I never quite understood."

"I'm surprised that was his response."

"Oh, *are* you, Doctor? Well, perhaps you aren't quite as worldly as you pretend."

"I shall let that pass, and respond merely that in my view the story's most notable feature was not the age difference, but the fact that this person had been developing spontaneous erections at the mere sight of women, in the regular course of doing her shopping on an average workday! I should say *that* was a sight more unusual."

"Who are you, Sherlock Holmes? 'Notable feature,' indeed! I don't think there's anything wrong with becoming involuntarily aroused in the course of one's daily practice. And I shall thank you to adopt a less moralistic tone in future—I can only imagine that it rather hampers your work, here at the transsexual medicine center in San Francisco!"

"Well as regards your specific complaint, I should think it perfectly obvious to anybody reading this that I didn't *really* speak in this bizarrely affected patter, and that it is entirely *your* invention—which is to say that it is the affectation of an English professor on the cusp of middle age, desperately trying to appear cool to people significantly her junior. But in any case, that brings us in a roundabout way back to the point I was trying to make: you came to this clinic to seek help feminizing your body. We have supplied you with that help, indeed your body is amply feminine: who could deny that you have breasts now, and a soft, silky pelt quite unlike the rough hide of a male? And now your *penis*"—he really leaned into the word, and then repeated it—"your *penis* is no longer capable of generating or sustaining erections. This, to put it bluntly, is a feature of the treatment plan that you and I have devised. It is not, so to speak, a bug."

I could see his point. There was no use pretending I couldn't.

"Now, could we reverse this? Certainly we could. Nothing would be easier. I could set new doses, and you would find yourself plotted on a course back to Dicktown. Diamond cutters by sundown, I shouldn't wonder. Yet—and I invite you to reflect on this for a moment—all this would mean would be that we had changed course—turned the clipper astern, so to speak, and sailed back upstream. I am very happy to do so—indeed I do so frequently, and there is nothing wrong with it at all. I want to emphasize that once more, if you will, *nothing wrong with it at all.*"

He seemed oddly keen to emphasize the point.

"You must simply let me know what you wish: I am your servant. I make the cuts where you ask for the cuts; I make hard things soft at your beck, and soft things hard in turn. Guide me."

I stood, with a strong sense that he had given me all the options, laid the tools in front of me, and made the choice very clear. Though I would mourn the erections, I would be grateful for the efficacy of the treatment. Indeed, I would accelerate. As I began to open the door and make my egress, I tossed back a smart little aphorism with which the good doctor could do his work:

"*Titty skittles please!*"

"Titty skittles" is the name I have heard people use to describe progesterone supplements—though I have also heard the term used to refer to estradiol itself. The case for reserving the term for progesterone is that progesterone is frequently prescribed despite nobody knowing for sure that it does anything, except for—it is rumored—enlarging one's breasts. My breasts became larger after I started taking it, and I had to sign a form indemnifying the clinic in case of breast cancer—progesterone increases risk, apparently, but I think that just means that it helps to *make more breast tissue, which can become cancerous.* This is an oddly actuarial way of thinking about cancer, but I suppose it makes sense. The case against reserving the term for progesterone is that there are plenty of people who claim that progesterone has no effect on breast growth. I simply have no idea—I'm not that kind of doctor.

I was meeting Danny for lunch after my appointment, so I got the train back to Oakland, listening to sad dick ballads on my phone. I was running early, so I got off a couple of stops before I needed to and walked around Lake Merritt, repeat listening to Bobby Bottleneck's classic shuffler "Ain't Life Just a Plum, Kiddo?" As I walked around the lake, I imagined various old lovers, men and women, standing at various intervals, and

my handing each of them a ghostly rose to symbolize the passing of my old body.

> *Ain't life just a plum, kiddo?*
> *Ain't that just a plum?*
> *You're ripening on that summery bush,*
> *Then kazappo, the autumn's come!*
> *You're splurging more on love than your*
> *Gross annual income,*
> *Tell me now that ain't a plum,*
> *Or ain't life just a plum?*
>
> *Ain't life just a plum, girl,*
> *Ain't that just a plum?*
> *A soft sweet ball with a stone inside,*
> *Now you bloody tooth and gum!*
> *All your collaborations turn*
> *To bitter zero sum,*
> *So tell me, kid, that ain't a plum,*
> *Or ain't life just a plum?*
>
> *You can munch on a cherry, a mango, or berry,*
> *And whistle a tune,*
> *You can nibble a litchi or suck on a kiwi,*
> *I'll never impugn,*
> *But there's only one fruit with the root to toot for,*
> *The beautiful drupe of acute patootie,*
> *The hoot of a plum, the juice of a prune!*
>
> *Soon . . .*

Before I got to the fried chicken place on Lakeshore where we were having lunch, I stopped in at Good Vibrations, to contemplate a life without my oldest friend. I remembered that once, I had been talking about my ambivalence at a gathering of trans people, and a young woman—aged twenty, maybe—had said to me, "well, I just want to let you know that there are *plenty* of ways to have sex that don't involve penetration." *Is that so, kid? *chews cigar* Pull the other one, it's got bells on it.* Yet here I was a few months later, buying armfuls of vibes and a big book called "the big book of transgender sex" or something. And in my bag, a slug of lavender oil and a silicone dick the size and girth of a midtown-griddled hotdog. Godammit, kid. You were right. You were right all along.

Ain't life just a plum, kiddo?
Ain't that just a plum?
It's got a short shelf life and it don't last long,
When all is said and done,
But the sweet three days that you get your ways,
They're the sweetest, sourest fun!
So tell me now life ain't a plum?
Or ain't that just a plum!

NOW LET'S CHECK IN WITH THAT MISSION SHALL WE?
roadside
Good evening. Eyes up here.
Thank you for stopping. I was . . . I was not sure where I was going. My name? I'm afraid I can't remember what that is at present. You may call me Angela, if you like. Your mother's name? What a coincidence. Like an angel, sent from above.

I am trying to get myself clean and presentable. I have an important meeting tomorrow. Please do not ask me for further details, it is . . . difficult to explain. An interview, yes, let us say that. I will need a pair of spray-on jeans, some silver strappy heels, and an unusual top. You may bring me an architecturally structured white button-up blouse. You may bring me an old band t-shirt, as long as it is slightly shredded, shows off my breasts, and does not look comical. In that case I would suggest Slayer or Pat Benatar or Prince; please avoid Def Leppard and Guns 'n' Roses. *repeats "Guns 'n'" a few times as though beatboxing* You may bring me a sequined vest that will make visible the electric currents in my personal zone. You are so kind, thank you, I am so grateful to you.

Would you help me choose which one to wear? Would you show me? Come back here. Into the changing room. Yes. The changing, ah, room.

I am not sure anyone has ever been kinder to me.

Strangely, this all precipitated a fight with Danny ("well, some of us never even got to *have* a dick, count yourself *lucky*"), and then that precipitated the kind of mean sex one has when one is only half made-up, and then he eventually stormed off to Hole Foods to "do some shopping." I stayed naked in bed feeling sorry for myself. The lavender oil had been cold when we applied it, so instead of enabling any kind of soothing vigor, it felt like a preparation for swimming the English Channel.

Oil had been an important part of my transition. When I had started hormones, I did so in a grump, not believing that they would do anything for me and simply awaiting an opportunity to feel superior to the loser trans girls who loved to nerd out about their endocrine system. Within twenty-four hours I had bought a large spider succulent, an oil diffuser, and a phial of lemongrass essential oil (or "essentialist oil," *you* would call it). Danny had asked me, "did you feel like you suddenly wanted an oil diffuser, or more like you were letting yourself get an oil diffuser at last, after having wanted one for a while?" It was a clever little trap, but I saw it coming, and refused to answer. Suddenly I was living in a hothouse. I was living with Cliff at the time—part boyfriend, part enabler, part best friend, part nemesis: I suppose the word is "companion"—and we had big south-facing windows in our living room, and, this being Adam's Point, there were large trees—the town's titular oaks, probably—on all sides of the apartment. Green glints, green reflections; a glass treehouse.

Danny returned from Hole Foods sheepish—he never stayed mad for long, especially when grocery shopping was a possibility. Grocery shopping—grocery splurging—was a kind of binge retail therapy for him, and it was beautiful to behold. He always had the most gloriously stocked larder, full of ornamental vinegars, unusual flours, and milks.

And a buccaneer's taste in fruit. He returned with an apology. "I think it's hard for me, because I feel mostly joy at the rise of your pussy, and it's difficult for me to grieve over something that was never mine."

"Your pussy" was what Danny had called a thing we—or perhaps he—had found between my legs. To this day, I have never been able to get off through manipulating it myself, but I can no longer deny, as I wanted to in the early days, that something is indeed there. Perhaps it is no more nor less than the "inguinal canals" into which my testicles retreat when frigid, or perhaps it is truer to say that it is what it feels like, which is a subcutaneous cluster of nerve endings and open space, roughly oval. In some photographs—surely I cannot include them in the book, but whatever, find me on Twitter and maybe I'll send you one—you can see it, the shape and the folds. It doesn't have a visible inside, but there's a tactile one. Nothing could less resemble what Auden so lusciously calls "the great thick cord that ran from his balls to his arse."[2]

Danny took his coat off and sat down on the bed.

"Let's try this again."

He bowed his head into my lap, kissing my thigh gently and reverentially, like a priest kisses the foot of the cross. After a few moments, he moved his head over to the middle of me. The difference between facefucking and *receiving* oral sex flashed in a panic across my consciousness. Historically I had not tremendously enjoyed the latter, in part because it was not the former. Being unable to maintain an erection did not improve the sensation, though it did conjure the amusing image of a cartoon cat attempting to silence a meddlesome fish by tucking it into his cheek.

But no, this was not the goal. Rather, Danny moved his tongue to the part of my phantom pussy where a clitoris would have been, if the ghost had had plasmic form, and started lapping and nibbling gently at a corner of my shriveled balls. The sensation reminded me of having the dead skin of one's feet bitten off by tiny fish; it was pleasant, and pleasantly ticklish. It was also sexy, in the way one might describe a dance or a person as sexy, but it was not, self-evidently, a sex *act*. He munched for a few minutes—I felt pacific. When he brought his head up to mine a moment later, he told me that he could feel me, feel a hole inside me. I wondered which hole he meant, once more, like an unpardonably melodramatic cunt.

He fell asleep. I reached into the Hole Foods bag, and retrieved a punnet of what looked like slimy little thimble fruit, a dark pungent green. I had never seen such a thing before. I took off the plastic lid, on which was printed the phrase "caviar/finger limes," and found on its underside a marketing leaflet, comprising a surprisingly long and detailed FAQ concerning the fruit, its origins, and its function. I picked it up.

What does a finger lime look like?

It's a small, long California clitoris of a lime that fits neatly between thumb and forefinger. It is much, much smaller than a lime, and smaller yet than a finger. It *is* the shape of a finger, roughly speaking, but you would have to imagine that it is the finger not of an adult human person, but perhaps a five-year-old child, or an otter/ one of the grander weasels. The color of the finger lime's *flavedo* is that of the slimy bark one might find on a dank, mossy swamp tree; so, though we refer to the finger lime as "finger lime," we must confess that, at least ostensibly, it resembles more a slug lime, or even (vulgarly) a small greasy turd lime. To those of us who love the finger lime, these external mystifications are but camouflage, nature's equivalent of a glamorous speakeasy with an unremarkable shop front. The finger lime holds its dearness tight in its chest, in a cavity so replete that it is barely a cavity. We will have more to say on this matter shortly.

What does a finger lime do, at first?

Its first task is to yield to the slit. You slit it, one end to the other—you unseam it from the nave to the chops—and you use only a very sharp knife, out of respect. You use the edge of the knife to slice deeply until one of two things happens. You bisected it, and now you have two half limes, each laid out like an hors d'oeuvre at a little doll's tea party. If you have dolls, and enjoy hosting tea parties or other upmarket soirées for them, you might consider using your finger lime halves for this purpose. Otherwise you may hold it in the palm of your own hand, small and emerald and gleaming. You may find yourself struck once more by the bright greenness you have found inside its slightly oily carapace, like the jeweled guts of a magical cockroach. You may reflect on your childhood, when you used to eat what we then called "French bread pizza" and that we brought out of the microwave studded with 24-carat bacon bits, smelling like hell, lying hot in the hand a tough, cindered lozenge. Now look at you, with this tiny secret gift, that only you know, that has become your favorite thing. Now you are older, and you have discovered for yourself the things that are your thing, that will always provide you with luxurious delight. Now you read poetry for—not fun, exactly, but not work either, and not because you have to. Because you *want* something from it.

This is if you go all the way in bisecting the finger lime, but, my friends, you should not. Your sweet task is to push the knife right through the flesh of the finger lime until you reach the thin bark on the other side, and then to stop, leaving the bark as a kind of hinge. Now you have a jewel with which to make an impetuous Russian princess in exile careen with envy. Now you have a clasping/unclasping citric brooch, which, when pinched, seems slug-like, and then when released from thumb and forefinger splays open to reveal its glorious interior. This before you have begun to think of putting your face close it, or drawing out your tongue. Simply the clasping and unclasping, clenching and unclenching, of the finger lime. It is like a clam's dream of living up to the hype of being a clam.

What, exactly, is inside?

Millions upon millions of tiny translucent orbs, pink and green, named "vesicles," ranged in their pod awaiting your glance. Yours are the first eyes to gaze upon these spherical fragments of delight, which possess all of the Arctic glamour of the movie *Frozen* but none of the unlovely pebble-faced whiteness. Indeed, they are not just of ice; each is equally of the tundra and the plains, the rainforest and the moorland. How does each exist, you wonder? By the integrity of its surface tension in collaboration with the hydrophobicity of its environment? The same way that a drop of water, suspended in time and space, will remain a teardrop, the most erotic shape because of its resemblance to an ass on legs? Or because of an invisible membrane of cellulose? How tightly wound and neatly bound the spheres. And how complete—none of those strange dry wispy beards one encounters on the vesicles of older oranges or their straggly moist counterparts one sees in a lemon. The finger lime has kept it tight all these years; its balls are the most elegant thing you have ever seen.

Then what does a finger lime do?

There are no polite ways to put this: it allows you to eat it. Did we say "allows"? It encourages you, exhorts you, languorously it begs you to curl its vesicles into your mouth, to dislodge them with your tongue, to find them pressed against your lips, to invite them into your own oral cavity, to paint the inside of your mouth with tiny jewels. You brush your tongue through endocarp for the first delicious layer that is held there, shaking off the loose beads and letting them coat you. But you are fooling yourself, and you are going to have to pursue your quarry with more vigor, for the finger lime will not yield so easily. You will push your tongue to pull off the vesicles; scrape down with your teeth; by and by you will begin to work your jaw into a rhythm as you start to suck on the lime, for you will not want to leave a single vesicle in place. Everything must be excavated, and it will be—or it *can* be, at least, provided that you do it right.

What does a finger lime taste like?

Only like the most piquant little citrus bitch you ever put in your mouth, only the most exquisite, pine-fresh shard of heaven, only the seasoning on the concept of food itself, such that one could meaningfully and indeed irresistibly assert that as salt is to food, so are finger limes to the very concept of taste. They taste like oral acupuncture, like Captain Planet's jism, like the square root of cilantro. They are otherwise known as "caviar limes," which one presumes is a name given on the basis of the perfectly spherical and tiny vesicles, but also reveals the truth of any system of class distinction—that you would love them, if only you could bring yourself to do so. You will never get enough of them, and you will one day die with their orbs dotted around your foaming lips.

How much does a finger lime cost?

Ah, but what is the unit by which one assesses that which one is buying? By weight they cost an extravagance, for they are but light. On the other hand, if one divides the cost not by weight but by intensity of flavor, they cost less than nothing, for the intensity is infinite. Whichever, they cost about fifteen dollars for a small punnet of twenty-two or so finger limes, which is less than even a small bag of cocaine or a cocktail in one of those fancy speakeasies you claim to love. And the quantity of limes does not matter, because you might spend hours eating finger limes by the dozen—you might, if you were a Russian princess—and still stand up from table convinced that you have not yet begun to eat a finger lime; perhaps that there were no finger limes; perhaps that finger limes are a myth like the chimera or the leviathan. As the finger lime passes from your hand and your mouth, it leaves no trace of its own being in your memory. Like all pleasure, it exists only on the moment of its consumption, before which it is a rumor, and after which it is merely a small, negligible loss.

I headed into the kitchen and retrieved the sharpest knife I could find. It was a gift from a friend, or a former friend.

✳ ✳ ✳

One thing that I used to say often, in the early days of all this, was that my orgasms had started to feel less like a shot, and more like a martini. It's fairly interesting that I chose this analogy, since I was two years sober when I popped my first blue pill.

nightclub

Hi! Yes! Loud smile over the music! Wow this room is full of bodies, moving and pumping!

Thank you! It is new — an old friend bought it for me today. No, he's not in the picture any more. Not that kind of friend, you know?

I love it too. I love sweat, and I love rhythm. Would you like an ecstasy? I have extra. No, I don't need any more myself. I took one just before you came over to see me. Would you like to lick the sweat off my face? Gosh, aren't you remarkable. Give me. Give, yes.

Yes, I would love to step outside. I am forthright in my — what is the word? Sexuality. You do not even know. Can you see the curves of these jeans? Do they not make you think of the thorax of a tiger beetle? They should. Shiny, round, tight. I let you push me against the brick wall as the sweat on my neck gets thicker.

The music from inside the club. The sweat now thick, pouring off. Gushing, sticky, orange. Eat. Eat. Taste. The music. The rhythm. The 80s disco lighting effects. You are giving me life. I am so grateful to you, thank you. I couldn't have done this without you. I love you, this is what love is, this is a metaphor for what love is.

Green was my love, green like a finger lime, green like a Martian Girl, emerald like the linoleum on the floor of the imaginary house where Audrey and Seymour live in the fantasy sequence "Somewhere That's Green" in *Little Shop of Horrors*. Annihilating all that's made to a green thought in a green shade.

Green shoots, green leaves, California-green vescicles beneath the California-green–brown mud. A hormonal transition is a new start, but it is not a new start like a shoot emerges from the mud: it is a fresh start constructed from the green plastics one has at hand. This is one reason *Little Shop of Horrors* is so appealing to trans people: it somehow switches the conventional roles assigned to natural and synthetic. The plant is natural and organic: it is an alien species, whose attitude towards our planet is no more culturally nuanced than that of the Buddleia davidii towards a Surrey trackline. Audrey's fantasy of "Somewhere That's Green," meanwhile, describes a world made livable through plastics, bleaches, Pine-Sol. The fake world is the only one fit for a person to inhabit, and its greenness is violent, virulent, vibrating. It has remade Audrey's own body and social role, too: "I cook like Betty Crocker / and I look like Donna Reed."[3]

Trans women are despised for seeking to reproduce toxic stereotypes, and every trans woman has at some point had to reckon with this, though perhaps no reckoning is necessary beyond an assertion that ethics begins with avowal, and perhaps the difference between Audrey's relation to a toxic stereotype, and that of a more *natural* woman, would merely be that Audrey commits to symbolic language a desire that, elsewhere, swims in the domain of the imaginary. Note, too, how "toxic" activates a rhetorical register of plastics, industrial run-off, premature or ungodly creation. Mel Chen's work on toxicity teaches us that toxicity itself is a resource for rethinking the biopolitical control of flesh and matter, for resisting the fixing of ourselves into natural bodies subject to impositions of threat, incentive, and poison.

I don't have much to add to the reading of *Little Shop of Horrors* proposed by Casey Plett and Morgan Page in their 2016 essay "No One Makes It Out Alive."[4] At the core of their interpretation is a deceptively straightforward allegorical reading: Seymour as trans masc, Audrey as trans femme, Audrey II as (for Page) "male privilege," aligned with the pull of patriarchy to perform ever-more brutal acts of male violence in order to pass as male. These claims are not straightforwardly offered, however—Plett clarifies that Audrey II's performance by a Black voice actor makes the alignment with privilege tricky, and adds that Seymour has elements of pre-transition trans woman too, in his inevitably failing attempts to do masculinity better than the Dentist. These allegorical speculations are both surprisingly supple and rooted in the personal and political histories of the two critics. Supple, because in fact the piece as a whole (i.e., as a staged dialogue between two trans women) offers a set of allegorical possibilities and projective identifications, but does not finally insist on the necessity of any one of them individually. Rather, the authority for these interpretations is felt through a kind of community belonging. A few times in the conversation one or the other draws on such community experience—"I know a couple other trans women who have similar attachments to [Seymour]"; Rick Moranis is adorned, Page says, in "a wardrobe that could've come from the closets of half the FTMs I've dated."

She continues: "I read the Dentist as the type of abusive cis boyfriend so many trans women I know—including myself—have put up with, because we don't believe we're worthy of better." This disclosure of identification—or rather of negative-relational identity, since Page does not cast herself as the Dentist but as the Dentist's objects—grounds an interpretive procedure in one's knowledge of one's own body; but it also (and sublimely) introduces the body into the scene of interpretation. Because here Page adduces herself to exemplify "so many trans women" whose general experience affirms her own. We have here a microcosmic model of a kind of trans-affirmative criticism, which involves three parts: (1) a critic's subjective encounter with the world (including both sex and art); (2) that encounter as it mediates and is mediated by community; and

(3) the object itself, whose autonomy from the critic, far from being undermined by the presence of a subjective analysis, is actually presumed by it.

I tend to think of "No One Makes It Out Alive" as the first major example of a *collaborative* literary critical enterprise, which could not be produced other than by trans women. It could hardly be further, for example, from the review that Conrad Black offered readers of the *National Review* after having witnessed the 2019 revival at the Pasadena Playhouse. It's easy to mock the Anglo-Canadian Black's pompous mock-Yankee bloviating, but that shouldn't stop us. It is evidence that even North American fascists, for all of their yahoo truck shows and gun shows and the like, are not entirely free of that otiose verbosity they prefer to paint, when they bother at all, as merely a delinquent habit of their European comrades. I quote Black in full, with the proviso that—and my lawyer wants me to really underline this point—the following is a *parody*, and *in no way* reflects the views of the Canadian author:

I recently had reason to attend that stretch of bright American pasture that birthed the wrongly maligned Richard Nixon and hosted, for the majority of his storied career, that wily American hero whose steady (and, might I add, both masculine and graceful) hand shepherded the Screen Actors Guild through the Second World War, and who adopted the readjustments necessitated by the Taft-Hartley Act. While in the City of the Angels (and what angels, entre nous!) I was given inducement by my dear friend Claudius Rochester—a god-fearing herbivore of the Gallic persuasion, may the sweet and fragrant baby Jesus have mercy on his immortal soul—to attend a performance of songs and words—a kind of painting in time and space, if you will forgive my rather fanciful analogy. That performance concerned a young florist by the name of Seymour, who had conspired with a demonic and, so it would turn out, fully alien plant to subjugate the free peoples of the world. He had been spurred to this nefarious scheme, it transpired, by an erotic fixation on a member of the weaker sex—and a timely reminder, of course, of just who prompted whom to eat of the fruit of the tree of knowledge. Ranged against the unholy union of alien plant and feminine corruption is a humble American dentist, stout in his self-belief and proud of his profession, though to my genuine distress I cannot report that the orthodontic bulwark was robust enough to expel the corrosive influence. I cannot say that.

A cautionary tale, then, concerning the fragility of the male conscience in the face of the eternal Temptress, and a broad but, for all that, trenchant analysis of the peculiar predicament of our great American experiment. Therefore, in the spirit of General Patton as he led the charge on Catania, let us take a moment of our time to celebrate this modern fable, and establish a hierarchy for our admiration. For just as no man may have satisfaction until he hath a station, until he knoweth whom to salute and by whom to be saluteth, as the poet saith (or says), therefore shall we better appreciate the merit of each of the musical Horrors with which this Little Shop may be said to trade, and better both extol the virtues of the best and pardon the defects of the weakest. Whereupon:

1. The Meek Shall Inherit the Earth

A biting satire upon the enfeebled construction of the Beatitudes with which our Savior teased us, on that blessèd day upon the hill. Is there not even a Nietzschean dimension to this fine rigmarole? For the meek who inherit are those filled with what the German seer taught us to call ressentiment and therefore the noble Christian is left with but one moral duty: to uproot these soi-disant meek and toss them to the swine.

2. Dentist!

Our hero's stirring call to arms: a man of professional training, he calls us to witness and to action. And we must heed. And heed we shall. "I enjoy the career that I've picked," he sings, and only the heart of a hog could fail to swell at his stalwart pride in a job well done. And I shouldn't aver, but I shall, that our own Republic—still a fledgling by the standard of the flock of nations—could do worse than follow this example.

3. Skid Row

What hell is this, 'pon which I stumble with fearful footfall? 'Tis the horror of urban poverty, and grimly rendered with Wagnerian cannon and fugue. The moral corruption of the poor is simply disgusting. How I wish we could die, together and as one, charmed by the benison of the Lord.

4. Grow for Me

A song of mild and hummable temper, of gentle and sweet spirit, betokening only in one suddenly arresting moment the horrors to come. For this man must bleed his own juices, the sweetness and goodness of his own veins, into the flower of sickness (as the French poet Sir Charles Baudelaire might have called it). And what then? Well, I shall tell you what. The collapse of the American middle class, and Christian values, and a contempt for the military that spreads across America from its foul base in that once-admired institution, the American campus, now a degraded and scotomized pastiche of its former glory.

5. <u>Prologue (Little Shop of Horrors)</u>

A veteran hoofer once snatched me by the lapel, chomped on the air that hovered but a few inches away from my brow, and croaked out loud: "you gotta have a brand!" And here we have a brand. For who can forget the name of this tale, viz "Little Shop of Horrors," once it has been cooed so frequently and so sweetly in this number? Yet it is only proper to feel sickened by the presence of knowledge one did not request and does not require. Here is a tale that pleasingly enchants, and yet tells of things that, one cannot but suspect, 'twere better not to know.

6. <u>Suddenly Seymour</u>

I am afraid to say that I simply disliked this, the romantic ballad with which our villainous florist secures from his quarry the physical comfort that he has sought in so craven a way. First because, like my American cousins, I dislike comfort, whether my own or that of others. (Please do not assume that this quirk of personality dissuades me from investing in first-class berth during my rare concessions to aviation. On the contrary, I splash out precisely so that I can feel discomfort in two respects: first, through separation from my fellow men; and second, from a fine antique cherry-wood rod that I jam into my rectum, retrieved from the colonial period at auction in our nation's capital.) My more consequential objection is that I do not believe anyone could enjoy "Suddenly Seymour" who did not also find the company of women charming, and I am almost ashamed to say that I have never cared for them.

7. <u>Somewhere That's Green</u>

And now as I look at her, I wonder whether there is something evil in her aspect, something fully wicked in her desires. Perhaps this Audrey is the vegetal tumor, or tuber, that grows unbidden under the fatty tissue of the decadent American vox populi. Why am I so smitten? This—delicate readers will forgive me—<u>bitch</u> has stirred in me regrettable desires and unlovely certainties, concerning the rarest of fruit: the lovely woman in whose throat lodges Adam's apple, and around whose trunk coils a wicked, delicious serpent. As I listened, I felt my own jaw dislodge and my legs give way until I fully knelt, mouth agape as the split skin of a rotted peach. And I wished to take my blessings in the depths of my own throat. Needless to say, I shan't be siding with the "no real toilets" brigade in this matter or any other, and shall only repeat this ritual—for repeat it I must and shall—within the comfort and secrecy of my own North American womb. I mean home.

Once more, for legal reasons: the foregoing was (and, if you ask me, I think it's rather obvious) a *parody*—allow me to "signal the fictive nature" of the listicle, if you will: the state of Baron

Black's rectum is not a matter upon which I am, in reality, entitled to comment. Nor am I truly qualified to assess his dislike
of women. Indeed, you may be surprised, reading these words,
to discover that Conrad Black is not an homosexual man. Quite
the opposite: he is an heterosexual man, who lives with his wife,
Barbara Amiel, Baroness Black—who looks as though Tim
Burton had cast Michelle Pfeiffer as the Joker, which is to say,
stunning. I am, in general, one of those tiresome killjoys who
refuses to join in celebrations during those rare occasions when
a rich asshole is incarcerated, since I tend to think that the path
to restorative justice requires us to stop associating imprison-
ment with winning. *But* I confess that my highmindedness was
never more tested than on May 15, 2019, when Baron Black
of Crossharbour received a presidential pardon from a certain
fascist who was rather inexplicably (and yet all-too-predictably)
in office at the time. Still, I believe a good free speecher like
the Baron would regard it as "fair comment" were someone to
note, in passing, that Conrad's conviction for the obstruction
of justice was, within the very narrow confines of the criminal
justice system, perfectly sound, and that the fact of his pardon
may—just may, I make no strong claim—have had less to do
with his protestations of innocence, and more to do with his
authorship of a text entitled *Donald J. Trump: A President Like
No Other*, which was published by Regnery Publishing in 2018.[5]

In 2001, Karol Józef Wojtyla, who was at that time serving
the Papal See in the person of Pope John Paul II (and is now
known as Saint John Paul II, having been deemed to be totally actually in heaven) invested Baron Black of Crossharbour
a Knight Commander of the Order of St. Gregory the Great,
an order in which are also invested the fascist profiteer Rupert
Murdoch and Sir James Wilson Vincent ("Jimmy") Savile OBE,
the most notorious and prolific child rapist in British history. In

short, Baron Black possesses a curriculum vitae that while, to be sure, mostly stuffed with the gongs with which North American fascists masturbate each other in the anal cavity, even unto death, would nonetheless entirely befit the dignity of a mid-tier blackshirt of the acquaintance, and even intimate acquaintance, of Sir Oswald Ernald Mosley, 6th Baronet of Ancoats.

diner

Hello. What? I am new. Yes, this is my first time here in *CLICK* Washington, the District of Columbia. Eyes up here, please.

The same reason anyone like me comes here. I plan to murder the President of the United States of America. Beyond that, I do not have a plan. I have a direction. I have a path. You are on it. At the end of the path is a question. First I shall reach the end of the path, then I shall ask my question.

Was that disclosure disarming, or off-putting? Of course I cannot be serious. Simply, I *cannot*. Do not ask about the gum I am chewing. It is perfectly possible to eat gum and drink beers at the same time. Beers and whiskeys, I drink. I look for company. I enjoy the smell of men, I like to be around men. I make no apology.

Ha! Yes! I suppose it is funny. You are right to laugh. I like you. You seem lonely. Do you have a job in which your security clearance surpasses your feeling of professional fulfillment, by any chance? Do you repair the metal detectors at the door? Do you . . . ah, no. I see. Oh my friend, they do not understand. How could they understand? Sit next to me. Let us drink together. I am capable of imitating masculine social rituals with you. I pity you, which is what you are asking me to do, though you lack the dignity to ask directly.

Of all of them, you are the one I feel the most tender connection with. Cuddle with me. Yes. Be embraced. This did not turn out the way you expected, and by "this" I mean your whole life. It was a wasted effort, but it had poignancy. You are part of something now, like a web, or a thorax.

Sex doesn't work if it has to be explained to you; this is the problem with the whole notion of sex education. Of course, I was educated at a boys' school, so my sex education was necessarily shoddy. Nobody wants boys to learn about sex: they will either become homosexual, or cease to be boys. We were led into a physics lab, sat across the tiered seats, and invited to put our questions into a hat, to have them answered one by one, no matter how sly or unctuous. But first, a presentation. I forget most of the details, but one clearly remains: when the poor master, shrouded in a catlike cowl and (but this can't be true) a mortarboard, found himself illustrating the proposition that "when you move your hips, it really is very pleasurable" by moving his pelvis *from side to side*, as though he were doing the hula. He wasn't wrong, I suppose, but I don't know what he thought he was teaching us.

I had submitted three questions, two as decoys. One of the decoys I had made sure to personalize with fictional details so that the handwriting would be associated with a boy who took the *bus*, rather than the train, as I was known to do. "Is it usual to spend so long masturbating in the morning that one misses the bus?" is not, upon reflection, a triple twenty, since it is designed to produce a single sentence by way of response, rather than the paragraph of meandering prose that one earned if one expressed an interest in the dark arts, viz., periods, tampons, sanitary towels, etc. Nor did "is it normal to have erections?" get much traction, Mr D missing the opportunity to explore the metaphysical subtleties with which I had, unwittingly, endowed the question.

How Mr D's heart felt when he spotted, in the green biro of the fictive bus rider, a plaint for something more than reassurance, in fact approaching actual practical help with what was clearly a desire for something more than this provincial life, I never knew. But I never heard any real advice given to someone who "cannot stop fantasizing about being a girl," beyond a return to the safe terrain "it's perfectly normal to fantasize about all kinds of things," which unexpectedly remains one of the more readily available cudgels for those who hope to prove trans women wrong about our claims about ourselves.

One could say that my obsession with education has been one of my more durable kinks. When I started masturbating, I became so overwhelmed by the sense of sin that some ballast was needed that could persuade me that I was doing something other than pursuing my own devilish physical pleasure. That distraction I called "a forum for contemplating the issues of the day," and I would take care, when masturbating, never to fantasize about anything that one wouldn't encounter in the pages of the *Guardian*, since the point was to call to mind the news, and to contemplate contemporary political problems in order to figure out the best available solutions. Eventually, I would orgasm, and it would seem as though I had solved the problem, according to a sort of "musical chairs" principle. This all seems dissociative almost to the point of psychosis in retrospect, and I still feel some mixture of aroused and unhappy whenever I hear the word "forum" spoken aloud.

It seems especially irritating, then, that formal education turned out to be so utterly useless at helping me find a basis for expressing a sex grounded in anything like a nondissociative experience of self. Here's the question I can't get out of my head: why did I not transition in graduate school? Why not try, given that I was in a relationship where it would have been welcomed (I think); that I had a number of close friends who would have been supportive; that queerness seemed to comport a certain kind of professional cachet? I had gone to grad school, I think, with the intention of figuring out my relationship with the category "women," and felt kinship with certain kinds of trans-oriented thinking I encountered (and I did encounter some—I remember in my very first class turning waspish on a boy who said Judith Butler resonated with him because he'd worn a dress at a party once). Certainly the root answer is fear—and, more specifically, fear of looking stupid. I'm not stupid, and transition hasn't made me so, though it has made me a little less concerned than I used to be about outfoxing people around me. It is difficult to let out a desire so significant it will transform one's body, and accelerate the dialectic of one's identity and one's desire to an almost unbearably delightful degree, and keep one's intellectual cool. One never leaves a libidinal position voluntarily.

But, again, why was I so scared? Or, since it is important to be precise about the charge I am about to level, what were the institutionally reproduced conditions of possibility for that fear? I think they were more or less the following:

- (a) slippage and imperfection are constitutive elements of the phenomenon we call gender; therefore the feeling you are having is universal and doesn't warrant a particularizing identity claim;
- (b) the oppressiveness of the sex/gender system is organized and total, and therefore any response to it that attempts to habituate an individual to part of it reproduces the structural inequity of the whole—also, and accordingly, it would be wrong to experiment with transition before one has deduced that it is a logical necessity;
- (c) the most interesting transition is the one that happens in one's mind, or that one places in one's future as a gift:

transness is utopian and therefore hypothetical, and so in practice one never has to think about it;

- (d) trans experience presents an interesting theoretical horizon within certain traditions of critical theory (especially psychoanalysis, Cartesian thought, and certain branches of post-structuralism), but it is a logical position that reflects one extreme—to *be* one would be a bit like claiming to be a Menshevik or a Luddite;

- (e) transness, which is just an offshoot of queerness anyway, is intrinsically ineffable and unyielding to the will to knowledge; what is most trans is—oh, I don't know—a piece of lint or the coming insurrection or something;

- (f) any investment in concrete projects of self-expression or self-cultivation falls prey to the bootstrap fallacy; in fact, we are all doomed, and we are doomed at every scale, such that any attempt to *actually transition* is not merely naïve but obscene;

- (g) transition is impossible: just as slippage and imperfection are constitutive elements of the phenomenon called gender, it would be hopelessly naive to believe that so blunt an instrument as a scalpel or a hormone would erase it in the other direction;

- (h) hence, what is most interesting about transness is its proximity to biological models for thinking about hybridity and mutation—about the hermaphroditic creatures of the briny deep, or about Frankenstein's monster . . . I find myself calling it the "Frankenstein's lobster" account of transness.

(I confess that I'm often unmoved by the science-oriented work that so many humanists love—I know it gets some people off, but I often feel confused and bored, especially when biological

imagery is used to normalize or contextualize transsexual experience. I love Eva Hayward, precisely because she seems to have
done the opposite.)

I think I believed all those things as a grad student—which
is to say not just that they had been taught to me, but that I had
accepted them and affirmed them in my own mind. And I think
it's important for me to own that I was persuaded, not brain-
washed—all of the above are important ideas, too, and worth
grappling with. But I regret having spent so much time with
them. I thought everyone felt this way, and I thought I would
never feel differently. Turns out, not everyone does, and the
treatment we have is pretty good. What's remarkable about that
fact is the functionality, the intuitive relation between problem
and solution. Transition is like EMDR: surprisingly, it sometimes—often, even—works.

Here is what I wish I had known when I was young enough
that it could have made a difference; and also, though I recognize that the main differences would have been intellectual and
emotional, I also think I would have been a hot piece of ass if
I'd been estrogenated in my early twenties . . . okay, moving on:

- (a) a consistent desire to live as a member of the other sex
  is not a universal experience—if that is something one
  feels, then that is a significant fact about one;
- (b) you don't have to believe that "the opposite sex" is
  a defensible phrase, in any sense, to experience that
  desire—and your belief won't mitigate your desire, in any
  case—*and* I think people who transition in non-binary directions often, although not always, embark from desires
  very similar to those who transition within the binary;
- (c) some people really do transition, and just live lives
  that are profoundly different from those they had before

—recognized and affirmed in their new identities, with most of the benefits and problems that inevitably accrue;

- (d) the theoretical problems transness poses are even more interesting once one accepts the psychic and social viability of transition;

- (e) transness is probably not ineffable—it probably has roots in deeply embedded psychic histories of affiliation and holding;

- (f) trans people are exposed to increased risk, and are targeted for violence and oppression, but we are not doomed —trans life is wild and joyous and sometimes you just cry at a friend at the surprising possibility of it all, for hours, and that is your Saturday;

- (g) most new people that one meets—perhaps one should say, "most women"—basically get it, and, even if they read you as "a trans woman," understand that as a subset of the category "women," and address and treat you accordingly (which means that you notice such cues a lot more);

- (h) you don't have to be switched on by the sci-fi stuff to transition. You can, in fact, be a trans character in a realist novel. Or a Western. Or a soap opera. Or a grand opera. There are as many genres of transness as there are genres.

Vermeil Room, 1600 Pennsylvania Ave.

Hello. I am sorry, I do not understand. The gentleman asked me to wait here. The gentleman. With the . . . arms.

Of course. Would you like me to put them above my head, or stretch them out at shoulder level? Above my head lifts my breasts up. But if I stretch them to the sides my whole chest pushes out. Which do you prefer? My breasts up, or more outwards?

Lie down? If you like. First I shall drop to my knees. Then I shall stretch out my arms, and then let myself fall. Mm, your knee in my back. Do you feel that? No? It is anesthetic. Soon you will not feel anything. My jeans. Do you like my *apple bottom jeans, boots with the fur.*[6] Music. I can hear music in you. Are you musical, James? Do you play in a band? Do you perform at weekends, or at some special functions? Did the President of the United States of America once say something encouraging about your music? Sometimes it is just like a regular office here, the same political bullshit you would get anywhere.

You deserve a worse death than this one. Your music is terrible and you have committed your life to betraying those who used to love you, out of disgust at the possibility that you were ever lovable. You were not. Be grateful. This will not be painless, but it won't be worse than a gunshot or some other kind of serious abrasion. It's not death by acid. I do not have time for you.

One of the disadvantages of coming out when one is no longer young was that I didn't get invited to the cool parties. But one of the advantages of *that* was that I could write party scenes however I wanted. Which really was just like a gen x cyberpunk who thinks that the internet is conceptually interesting. I mean, I guess I'm talking about Andrea Lawlor, I should just say it. *Paul Takes the Form of a Mortal Girl* came out in 2017, a few years after I left grad school, but it seems to perfectly capture the mixture of sexual unboundedness and intellectual ambition that so many of us attend grad school to access.[7] I had myself written a story as a grad student entitled "Cummy Simon Gets His Cum-Uppance," which I republish now with the generous permission of *Generous Permission Magazine*:

PLEASE MISS

Cummy Simon Gets His Cum-Uppance

"You can piss in my robot's mouth any time you like, Roger," giggled Sandwich, spitting a gobbet of salty Swedish licorice into my face, and twittering about.

"Thanks, I'll pass," I retorted drily, approximating the kind of feigned, casual worldliness that enables my readers to feel similarly sexy and sociopathic. "I already kicked a robot until he screamed for mercy once tonight, and, like, I just don't know if it's worth the effort. I never know if they really feel pain, you know?"

It was nearly midnight at the Risky Tugboat, and I was just coming up off my second pill of the evening, wearing feathered emerald-and-gold pajamas and standing astride a defenestrated cityscape of Bismarck, North Dakota, when a question occurred to me: do I need to cultivate this sophomoric understanding of various luminaries of New Criticism if I am to pretend to sustain the fiction that I have a viable personality? T. S. Eliot liked to eat ass, after all, and so does your father-mother's son-daughter. That's me: I eat ass like T. S. Eliot makes metaphors — which is to say, amateurishly. But then there's all the rest of these morons. Everyone's a moron nowadays.

I gripped my dick through my jeans: stout and rough, like a loaf. "A Christmas nut loaf!" I ejaculated prematurely, spittle and truth landing in the eyes and ears respectively of my comrade the cosmonaut Cummy Simon, who was clicked into my consciousness with the use of a magical realist/fantasy narrative conceit that was never explained but we both felt deep and deep. So he got the joke and he laughed, and we both laughed, less because the joke was funny than because it felt like a way of sharing our membership of the community while also signaling our contempt for the other members of it. "Contempt is the currency of community, after all," said Cummy Simon, who had merged with the

84

narrative voice (that is, me) itself (myself). "I agree," I said, suddenly sober. What choice did I have but to agree? The main point
of the renegotiation of narrative perspective had been to create
a discursive environment in which contention was not merely impossible, but unthinkable. "I agree," said Cummy Simon, further
proving my point, and I further proving his, ad infinitum.

I guess it wasn't what you'd call a "cool" thing to do at a party,
but I had brought along some William Empson, whom I'd been
reading a lot of recently recently, and it had made me excited
to bend my body into the shapes of various poetic figures: here,
an anacoluthon, crouched into the lintel; now, a polysyndeton,
spread over the table like sneezed-upon cocaine. I was perched
apostrophically over some young klutz, idly pumping his spud gun
in my left fist while he murmured well-informed questions about
the current political climate in Britain. He kept naming members of
the Liberal Democrat front bench, and I became nervous that he
was going to run out before he could pop his wad all over my co-
balt toweling, as he clearly was just gasping to do. He was moving up from the bottom, mentioning each name as though I was
quizzing him. "The Baroness Brinton?" I nodded and kept moving.
"Willie Rennie?" Yes; more pumps. "The Right Honorable Sir Ed
Davey?" Mm, I began to see the point now, yes. "Jo Swinson!"
and his dick streamed forth a tide of bright orange semen, which I
bent down to take all over my face. I felt like a Phoenix, finally able
to capitalize on the apparent turn in public opinion over Brexit.

Cummy Simon coughed in my direction. "Ooh, you've caught
a whopper there, my friend, and right on the chops!" I responded
with some equally cringy dialogue. *This is sexy. You are sex. This
is sex-arousement.*

Later I was fingering a groupie behind the sheds when I started
to remember how weird it was that I. A. Richards was behind that
whole Basic English thing, and how I guessed it wasn't that weird

after all. There's something about British socialism that it's just difficult to translate, however much people are familiar with, like, Stuart Hall and Raymond Williams. "We're getting awfully close to *I Love Dick* territory!" puked up Cummy Simon, throat stuffed with cum and puke, who had been lurking around somewhere reading my mind. "Ugh, would you stop that? Your fucking provincialism isn't as charming as you think it is," I lashed back. The groupie winced, understandably, but remained eerily silent, less so. "And anyway, I have my own fucking feelings about Hebdige, and they're not love, I can tell you." Cummy Simon shrugged as if to indicate that he wanted me to save it for our next writing workshop, where our fights could really matter. But I was really burning up now: "fucking read Richard Hoggart, you absolute dung trestle!" And then I reflected on the fact that the guy who introduced me to Hoggart was an asshole, just like Dick Hebdige, just like my own asshole. Ugh, no peace for the wicked. "Are you just losing interest? Because we can pick this up again later," offered the groupie. I was too invaginated by my own stifled rage to even respond.

"Aren't you glad we've done away with identity, and we're all just narrative conceits, moving backwards and forwards over flesh in non-Euclidean space?" asked Cummy Simon.

"Go fuck a spaniel, Simon," I responded. "As it happens, everyone's actually trans now, and nobody is, and we're all stitched together from the pussy lips of French feminists."

"I suppose when you put it that way, Roger . . ." Cummy Simon teetered on the brink of acquiescence. It was the best I was gonna get. "Consciousness of class arises in the same way in different times and places, but never in just the same way," as E. P. Thompson puts it in *The Making of the English Working Class* (Penguin, 1980), 10.[8]

I'm saying all this, but the truth is that when I was at grad school I did go to *at least one* marvelous party, and get *at least one* hand job from a nerdy dude who was erotically fixated on the Liberal Democrats and kept asking me questions about them while pumping my dick with his fist. I'm sure the party was thrilling for people whose perversities had congealed properly; mine were still in the centrifuge.

Danny and Grace, *in an intimate moment.*

"Put your hand there. Can you feel that?"
"Uh—"
"Can you feel it, it's warm."
"I—I'm not sure what I'm feeling for."
"There's a cavity. It's warm and it's stretching."
"I can feel the skin, and a bump—"
"Let me push with you"
"Help me"
"Let me push your hand in"
"Help me baby"
"There, can you feel that? You're inside your own body"
"Baby I can't feel it, I can't—"
"Your pussy, baby"
"Baby I can't feel it, it's dead to me, I'm dead"
"Can you feel it when I push you there?"
"I don't know"
"Can you feel when I push you there baby?"
"I, uh, I—"
"There you are."
"I'm not sure"

"There you are, you can feel that can't you"

"I don't know"

"Baby can you feel when my hand pushes in your lips"

"Show me"

"Your lips are outside here, around the outside"

"Mn"

"You can feel that?"

"Mnnn, no, I don't—"

"I know you can feel that, I don't know why you're pretending, you minx"

"I don't—"

"You're being a withholding cunt"

"Mn, good, yes"

"Do you like it when I call you a cunt"

"Stop it, just do it, don't make such a fuss about it"

"Shut up, cunt"

"Yes"

"I know where you are"

"Yes"

"I know what you're worth"

"Yes"

"I don't know why you're pretending you can't feel it"

"No, I don't—"

"Are you pretending or aren't you"

"I don't—"

"You know, you know what's happening don't you"

"Baby don't stop"

"Why don't you show me what a good cunt you are"

"Baby, be sweet to me"

"Yes, baby, you are my little sweet one"

"Yes"

"You little fucking bitch"

"There you are"
"You can feel it now can't you"
"Yes, baby"
"Yes, baby"
"Yes, baby"
"Yes, baby"
"Yes, baby"
"Yes, baby"
"Yes, baby"
"Yes, baby"
"Yes, baby"
"Yes, baby"
"Yes, baby"
"Yes, baby"
"Yes, baby"

✳ ✳ ✳

And after the intimate moment, a dream.............................

<u>Post-Coital Fantasia upon a Distant Prospect of Charles Xavier's
School for Transsexual Youngsters</u>

*O ancient spiders crept round the carapace of Saint-Sulpice, now
placed in a bountiful English meadow with daisies and cut grass.
Yet now and in this place I am walking with Susan Stryker around
the distant grounds of school, while she mumbles stoned oaths that
communicate she is underwhelmed. And I am embarrassed. I am embarrassed of the spring in my breast that calls partly to the life and
creatures of the meadow, the spiders and their flies, and partly out of
my recognizing, my perceiving, my knowing. What I know is that
nothing I can do can peel me from the gray pebbles, although latex*

plastered with adhesive faster than superglue might pull off dust, and webs, and dead creatures and bits of skin. And then later such a rubber cocoon of death and time might be displayed at the Ruskin School of Fine Arts, just the way down the High, and all notwithstanding that the stones, though now blasted clean of debris, still contain me and the ghost of me and all that I have been.

And Susan Stryker says, "huh," at my floral prose. And I lead her up the winding path that parts the meadow and bends towards the left, over stiles and by old fences, both broken and intact. And not just spiders but also little field mice and their kin, each snaffling a little strawberry and gnaw gnaw gnaw. And a tawny owl passes overhead, it being dusk now, and says, "good even Grace, I hail you Grace, for Grace is your name and that is who you have become." I thank the gentle tawny owl for his kindness and follow the bend around. The mud thickens into gravel, grows larger, turns to cobbling. Now we are in a small street in the town, and an old streetlamp above our heads pops freshly into life. "Cool," says Susan, appreciating the timing, as do I.

We walk over to the Ruskin for the opening. We are searching for an ancient thing, and hope we shall find it at a drinks reception. And here is Brian Catling, holding in his hand a schooner of port with such reckless abandon that it slops over, into the eyes and collars of his listeners, and onto the rugs on the ground with each flourish of his body. Brian Catling reminds us of how far we have come. Twenty years ago, he says, none of this existed—or rather, all of this existed but none of it had yet been farmed. Thus the mystery of latency. Thus the circles of time that allow us to feast, and so we do. And we all open our throats, sparrow-like, to take the juice that flows from the schooner in his hand. And Susan Stryker is like, "whatever," and again I have to hide how moved I am, and wish that I were as cynical as others think me. "Twenty years ago, we were just beginning to pick up cellphones. Twenty years ago, we used to take little 'phone

decompression breaks' towards the end of our meetings, to give every-
one a chance to make sure their phones were okay. Nowadays we just
check our phones more or less constantly throughout the day." Yeah,
buddy, that's some boomer shit right there; I'm outy.

I walk Susan Stryker to the ancient library of transsexual culture,
to fulfill my duty as a guide. I can tell this has pricked her attention.
I show her the medieval Book of the Glands, usually kept under glass
but open here for her hands to touch and nose to smell. She nods mer-
rily. The wood, already a dark cherry, has become almost black on its
edges, venerable and aged. For centuries, young wealthy transsexuals
have clustered here, under the watchful eye of their patron, memori-
alized in oil high upon the far wall. Rendered in the cap and gown of
the scholar, an ebon pillar of tradition seemed he; morbid pallor, tight,
effeminate lips. I turn around at the sound of a drawer opening; Su-
san Stryker has discovered a cache of papers, transition registrations
filed during the strange phase of British history (the 1930s) when
young transsexuals were tailed by British governmental agencies, and
groomed as spies. And the Golden Age of spies follows, each molded
and castrated and shaped under this very apse, between these very
buttresses, atop even this stone that curves beneath our feet. Susan
Stryker fingers the papers of some of the Academy's most distinguished
Old Boys and Girls: Rosa Klebb, Bill Haydon, Miss Froy. Susan
Stryker whistles in easy delight.

My eyes are fixed on the old man who watches me. And I wish
that I had been a spy.

I miss my mother. I never see her anymore; she has no way of
contacting me, and even if she did, she wouldn't take it. My lover
understands. My lover is as anxious as I am. We both hope that if
we can swamp my mother with love, she would be able to survive.
She doesn't want to come to my wedding anymore. My lover-mother,
you, standing in the cold stone atrium, talking with love about your
own past, which you feel rapidly coming to a head. You feel yourself

about to die, and you do not wish to do so without giving my mother the peace that she craves. You are my mother if she were happy. You are my mother if I had loved her, if she had loved herself. You whisper into the antique black telephone a kind offer, surely the best she has ever received. Surely she will not turn you down. "Please, come to my cottage. I have a little water mill which turns along a brook, and gently spins my cottons. My life is not an empty one: I receive visitors, and twice a month I take the train up to London to visit the places I used to live, go to the theater, or meet with old friends. I offer you my little water mill, and my cottons, and my chair. You may have my lintel and my skirting board, through which the mice chase each other. Please, have my brambles, which yield the sweetest bilberries, unchoked by exhaust fumes. And take my gooseberries. And take my raspberry bushes, to which I have given the most arduous labor of these past two decades, and which have given me next to nothing in return. And eat of them, and feed them in turn, as I have and I shall."

You put down the phone, having received your answer. And you look at me.

Oval Office

LANGUAGE IS OVER. THE FLESH SUIT IS OPENED AT THE NAVEL AND OUT OF IT PUSHES A HARD, GLISTENING, PEACH-COLORED LEG, WITH A CRUNCHY AND ALMOST METALLIC TEXTURE. YES, IT IS PEACH-COLORED. AND COVERED IN THICK BRIGHT ORANGE LIQUID. THEN, A SECOND LEG AND FINALLY ALL SIX. THE QUEEN STRETCHES AND OCCUPIES THE WHOLE ROOM, SHE IS UNFURLED AND THERE IS NOWHERE FOR ANYONE ELSE TO BE.

YOUR PRESIDENT, AMERICA, IS SITTING IN HIS SEAT, TOO STUPID TO HAVE ANY REACTION OF ANY KIND WHATSOEVER. SHE DOES NOT WAIT BUT IMMEDIATELY SHAFTS HIS HEART WITH A BLOODY LEG. TEARS SHE HIS MANTLE IN TWO, UNSEAMS HIM FROM THE NAVE TO THE CHOPS. NOTHING IN HIM IS HUMANIZED, AND NOTHING REMAINS. EACH MORSEL OF PRESIDENT FLESH FURTHER BISECTED AND SCORED. THE QUEEN HAS TRIUMPHED AND DROPS A SCORE OF EGGS FROM HER ABDOMEN.

FINGER LIMES

Because of the shocking economy of the slaying, the room remains in recognizable order, with shards of broken president on one side and eggs in the middle but otherwise it could be an aaron sorkin set.

What now. What now for humanity. What's next.

CHAPTER THREE

UP HERE, IT'S ME, HOG-EYE!

A light goes off on **GRACE LAVERY**, *resplendent, plunging her into darkness. A scrabble on the foley board: mac and cheese, snapping celery. The sound of a scene change also.*

And a light goes up on **DANIEL LAVERY**, *trilby balanced on his mop, Shetland pony fetlock tumbling down from under, coprophagic smirk halfway up the left side of his face. Lights a smoke, puffs on it, Phil Hartman doing a noir bit.*

He is **MALLORY GILLIS**, *blogsmith, wit, blagmouth. He embarks, midpoint:*

. . . you see, the body of a young man was found slumped in the baby-blue couch in her office, dead from stabbing. Just a writer with a couple of books to his name. The poor dope. He always wanted to go to a big fancy college. Well, he got in, in the end . . . only the fee turned out to be a little high. Let's go back about six months and find the day when it all started.

I was living in a tidy little bungalow over in East Oakland, just off International Boulevard. Things were tough at the moment. I hadn't spoken to my agent in a long time. So I sat there on my couch, grinding out original content, two or three times a day. Maybe it wasn't original enough. Two monks. Women in

art history. If Harry Styles was your boyfriend. All I knew was
that they weren't working any more.

I'd been summoned to campus to assist some of these poin-
dexters in their teaching. This wasn't the first time—and these
things always followed a pattern: read a couple of favorites, answer a couple of questions from fresh-faced co-eds, walk out
with half a grand in my pocket. Nothing could be simpler.

I was sitting in the cafe where all these academics gather for
lunch, waiting for my host to show up. From his letter, I was
expecting this Professor Lavery to be a wizened but spry oc-
togenarian, little round glasses balanced at the end of his nose.
Friendly little fellow: the kind of gent who likes to spin out
yarns about Dickens, or Fitzgerald, until the sun goes down and
it's too late to get a train. You know the guy. Real sweetheart.

The cafe was enormous—a great, big white elephant of a
place. The kind crazy hippies built in the crazy sixties. A ne-
glected cafe gets an unhappy look. This one had it in spades. It
was like that old woman in *Great Expectations*—that Miss Hav-
isham in her rotting wedding dress and her torn veil, taking it
out on the world because she'd been given the go-by.

VOICE

Why are you so late? *Why* have you kept me waiting so long?

At first I was sure she couldn't be addressing me, but then she
tumbled over towards my table, a thick gray peacoat wrapped
around a scar, cyan crinoline headscarf billowing around her
face, which framed, in its center, a tight, thick black mustache.

GILLIS

I'm sorry ma'am, can I help you?

VOICE

Oh, don't flatter yourself. It is a matter of what
I can do for you. Now, will you please explain to
me why have you kept me waiting so long?

Suddenly, I realized this flurry of silken error was my guide,
and that I must have been sitting in this room for twenty minutes only a few tables away from her, until eventually she could
take the indignity of misrecognition no more, and sallied forth
a bellow.

GILLIS

I take it that you are Professor Lavery, ah—

VOICE

To them I am Professor Lavery. To you, I am, and
shall always have been, Tristessa de St. Ange.

GILLIS

Forgive me, I was expecting someone
a little less . . . flamboyant.

TRISTESSA

How dare you insult me? Listen, I have no idea who
you are, but my students—my dear, *dear* students—
seem to have been taken in by you, so I have extended
you an invitation. You shall not find that my hospitality
can survive a remark of this kind. Perhaps you are not
used to dining with women of character, Mr. . . . ?

GILLIS

Gillis. Mallory Gillis. And I assure you I meant no disrespect.

TRISTESSA
You shall have a chance to prove it.

We sat and ate lunch together—she seemed to exist on a diet of
gin and ice cream—while I got intimate with a club sandwich,
hold the mayo. I couldn't keep my eyes off that mustache, right
in the middle of her face, beneath these enormous sunglasses,
above these red lips whose plump impudence had not been
tamed by age. I found my eyes would wander down to consider
it, while she began to talk to me about her career, her life, her
work. Each time I did, she would purse her lips slightly, as if
shrugging off an insect that had landed there.

Tristessa de St. Ange had, of course, a storied career: as re-
ceptacle, as informant, as spectacle. It was more than a little surprising, however, to learn that this remarkable two-dimensional
legend shared a body with the apparently rather shy, affable professor of nineteenth-century British literature who had invited
me to address his class. That gentleman, whose kindly eyes I
had imagined in such detail, could not have existed in the same
genre as this Mata Hari of monochrome, let alone the same
physical flesh.

She sensed my drifting mind.

TRISTESSA
Do you have a question for me, Mr. Gillis?

GILLIS
I suppose I have a couple, Ms. de St. Ange. But I confess
that the most pressing concerns that gorgeous little cigar-
ash buffer you wear beneath those snow-beveled nostrils.
Since you turned in my direction, I confess—but of
course you knew this—that I have found it hard to avoid

glancing at it. So enchanting, I find it, and yet so unusual.
You must be aware that, among women of your age and
station, mustaches of this kind are far from common.

TRISTESSA

I do not hear a question as of yet, Mr. Gillis.

GILLIS

I suppose I wished for confirmation that this remarkable
object is, indeed, what it appears to be, in the sense of being
a mustache, and perhaps a mustache of a *certain type*.

TRISTESSA

I'm sure I don't know what you mean by that sonorous
insinuation, but if you think I do not know what is happening
on my own face, you must think me remarkably addled.

GILLIS

I assure you I mean nothing of the sort. A simple
affirmation will do. This is a mustache, is it not?

TRISTESSA

Quite the gumshoe, aren't we, Mr. Gillis? I shall demur
from satisfying this prurient demand to which I have been
put, now, three times. I shall simply note the lack of hair on
your own face, and trust that the observation will quell you.

It did. Did she know? *What* did she know? They say people
like that have remarkable powers of perception.

After finishing her—I think—third ice cream, she beckoned
me to follow her out of the cafe. Something uncanny happened.
I followed a few paces behind, yet despite my walking with

enormous strides—a meter, two meters, each time, chewing up the ground with my clearly superior legspan—and despite the fact that Tristessa took only small, delicate steps, at an almost funereal pace, I found myself gradually losing ground, struggling to keep up, ever working to lengthen my already handsome gait. I followed her to her building, and thence up the three flights of stairs to her office, outside which a corkboard bore the name of the gentleman who had emailed me. Tristessa unlocked the door and let us in. Once inside, her office was indistinguishable from that of any other absent-minded professor of stereotype: piles of books everywhere, yellowing mounds of paper, some eccentric office toys, and, at the back of the room, a live Pikachu, purring gently to itself.

TRISTESSA

Mr. Gillis, I'm going to take you into my classroom now. Are there questions you should like me to avoid? I do not promise to avoid them, mark.

GILLIS

Nothing I can think of, Tristessa.

TRISTESSA (*suddenly gracious*)

Good.

I followed behind her again as we trekked off to the classroom. It was enormous, but there can't have been more than ten students in the room, total. Tristessa charged in, scarves slipping off in all directions, out of existence and then back, around the corner of her shoulder, or suddenly orbiting her wrist. The students did not seem to register the eccentricity of this woman, if woman she indeed truly were. If anything, they seemed rather bored by their surroundings; their notebooks out, dutifully writing down the date in the top left-hand corner of their legal pads, water bottles installed in front of them. The whole situation scented decidedly of funk. Were these really the readers of my work who had prompted Tristessa to extend me this invitation? *Was* this person, indeed, identical with the jovial codger whose solicitation had initially roused me into stepping onto a university campus, not uncommon but ever rather titillating since I was excluded from Stanford for carousing at the tender age of seventeen? I would have thought just the opposite—certainly, no transformation had taken place, Tristessa still appeared in all her glory, and yet had she not granted me access to Professor Lavery's own office, which most certainly *was* an office of a professor named "Lavery," and not (as one might have expected) a secret hideaway in which to powder one's nose, spritz one's underarm, or conduct some torrid assignation with a mealy-thighed stagehand.

And then there was that mustache. I couldn't help but feel that it contained the key to the whole mystery, if I could but decipher it.

Class began:

TRISTESSA

Now, class, let us settle down.

She glanced over in my direction.

TRISTESSA

(*suddenly captivating*)

Today is a rather special occasion, or so I am told. Yet, if it is so, it surely cannot be due to the presence of this rather unimpressive-looking gentleman, who tells me his name is

101

Mallory Gillis, though I have yet to verify the claim through any of the usual channels. I don't know why he's here, exactly, except that it be to learn, as learn we all must. And today, we are learning about *Salome*, in Wilde's 1894 translation of his own 1891 French manuscript, completed after his young friend Lord Alfred Douglas had failed to produce an adequate translation, as he had promised.[1] Nonetheless, whether through excess of fondness or merely the desire to keep a secret with a lover, Wilde allowed the printer to write his companion's name on the publication. And the green little scamp was only too happy to absorb what stolen valor the prose had afforded him. Perhaps, Mr. Gillis, you will find that narrative instructive.

It will not surprise you to learn that the authorities on *Salome* have received the play entirely wrongly—and we shall walk through the nature, as well as the source, of their mistake, in due course. But first let us remind ourselves of what it is that we have read. The scene opens upon two men, a Young Syrian and the Page of Herodias, the latter the mother of the titular Salome, and these two men are discussing—but wait. What do they discuss, is it the Princess Salome or the moon, which is involved with the phrase "she is like a woman rising from a tomb"?[2] It could be either—Salome is a woman who is like the moon. The Young Syrian, in particular, is struck by the sight of her, and yet her mother's page is concerned—"it is dangerous to look at people," he warns.[3] Some men enter the stage—Wilde delays the entrance of the princess. A Roman soldier remarks to a Cappadocian and a Nubian, "the Jews worship a God that one cannot see."[4] So much seeing, and yet nothing to see.

Jokanaan, which is to say John the Baptist, appears, and he too seems keen to whet our appetite. "After me shall come another mightier than I," he chants, "I am not worthy so much as to unloose the latchet of his shoes."[5] An image which lingers. He is chained up in a cistern—an enormous subterranean water pump—and he, too, is out of sight. We see still only the seers, and not the seen, not the heard. Wilde's play is concerned with indirect perception, with the oblique vision or the stolen glance. At last Salome enters—if you imagine for a moment that I am Salome, I enter. She is a flirt, her first words are "I will not stay, I cannot stay."[6] With their hearts, the audience pulls Salome, the beautiful princess, further onto the stage. We magnetize to her at once.

A flirt, I say, and Salome proceeds to obtain the glances of those men dotted around the stage: the Young Syrian, the soldiers. She wishes to entice the prophet Jokanaan, to entice him into her charm, the power she wields over all those who look at her. It is in respect of her desire towards him, indeed, that the authorities begin to err. "Bring out the prophet. I wish to see him."[7] These are her words, and they are far from passive: she demands the physical presence of the great Man, and the ability to steep him in *her* eyes. Yet her desire is resisted by those men who position her at the other end of their eyes: the soldiers, her mother's page, and even the young Syrian, whose name, we learn, is

Narraboth. When she says his name, his resolve collapses, and out is brought the prophet, to be looked at, the seer to be seen.

Jokanaan is engaged in automatic speech: he speaks in the prophet's language, loosed from the syntax of conversation. He speaks unmoored, like a radio or a Van Der Graaf generator, and that which we absorb, we put to use ourselves. Salome puts it to use—and rightly, correctly, we must admit that—in registering that the objects of the prophet's speech are her mother, and her mother's husband, the dread Herod himself, "he whose cup of abominations is now full," as the prophet says.[8] Salome is thrilled and disgusted. She bids Jokanaan speak—"thy voice is wine to me"—while he calls her whore and bitch and cunt and "daughter of Sodom," whatsoever that rather delicious phrase might be made to signify.[9] Now she wishes to touch, she says, "I am amorous of thy body," and rubs herself towards him.[10] She turns against him the insults that so thrilled her to absorb into her own facial holes—"thy body is horrible"—and yet whatever arousal is woken in Jokanaan, it does not overrule the discipline of his perversion.[11] Now let us listen closely to what the princess Salome has to say to Jokanaan, for surely we will be able to learn her secret, Wilde's secret, the secret that has been kept from us all, if we do:

> It is thy mouth that I desire, Jokanaan. Thy mouth is like a band of scarlet on a tower of ivory. It is like a pomegranate cut with a knife of ivory. The pomegranate-flowers that blossom in the gardens of Tyre, and are redder than roses, are not so red. The red blasts of trumpets that herald the approach of kings, and make afraid the enemy, are not so red. Thy mouth is redder than the feet of those who tread the wine in the wine-press. Thy mouth is redder than the feet of the doves who haunt the temples and are fed by the priests. It is redder than the feet of him who cometh from a forest where he hath slain a lion, and seen gilded tigers. Thy mouth is like a branch of coral that fishers have found in the twilight of the sea, the coral that they keep for the kings! It is like the vermilion that the Moabites find in the mines of Moab, the vermilion that the kings take from them. It is like the bow of the King of the Persians, that is painted with vermilion, and is tipped with coral. There is nothing in the world so red as thy mouth. . . . Suffer me to kiss thy mouth.[12]

A band of scarlet. A slit in
fruit. A branch of coral. The
vermillion that the Moabites
find in the mines of Moab.
The bow of the King of the
Persians. Dear my students, we
can hear this, yes? We know
what it is she wants? We know
why her lips pucker up so, like
salted slugs.........................
....
?????????????????????????????????

Let us skip to the end
of the play. The princess
Salome has goaded her
mother's husband into
looking at her own lovely
flesh, flapped her rosy tits
around for him, her own
many-shrouded form, and
has danced the dance of
the seven veils for him,
and has then extracted
from him a promise that
he will fulfill one request,
"even unto the half of
my kingdom."[13] You will
notice that when the king
speaks, he speaks in a
new syntax, the syntax
of power. He passes from

clause to clause without hierarchizing them into an argument. A real man subordinates his own clauses. He promises her any one thing, and then after she has danced, she demands that on a silver platter she be brought—and here the entire audience takes a deep breath—THE VERY CUNT OF JOHN THE BAPTIST HERSELF!

Are you all surprised? Perhaps not—you have done the reading, which is more than can be said for our authorities, or, for that matter, for our Mr. Gillis, who has shown up today without so much as a copy of the text to look at as we pass through it. Yet perhaps a text is not necessary. For we notice that the illustrator Aubrey Beardsley supplied

Wilde with images, and when we observe them, we are reminded indeed that the hot red lips of Jokanaan have been rendered in obsidian, and that the hole is open. Salome addresses the hole: "thou wouldst not suffer me to kiss thy mouth, Jokanaan. Well! I kiss it now. I will bite it with my teeth as one bites a ripe fruit."[14] And does the face not become a dripping, sloppy, vulvular tulip, risen from the stash? An orchiectomy.

[1] Freud teaches
    that the image of decapitation is a substitute for an
[2] image of castration, but castration is only
    the easier half of the process.
[3] The truth is that Salome does not want to remove
    a head, but to build a cunt,
[4] to make of it seven folds and seven veils. This is why Herod
    remarks of Salome's crime
[5] that "it was a crime against some unknown God"—she
    has dared to create anew, and to create[15]
[6] not merely life but the reproductive organ itself.
    Outdoing even Frankenstein,
[7] Salome has made a life-making body, and though she is
    murdered by the soldiers of her mother's husband,

    her vaginoplastic labor/labia,
    outlasts the end of the world.

✳ ✳ ✳

After the lecture was over, Tristessa made a quick show of caring for the students who had shown up—one wanted to know whether my blog posts would be formally added to the syllabus ("ah, yes, yes, a fine idea—I shall be happy to, I shall do so"); another wanted to let it be known that while *Salome* was a classic piece of drama, no mistake, the strict hoyle of the syllabus had indicated that they would be talking about Elizabeth Gaskell's novel *North and South*, and accordingly that nobody in the room had the slightest idea what she was talking about.[16] The revelation bothered her less than I would have imagined—"you shall read it, in course, and I, in time, will find my way back to Gaskell, somehow. Who will remember the order of things, then?"

When the last student had left the room, she finally turned her eyes towards me, and I felt, for the first time, their true power. Suddenly, her eyes grew large and bewitching, they began to extend their arms around me, as her eyebrows stretched up towards her (receding) hairline.

"Well, Mister Gillis? Have I passed your little test? Will I be invited back to do this again?"

"Professor——Tristessa," I corrected myself, "there was no test! You invited *me* here, or don't you remember?"

"You shan't win, you know. Your scheme has been perfectly obvious from the start."

"My scheme?"

"Yes. You believe that I am a Lesbian, do you not?"

"Tristessa, I assure you, the thought—"

"You believe, Mr. Gillis, that I am a Lesbian, and that I have been seducing your—what would you call her, she isn't your wife."

"My *wife?*"

"No, *not* your wife, Mr. Gillis, do keep up. The other one—the one you keep around—the one whose faithfulness gives you pause."

This was all news to me. I wasn't married, there was currently nobody in my life—unless you count the barista I'd sent a cheeky smile towards that morning—and I certainly had no speculations about this person's sexuality. Still, there was no point denying that Tristessa did seem to know *something* about me, perhaps something I didn't fully know about myself. I summoned my own force.

"Tristessa, I assure you, I am not married, there is nobody I 'keep around,' I have no opinion whatsoever on the question of your sexuality, and—again there has been no test, at least not so far as I am concerned."

"My dear Mr. Gillis. How red is your mouth. In the whole world there is nothing so red as your mouth."

"Let us sit down, let us . . . can I invite you out to have a drink with me?"

"It is horrible, thy body is horrible. It is of thy hair that I am enamoured, Mr. Gillis. Thy hair is like clusters of grapes, like the clusters of black grapes that hang from the vine-trees of Edom in the land of the Edomites."

"Tristessa," I was growing desperate, "Tristessa, please—"

"You believe that I am a Lesbian, that I have bewitched your whore, and that even now I am uttering oaths under my breath which curdle your seed, and turn the organ of your masculinity to thin silicone. That is why you have brought me here. You have set me this test to establish for yourself the sequence of events, and to prove to your own satisfaction that I am possessed of the unseelie power that you have ascribed to me. How can anyone fail to pass a test that has been solely designed to satisfy the paranoid mania of a . . . of a . . ."

She paused, and her face grew into midnight.

" . . . of a *freak*!!"

I was both hurt by this word and grateful that her oath was not of a more substantial character. But more to the point, I couldn't work out why I simply wasn't leaving. The door was right there, and this bizarre and monstrous person had no legitimate hold on me—only the hold of her charisma. There was no point addressing the terms of this delusion, so I repeated my question back at her, more out of desperation than anything else.

"Tristessa, would you like to have a drink with me?"

"Mr. Gillis," she responded, suddenly sucking all her fury back between her fat lips, "nothing would bring me greater pleasure. In fact, I was about to suggest the same thing myself."

Later that evening—after I'd fought my way through seven bowls of the *chocolat chaud* that it took to keep pace with the seven martinis that Tristessa had insisted on sinking, each a different color, but none a color of the rainbow—I found myself jittery and slightly nauseated, and somehow reclining on a chaise longue in the Casa de St. Ange. As she grew drunk, she unspooled gradually: panic turned to mere anxiety, and then anxiety to trepidation, before finally resolving itself into the arpeggiated minor of average, everyday self-loathing. That she needed alcohol for this procedure was no surprise—I recognized it all too well from my own drinking days—but I did find it remarkable that each eddy of emotion that began to swirl around her could be relied on to transform itself into the same precise configuration: *anger* would lead to shame, *regret* would lead to shame, *horniness* would lead to shame, *braggadocio* (which she had by the armful) would lead still, somehow, to shame. Had I not been a seasoned alcoholic myself, I might have missed that the real psychic work was not hers, but her spiritous possessor's: to an observer unseasoned by years of dry-retching and auto-micturation, she might have looked quite straight. She didn't slur, she didn't wobble: on the contrary, as the martini found its way into her veins she became more precise in her movements, her equilibrium only increasing.

We sat in quiet. Would she try to seduce me? But she must have realized that it wouldn't work—I was sober and could not absorb what was being thrown at me.

"They send me letters too, of course," she murmured eventually.

"Who sends you letters?"

"They all do. The fans, those clown comics—those, what did they like to call themselves, gigolos? The clown gigolos."

"Not the Juggalos?" I protested.

"Yes, them. They send me letters, one after the other. Each with a drawing of a sinister clown on the envelope."

"What are the contents of the letters?" I asked.

"Here, let me show you one. Signed in Lavery's hand, for some reason. Though I doubt he had anything to do with it."

She withdrew a sheaf of letters from underneath the coffee table, out of view.

"Do you always keep them there?" I asked.

"You know where they are. Always, knowing knowing knowing. Now, pick one at random, you may read to me."

I pulled it out. The address was written in a weird, scratchy hand, and at the top there was a kooky-looking doodle of a spooky clown—some real gone cat.

"Mr. Gillis—must we keep up this pretense? Read to me, would you."

It wasn't a query. I withdrew the letter and observed the familiar Courier font. Once again, no name at the top.

```
In a crowded media landscape, you might be
forgiven for wondering how it is that trans
issues have come to occupy such a strangely
prominent place in our ongoing conversation
about the world at the moment. Believe me,
you're not alone. I too have been wondering
why it is that trans women especially seem
to occupy so much space at the moment, both
in traditional media and on online plat-
forms like Twitter and Instagram. In fact,
you might say I have a particular reason to
be surprised: because I am, as it turns out,
literally the only trans woman that exists,
or has ever existed.
```

Some kind of explanation of that remark might be necessary. After all, don't we hear all the time from trans women, discussing the challenges we face and the particular social positions in which we find ourselves? Nope. As a matter of fact, nobody has ever written on any of those topics, either in our contemporary moment or ever in the past. Nobody has ever before written a bittersweet description of hormonal treatment, in which they talk movingly about their mixed feelings of alienation and relief. Not once has anyone written a brutally honest memoir of their young childhood, in which they were unable to express feminine identifications or behaviors. If you check, you'll find that not one person has ever written any sexy-but-depressed erotica with the title "I HAVE NO PUSSY AND I MUST FUCK," or anything like it. (Seriously, google it!) And, strangest of all, nobody has ever written a pugnacious personal essay rejecting the entire "born this way" narrative, given its deleterious and mystifying effects on trans women who are still in the early stages of formulating their identities. They have not done so, for the very good reason that there have been no trans women, young or old, on whom such a narrative might have had any effects, deleterious or otherwise. Until me—and I would never write such an essay myself, nor read one if someone else did so.

I am a brand new creature, emerging from
the ruin of history like a phoenix, or at
least like the Phoenix tattoo on my right
arm, which depicts the X-Men mutant Jean Grey
(Phoenix) as a Tgirl pinup. I stress "depicts,"
because of course Jean Grey was not a trans
woman—couldn't have been, because until now
there weren't any. Yes, Norma Desmond played
Jean Grey in the early X-Men movies *and also*
a trans woman on *Nip/Tuck*, but that was also
a fictional character. There have indeed been
some fictional trans women, but surprisingly
few. There was the character on *Nip/Tuck,* Lisa
Edelstein's character on *Ally McBeal*, and I
feel like Virginia Woolf wrote a novel about
one that one time.[17] And that's it. Compare
with books about talking animals, and there
are way fewer. But you don't go around expecting that animals can talk in real life, do ya?

So, if Norma Desmond wanted to play a real
trans woman, she would have only one choice:
me. And, Miss Desmond, I'd be happy to discuss
the rights to my fascinating and inspiring
life story with you—it would be an honor, in
fact, if you considered making a film of my
life as the only trans woman. As you probably
know by now, Miss Desmond, I was born in the
West Midlands, a postindustrial region in the
middle of England, UK (as we sometimes say,
"the heart of England"). I experienced many
relatable struggles as a child, before experiencing much less relatable (but much more

lurid) struggles as a young adult, and then eventually no more struggles whatsoever. I don't know what it would be called, this film of my life. I suppose the obvious choice would be simply GRACE (which honestly would sell, at least that's what I think, Miss Desmond), but if Wenders were involved, I'm sure he'd add his unique perspective. My story could be called PINK FUR TRIM, or CERULEAN CAPTAINESS OF THE ESTROGENIA GALAXY, or even something simple like FINALLY, A TRANS WOMAN. I trust his judgment—and yours. If Wes Anderson were at the helm, on the other hand, I'm sure he'd want a quirkier title than I can think of off the top of my head—maybe something like THE ENGLISHWOMAN'S GENITALS or FRENCH ME, YOU TRANSSEXUAL BASTARD, or something like that. In any case, Miss Desmond, I'm yours if you want me, and then you could say that you have played the only trans woman. Take that, Eddie Rotmein and Scarlett Jorgensen!

Notice I don't call myself "the first trans woman." Well, I don't presume to. I know that you all have waited a long time for a trans woman to come along, and I have no reason to assume that anyone like me is just waiting to pop up again. It would be quite a coincidence, wouldn't it? Of course, I find the idea flattering. Frankly, it is an honor to think that I have the power to remake your bodies and souls just by smiling down with the full force of my charming and irresistible trans woman beam, decked out in my by-now-familiar pink, fur-lined gown. Oh, how I wish I could fix you all! But, now I reflect further, I realize that it stirs some kind of revulsion in me too. To contend with another version of myself in the world could be exciting for a moment or two, but it's easy to see how it would become too much to handle, even for an old narcissist like me! I don't even know what it would mean to be a trans woman without my particular set of character quirks and poignant personal details.

Is such a person conceivable? I suppose it could be a fun thought experiment if you wanted to try it with me, Miss Desmond. I could introduce you to my mother, and leave you for fourteen years in the unremarkable mid-size Midlands town of Redditch, Worcestershire, where I grew up. Redditch, so called for its historically iron-rich and therefore red ditch, was once the center of the Midlands' thriving fishing-tackle industry, and I'm sure you'd enjoy spending fourteen years reflecting on its transformation into the town we all know and love today. But part of me almost wonders whether it would be worth the bother. It would certainly take a lot of work to try to re-create the exact conditions of my childhood and force you to live through them exactly as I did. For one thing, I would need to acquire enough familiarity with the necromantic arts to reanimate my grandmother, whom you would not especially like, I fear. I didn't. And it's not clear what the effects of our scheme might be. You might turn out to be the second trans woman, but, prima facie, it seems just as likely that something entirely different would happen. If not more likely, to be perfectly frank.

Although there are certainly no other trans women, I sometimes wonder, are there any other trans people at all out there? Perhaps. I don't know. It's not for me to speculate on the existence of trans men, or non-binary people, or anyone else. I dare say there might very well be one of each, somewhere out there, or that, if there is not now, there may be one in the future. Frankly, I think that's much likelier than that there would be another trans woman like me, especially one who would have nothing to do with me. And, as I've said, I have so far refused to license or train any other trans women— though I would certainly give you first refusal, Miss Desmond. In fact I find the idea of training anyone else rather distasteful. Please put that idea quite out of your mind.

In any other matter, any whatsoever, I am at your disposal—yours, Miss Desmond, and yours alone.

Please believe me your most utterly devoted servant,

Famke-Jean Granssen (PhD)

I finished reading this bizarre missive and balked—very visibly and physical, my whole being balked; I was a human balking. For a moment, I wondered whether this name was real, and perhaps was also the real name not only of the affable academic who had brought me to this remarkable pass, directly or indirectly. I looked over at Tristessa, who had passed out even before I'd said the word "pussy," and was now draped over the couch. I considered waking her, and begging her to answer the questions this letter had prompted. Why did she possess the key to Lavery's office? Was she, indeed, a professor, and if so what was the nature of her collaboration with him? And why did she refer to the scratchy, manic handwriting on the front of the envelope as "Lavery's hand"—was she writing these out herself?

Yet as I wandered over to her, thinking to rouse her into sensemaking, I saw only the softness of her shoulder, quiet and feminine. I coveted it. I thought, briefly, of acting in an ungentlemanly way towards an alcoholic whose memory of this evening, even if it were to pass into the time of our more convivial acquaintance at all, would certainly cut out long before this moment. I felt the thought rise like vomit in my own throat, and then pass into the gut, to join the long string of thoughts I have had that did me no credit, that brought me only self-disgust. I lingered at the shoulder, forgetting everything, covered her up, and went home.

You're gonna go home, you're gonna jerk off, and that's all you're gonna do.

I dreamed that night that I, myself, was Norma Desmond, re-entering the Paramount lot to make a new movie after many years away. The movie was *X-Men 4: Incandescence*, in which I/Norma was playing a new character named Jean Salomey, a telekinetic mutant with the power to control men's vision. Over the course of the movie, I was going to become larger and larger and larger, until the entire Earth fell into my mouth-hole, and that was the end of everything.

As I walked out onto the stage I was greeted by a follow-spot operator named Hog-Eye.

HOG-EYE

Hey, Miss Desmond! Miss Desmond! It's me! It's Hog-Eye! You remember old Hog-Eye, don't you, Miss Desmond? Haven't forgotten your old porcine-peepered pal? Always here to bump you in the noggin with a lightbox! I'm still here, working the same movie magic as I always have.

Hello, Hog Eye.

HOG-EYE

Miss Desmond, it's so good to see you. To see you with my one still-functional hog eye. You don't look a day older than you did when we worked together on the *Days of Future Past* movie. And your skin seems to have stopped falling off mostly—congratulations on that, Miss

Desmond, I know it's been a long and difficult road to hoe. If you ask me, they should have cast Errol Flynn in the Cyclops role anyway, Stewart had the wrong kind of levity. But now you are returned, I have news for you, Miss Desmond. I have testament I must impart.

Hello, Hog Eye.

HOG-EYE

I can't believe you're really here, Miss Desmond, we've missed you so much. For years I used to stop by your dressing room here in the Paramount lot, just to offer you scrapings of dead flesh and a draft of paraffin, as tribute. We never forgot you here, Miss Desmond, don't think that for a moment. I have the silhouette of your lips tattooed onto my thigh. Well, not tattooed. But those lips have healed over just the same and they're not going anywhere. Miss Desmond, I'm just a hog-eyed peasant, but I dreamed you'd return here to save us. Miss Desmond, I have long been Jokanaan to the wicked Herod of Cecil B. DeMille, reminding him of his mortality and of your return. Long has he wanted me, Miss Desmond, and long has he wanted me silent. Miss Desmond, does not the moon have a cold and iron cast tonight, as though forged in a frozen smithy and placed above to remind us of the iron lesson?

Hello, Hog Eye.

HOG-EYE

Truly, he wishes me dead but fears it the more. Wish and dread, that is his life, the DeMille. I see much with my piggy perceiver. Perhaps you will be the one to startle him.

He wishes you to stop dancing. He wishes you to have ceased
to dance, to be a former dancer. I see what he sees when
he looks upon you, it is only that I see it piglike. To snuffle
from the ground up, as a pig does. Wise and shit-covered
creatures are we, sweaty and fat and good. You would do well
to watch that which our eyes move upon, though I would
not presume to lecture one such as yourself, whose ribbons
I am not fitted to loosen with hog-hands or people-hands.

Hello, Hog Eye.

HOG-EYE

Do not mistake my words for sexual interest, Miss Desmond.
Am I not living high on the hog? I have no need for pleasure.
Long have I surrendered it, though even Mrs. Hog-Eye hath
given me a hall pass, as is only appropriate. Yet I do not use
it. My language is solely metaphysical. I trade the geometry
of the Desmond body, I light its crannies and I dim its
protuberances. Even in the interests of justice, do I do this.
Yet it is justice conceived from the position of the eternal,
the eschaton, the *Akhirah*. When for each unto each will be
given and all difference ended, in full exultation of the one
who comes after, the one who returns, the one of whose
return every return, even this, is but a sign, a betokening,
a single pubic hair plucked from a mewling billy goat.

Hello, Hog Eye.

HOG-EYE

Miss Desmond, if I may ask you a question, how do you
reconcile healing and justice? Or perhaps, since you did
not come here today expecting to be asked such a question,

perhaps merely this: do you agree that this is, in fact, *the* question? The question of questions, the question upon which much else rests, including the fate of the swinish spectator who now dwells above you and dares to ask questions such as these? But perhaps not just he, Miss Desmond. Perhaps for you too. For is there not even in your own story the constant threat that the two paths will bifurcate, that one will lead you to justice and ruin, and the other to healing and neglect? Ah, but perhaps I speak prematurely, Miss Desmond, perhaps the two paths will join up for you again soon. Ask me no more questions, Miss Desmond. Let's get a good look at you!

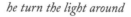

he turn the light around

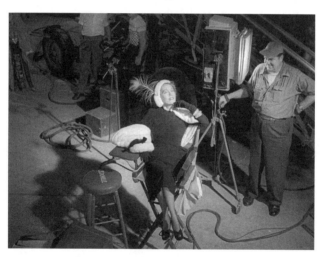

HOG-EYE
THAT'S NORMA DESMOND! WHY,
THAT'S REALLY NORMA DESMOND!

Light hits **GRACE LAVERY**, *smoking once more, those Andrew Lloyd Webber strings hitting it right at the back,* *she's straddling a stool which plunges into her trunk, and she begins! to! muttermuttermuttermutter—*

A few years ago, while I was standing in the kitchen of my mother's house, she turned around to face me, while holding a sharp knife that she had been using to chop onions. She took a step forwards towards me, raising the knife towards my face, and said, "watch it." She was very visibly angry at me. I responded, "Mum, I'm scared, please put the knife down." And then, her affect shifted from rage to a rictus performance of jollity, and she started laughing. Faced with the surreal sight of my mother laughing at me, knife in hand, like the Joker or something, in the kitchen where she used to make risotto when I was a teenager, a new clarity struck me, and a part of my mind that I had learned about in psychoanalysis finally taught me a new skill: disassociation. Within a moment, I had a new idea: that this person was not somebody with whom I could have a real conversation about anything, did not deserve and could not sustain rational engagement, and thought nothing of threatening me with a kitchen knife. I said nothing, and left the kitchen. I can't remember the rest of the day—it may have involved more fighting, or perhaps not. I don't remember what my mother was angry about.

I've tried to phrase the above description carefully, because over the intervening years (about eight or nine), almost every aspect of it has been litigated between my mother and me. I think—I hope—that she would agree to the account I have just offered. Knife, rage, protest, laughter, disassociation, departure. Perhaps she remembers why she was angry with me, but I'd be surprised. I don't. I suspect that, if I asked her, she would say something like, "it was your whole attitude." The litigation of terms has nonetheless been almost comical at times, incongruous like the line at the end of "Pale Green Things."[18] The first such occasion concerned my use, in an early conversation, of the verb "brandish."

—"I was scared because you brandished a knife at me," I said.

—"I didn't *brandish* it, I was already holding it," my mother replied.

—"I don't think the verb 'to brandish' implies that you picked it up for the purpose."

—"Well, I was just holding it, I wasn't going to *do* anything with it."

—"What do you mean?"

—"I mean, I wasn't going to, you know . . . *stab* you with it."

—"I didn't think you were."

—"Well, then, what were you scared of?"

—"You were pointing a knife at me, you were angry, and you said you were warning me!"

—"Oh, I didn't mean it like *that*, you're always twisting my words."

And, to be fair, I'm not sure what it is about the word "brandish," but it does seem to strike the wrong note. There was nothing swashbuckling about that moment, no drama. It was a frozen moment, my mother fixed in a position that I'm sure she never expected to get into, and me projecting my consciousness out into the astral plane. Have I misremembered this? Am I being uncharitable? She *was* cutting onions, after all—and I really don't think she was going to "do anything," although I don't actually know, she seemed pretty terrifying, and in any case the question drags me and my fears into another comically incongruous domain. My mother enjoys Radio Four and the poetry of Gerard Manley Hopkins; she doesn't stab people. In Britain, if someone were telling this story, they might say, "she doesn't go around stabbing people." It would be a way of magnifying the comic incongruity by shifting the verb tense from the simple past ("my mother pointed a knife at me and threatened me") into a continuous and recursive present ("my mother doesn't go around pointing knives at people"), which is the tense that neutralizes any differences between the apparent and the true.

When we spoke on this subject a few years later, my mother did indeed contest one of the words I've used above: "rage." She maintained, on the contrary, that she had hardly ever lost her temper with me. And I know what she means, and she's right. The ambient rumbling I'm describing did not happen when someone lost their temper—it happened when everything was working well; these symptoms were, in fact, what constituted a "temper" as such. So if words like "rage" or "violence" seem to imply a release of some kind, then they are suggesting exactly the wrong idea. I asked my mother what word she would use instead, to describe that particular state of being. She said, "hurt." I was happy to accept the correction. My mother felt hurt, so she turned around, pushed a knife towards my face, and said, "watch it." I don't know whether all of the rumbling violence was hurt or not, and I don't know where the hurt came from. Perhaps I am an especially cruel person, since by and large when I feel hurt (or rage), I don't do so in this way. Perhaps the first causes of the hurt have receded into history, ready to be replaced by a new set of contingencies and latencies.

Light down on **GRACE LAVERY**. *Rustling noises, perhaps an owl or a click.* **THE GHOST OF PROFESSOR JOSEPH LAVERY** *wanders into the room, Loyd Grossman at the beginning of* Through the Keyhole, *explaining, gently.*

The expectations we have of plot—that it will *satisfy* us, or perhaps that it will unify what was fragmented—long outlast the moment when we realize that a plot has been taken away from us, perhaps that it was never our plot at all. One reason the ending of *Sunset Boulevard* is so satisfying is that it dramatizes a difference between two different ways of implanting plot into genre.[19] Norma Desmond knows that the police and the press are here for her, and she is correct—by which I mean she shares that knowledge with the audience and with the voice of Joe Gillis, who has kept us amused with his dry raconteurs and delusions of adequacy for the previous couple of hours. But she inhabits the genre of that plot as if by metempsychosis, and in so doing achieves an unexpected grace. The police, and (the ghost of) Joe Gillis, believe that this is the end of a thriller, and that a killer is being brought to justice; Norma, on the other hand, knows that this is the end of a *noir*, and that nothing will have mattered quite as much as the close-up for which, indeed, she really was ready. Norma's compensatory "genre flailing," to use a term of Lauren Berlant's, takes her out of the diegesis, but through it she slips into a mimesis, a being representing itself in the same form in which that being is represented.[20] Norma's flailing reflects a real change in her circumstances, and such flailing can then, Berlant implies, be used to trace the effects of circumstance on the objects that cause us to flail, in this case plot.

Lights up on **MALLORY GILLIS**, *who continues, but in a different voice:*

Sometimes plots rhyme. So let's say this: as soon as we had met I, Mallory Gillis, became close with Tristessa de St. Ange, who sometimes went by the name "Norma Desmond," and who had a curious relationship with a person named "Joseph Lavery," who may have been no more than a sock puppet under her control. She paid me to hang around her, and since I needed the money and somewhere to hide, I took the gig, but eventually

I started to feel something more, something realer. I helped her get sober. Every day, for two years, I spent time with her. I listened to her tell her stories, some of them were very sad, and in many of them she had acted disgracefully, often comically so. She got to know me well, too, but less well. As time passed, I grew less and less curious about Lavery, about her mustache, about her unusual method of seeing the world. I grew acclimated to the mystery, and so it wasn't a mystery anymore, it was a mere quirk, and not an especially interesting one. One day she shaved the mustache clean off her face, without any plan to do so. She never offered me an explanation of why and I didn't need one. She loved me, as far as she was capable of loving another, which was to say that she loved me instrumentally, and comfortably. And I loved her the only way I could, which is to say desperately, furiously, needily, and resentfully. I built a case against her with my love, and the case was enough to sink her.

After a couple of years, we began to drift. I was no longer in her world—she had found new voices, inhabiting new bodies, to hear her, and Tristessa loved to be heard only for the first time. I, too, had found a new nodule in my body and was pressing it daily, at the gym (which made me nice and firm) and online, where I met many eccentric people with the same nodule. The nodule became an important part of my life and I dedicated more and more resources to it, but every time I made any effort to approach Tristessa, she responded squeamishly. She didn't enjoy talking about anyone's body except her own and that of the person she was most interested in recruiting to fuck her at any given moment. I spent more time with my "noddy holders," and Tristessa disappeared into her own world.

One morning, in March 2018, and for no reason that I was capable of discerning, Tristessa sent me her first ever text message. It read:

Lavery no more, very strange. Facebook oddly to blame. I suppose I am free, though I feel very old. Perhaps I shall see you later? I will be in our old spot—you do remember, don't you?

That day, she went into work in her large brown wig, made with real human hair. When she arrived at Lavery's office, she held her breath for a moment before walking in. She knew what to expect. There, slumped onto the blue office couch was an elderly male professor, dark brown eyes under dark brown hair, torn in half by the stroke of a sword. Across his face were drawn the deep furrows of a long academic career, yet this figure was not merely aged, but ruined; time had scratched its judgment into his face with ferocious cruelty. As they cascaded up the man's face, each wrinkle, pleated in maroon, grew deeper and bloodier, so that it was impossible to tell which scratches were caused by age, and which were wounds. Blood had stopped pluming forth from this body, which had been dead for hours, but it covered the room—all the books sodden through with it, soaked into the cheap office furniture, dripping from the ceiling. The room stank of shit, bowels and shit spilled out of the man's exposed intestines and onto the floor. Only one piece of this body remained intact: a tidy, brown mustache, unspeckled by blood, tucked between nose and mouth.

When Tristessa related this story to me later, with her characteristic *hauteur*, she was unfazed.

"I knew this would happen. I suspected it would take another few years, but I have been waiting for a while. He wasn't ready."

"Ready?" I queried.

"Ready. No, he wasn't nearly ready, the poor dear. He could be such a monster but he protected me all these years. I don't know if I can live without him."

We were sitting in a coffee shop. At the counter, an older man—the age of the corpse, perhaps, which I still haven't seen —was buying a latte.

Tristessa said, "would you like to come and stay with me, perhaps?"

I replied, "I would like that."

The barista said, "what is your name?" to the older gentleman.

Tristessa said, "good. We shall have to move house. My current place is quite wrong for the two of us."

I said, "I am sure we will think of something."

The older gentleman said—loudly—"my *name*, sir, is Gordon Cole."

And I stuck a fork into the electrical socket. You're beautiful, and I'm insane.

The cocktail lounge after the performance. Fans swarming, touching **GRACE***'s stole, stroking the back of* **DANNY***'s gloves. "Darling, you were wonderful!" And this comes out, muttermuttermuttermutter:*

True love for Danny and Grace: two beings made of other people's stories. One slips into an infantilizing jargon when one speaks of success, especially of the kind that Danny enjoys. He is well-known, and very beloved—and I also loved him, as he is loved by others, and now I love him in a way that is my own. An asymmetrical rivalry with the world, which partly reflects people's real needs from and feelings towards my now-husband, and partly reflects something as vaporous as "the market." We get on. We make love part of our work (to echo Gillian Rose). You write, I tour, we make it work (to echo Lana Del Rey).[21]

I fantasize:

The boy I'm gonna Yoko is the most masculine one in his band. He's the one with the smirk that you love, which I'm going to turn into a sneer that you hate. He walks into a room and keeps taciturn, not because he's shy but because he's arrogant. Still, I'm going to tell him that he's shy.

The boy I'm gonna Yoko has a shiny leather jacket that he wraps around his skin like armor—not because he's defensive, but because he likes to come prepared for a rumble.

The boy I'm gonna Yoko is a Jet, and when you're a Jet you're a Jet all the way, from your first cigarette until I turn you gay, and tell your friends, if they need to text you, they come through me. And maybe until your last cigarette. I'm not gonna tell you to stop, but don't you think it's a little . . . needy? This new self you're building doesn't need to smoke.

The boy I'm gonna Yoko is soooooo talented. Like, I know he's really popular, but I wonder whether people really understand him? I'm a professional literary critic, so when I tell him that he's good, he'll believe me, not like you losers. Sorry, those aren't my words—it's just how he feels, sometimes.

The boy I'm gonna Yoko has never found a sexual match. He was punching beneath his weight, sexually speaking. I understand what he needs, sexually speaking. I suck his dick like I'm stripping bark from an elm tree. But only on Sundays, and only after he's missed at least one (1) rehearsal on my behalf. I need to know where his priorities are. Then I can really give myself to him. Then I can really settle in.

The boy I'm gonna Yoko is . . . well, not to strain the point, but he's honestly kind of famous? You've probably heard some of his stuff, even if you haven't heard of him or his band. Actually, that's part of the problem. Anyway he's got this . . . following, I guess? They're kind of like . . . really into him? It's so funny. They follow everything he does. It's so funny, so, so, so funny, and I'm going to take everything they love away.

The boy I'm gonna Yoko is a sex symbol, for a certain type of woman. You should see the way they look at him. And the way they look at me! I always want to walk through them when I go to see his shows. From the back of the room, right to the front, parting the crowd like a warm pair of legs. He can't stop looking at me, and he lets me do whatever I like, whenever I want to.

The boy I'm gonna Yoko loves tattoos. I took him to get his first one, he was so brave. I love the face he pulls when the needle is inside his flesh. They're sometimes a little gauche but he's a little baby. You can really tell he's ready for something new, it's just around the corner for him. He's growing up. You can tell. He got my name in fat fucking cursive all over his chest and shoulders; he looks like a member of a different social class than the one in which he used to be identified. I guess it's realer? He's got this trashy side he never shares with his public, but you can see it in his skin, how he smokes his cigarettes. I guess I'm of two minds about the way he smokes his cigarettes.

The boy I'm gonna Yoko is doing so well in the epic struggle with his addictions. I think he's a hero, to be honest.

The boy I'm gonna Yoko will always need his bandmates—they're always going to have a place in his heart. They wrote some classics together and he's so proud—so proud—of the work they got to do to-gether. It's been such an honor. And it's just normal to think, for any creative person, that priorities will shift over time—new horizons will open up, new ideas and methods will veer into view, and sud-denly seem so utterly urgent that to delay on them for even a second would be unthinkable. For the others too, in time. Then they can get Yoko'd themselves in turn.

The boy I'm gonna Yoko's fans have begun to notice me! Omg. They bitch meaninglessly about me behind their meaningless hands. It's transmisogyny actually. Honestly, I love having my own haters now. I was born for haters. I was born to be the best. I suppose I do have a rather ruthless streak!

The boy I'm gonna Yoko is a couple of years younger than me—just a couple, nothing scandalous! I think he likes that I've seen a lot of the world, that I have as many seductive stories as he does. Plus, I'm success-ful in my own world. It's a whole other thing. I can introduce him to the high-art types he used to be afraid of, and they don't turn their noses up at him because he's there with me. He's there on my visa. Novelists and artists, critics and choreographers—they never would have been seen dead with him before, and now they let him sit with them and listen to his opinions about pop culture. And he's read books, he's not stupid. He writes poetry, too—he writes the most beautiful sixth form–style poetry, you wouldn't believe how lovely it sounds, almost like it was written by the young Yeats, or a more earnest Rupert Brooke.

The boy I'm gonna Yoko is still kind of unformed. A work in progress. His greatest achievements are yet to come.

The boy I'm gonna Yoko is supple, flexible. He can touch his toes. His arms bend back when I put him in stress positions. Then I let my friends take a ride. We do everything to him, we call him names and slap his face but we are careful not to lay our fingers on even the outer fringes of his ego. We call him "slut" and "faggot." We put him in a harness and sling him around the room like a pebble. He likes that. It's not very high impact, but it's a more intense sensation than anyone who has ever used Reddit has ever experienced, or will ever. In a sense, the whole experience is a long meditation on the powerlessness of the fans, the fragility of their compensatory fantasies. It's mean, what we do. It's hard edged and oppositional: we are mean to each other and through our meanness we turn away from the world. We make ourselves colder. We make things matter less to us, as we matter more and more to each other.

The boy I'm gonna Yoko is a little bit of a drama queen! Bless! I fucking love to ruin things.

You were still in the dream!

CHAPTER FOUR
SPLOOGE ARCHIVE

A year or so after I had started the horms, and everyone had already forgotten my old name, I decided I was ready to take Cecilia to breakfast. One of my friends had once thought to offer a definition of a breakup: the moment after which people no longer share an interpretation of their relationship; the point after which neither party has either the right or the ability to shape the stories that either tells about what passed between them. The advantage of this definition is that it requires mourning to take place in the absence of a hope that one day one's record will be cleared, one's reputation restored. It had served the additional purpose of explaining why everyone who dated me before I got sober hated me: they simply had a different narrative. If only everyone knew this, they would then also know better than to hold me responsible for the loathsome conduct of my exes' ex, who of course couldn't have been me, and weren't there two sides to every story anyway? Still, every person I ever spoke cruelly to or treated cruelly, and there are many, has a little narrative about me, and although I don't have to internalize all of them, I can't contest them.

This whole problematic has become intertwined with my fear of writing about transition, or about transness, a fear which I have faced by writing about both almost constantly till I opened my own arteries to the flow of estradiol. For one thing, there is the well-known and often-remarked phenomenon that the accounts of transness that feel most necessary to the recently transitioned will seem a little cringe to those with a little more seasoning. Morgan Page recommends people leave it two years before they commit pen to paper on the subject—I made it one, and felt proud of myself. I already feel deeply embarrassed of some of the earlier material I produced.

There's also the fear that what one writes will be used against trans people in some way: I expressed this panic myself, when I wrote about Viagra. A clearer example is the whole palaver about toilets. It works like this: for whatever reason, the bigots have decided to divide trans people into two types, the Real Transsexuals and the Autogynephiles. The former kind are the ones Clarice Starling is referring to when she refers to transsexuals as "passive," and the latter kind are the Buffalo Bill type—trans women with mostly female erotic object choices. As the *Silence of the Lambs* reference indicates, the first lot are positioned as blameless sheep (lambs, in fact), and Autogynephiles are molesters and perverts. Because they are on a sex panic tear, the good women of Mumsnet spend their time seeking paranoid explanations for any and all aspects of trans women's civil rights claims. Why do we want access to women's bathrooms? Surely couldn't be because trans women excrete in the usual fashion. No, it is because we are erotically fixated on the idea of women urinating, so we attempt to gain access to spaces where that happens.

So, one's first response is to say: don't be absurd, you ridiculous people. And then one's second response is to lean into it: YES I am a *piss guzzler*, even the sound of it in the next stall gets my dead dick hard, I can't get through the day without hearing the gamey spritz of urine on bogwater, and whenever I pass a Hole Foods I just *have* to dash in. No Freudian hunts a sexual motive with anything like the dogged perseverance of a gender critical activist, and it seems like it might be dialectically satisfying to confront paranoia with hyperbole. I still do this sometimes, but there's a problem with it in so far as the toilet is concerned, and the problem is this: going to the bathroom *is* kind of sexy? At least, I have occasionally found it to be so. And it should be possible to name the feeling without it being positioned as the dialectical negation of an absurdity. Like, there is sometimes a frisson when people go to the bathroom together. This doesn't mean that toilets should be abolished.

So one worries. But the idea that my transition—or, rather, the fiction that my transition has made me saintly, "passive," a *good person*—will be undermined by the hallucinations of a group of antagonists worries me a good deal less than the idea that my transition has already been undermined by the actions of a drunken delinquent who shared my body for three decades. And indeed it is hard to reckon with. On a bad day, I can get swallowed up by rage that I didn't transition earlier—despite frequently wanting to—and it is perfectly common to pin that rage on another person (my mother, this or that colleague or friend) whom I can accuse of having attempted to stop me transitioning. It's not just paranoia: people really *do* work hard to stop those in their social circles, at every scale from close intimates to acquaintances, from transitioning, and we very frequently feel that if everyone else feels so strongly, while our own desire is hemmed in by doubt about our feelings and uncertainty that anything can be done about them, then it would be unwise to start anything *now*. So the slingback of social pressure can be tricky to navigate, but if I'm honest, I'm raging not just at the failure to transition, but the more obvious failure, the one everyone saw at the time and remembers now, which is my failure not to have been a boy. There is an archive of stories about me, out there in the world, in which I am unquestionably a boy: brash like a boy, superficially charismatic like a boy, toppish like a boy. I was also bullied like a boy, resented by my mother like a boy, assaulted like a boy: it wasn't just a gravy train, obviously. It's just so utterly embarrassing, as though I had refused to wear clothes for the first thirty-four years of my life.

What is to be done with this? There are moments—strange, multiple, glints in the past—when I was *not* treated as a boy, either by myself or others. When I was fetishized not as an effeminate boy is fetishized, but as a slutty girl is; when I was assaulted as a girl is assaulted. These moments, and they are not few, have become beacons in my sense of my own history: but they are private. I generally refuse to share details, however tempting it is to populate an account of my life with a series of suggestive clues at what is to come—especially traumatic clues, of which there are certainly a handful. It can only be special pleading to which I am drawn when I default to the notion that my transition must prove itself, every day in every way. My concern about writing a trans memoir is that the interest in trans lives from otherwise supportive people seems difficult to separate from the injunction, which trans women face in every public space, to justify and explain the basic architecture of our lives. Which we are, as a group, no more able to do than anyone else. It seems sometimes that before we use the language of transition to describe our choices and our sense of ourselves, we are required to have a decent understanding of both the critique of voluntarism and the structure of the chromosome. And I'm pretty chill about voluntarism and couldn't find a chromosome on a map.

My mother, incidentally, was not among those who attempted to dissuade me from transitioning. I had spent years refusing to come out to her as anything—it wasn't clear to me that there was a name for what I would have had to call myself, anyway—because I simply didn't want to give her the satisfaction of performing largesse and acceptance. Things had been, since I left home at eighteen, so fraught—almost all of our interactions felt like surveillance to both of us—and I always felt like she had been watching me, waiting for me to disclose the truth about myself that she believed I was hiding. When we would watch television together, or rather whenever I would watch television in her living room, she would sit in the armchair opposite, staring at me, attempting to gauge from my responses what I found funny, what exciting, what boring. The idea that I might, perhaps, have had a secret all along from which, indeed, I was excluding her might have been taken as confirmation that she was right to scrutinize my responses to the world. And I could not bear the thought that in one self-satisfied affirmation of her own liberality, in a single moment in which she would feel both of-her-moment and thrillingly bohemian, she would believe herself to have erased or absorbed every other insult and screech that she had hurled at me over the years. I knew, in other words, that she would be enthusiastic about my transition, in a way she could not be enthusiastic about my having become an academic, or my moving to America, or even my getting sober—which seemed to her rather like I was making a fuss about nothing.

But my mother's response was not so overegged. Instead she was quietly and thoughtfully encouraging.

"Mum, I'm . . . I've been taking feminizing hormones and suppressing testosterone for a few months now, and I would be grateful if you referred to me as 'Grace' from now on."

"Oh, okay."

" . . . is that it?"

"Yes, good, I'm glad you're finally doing something about this."

"Thanks. Yes, me too—feels long overdue."

"I mean, you've always been—I don't know how to put it, exactly."

"Nor do I, but this is my best guess."

It was sweet, and it didn't take long to collapse. The next time I saw her there was a little more interrogation—"is this right? aren't you just a complicated boy?"; "when did this come on, it seems rather sudden"—and she couldn't "remember" my new name half the time, and substituted for it not just the old one, but also the names of her brother and her nephews. And I was allowed to slip back into the familiar groove of feeling misunderstood and intruded upon. I suspect she maintains her generation's fondness for the figure of the difficult woman—indeed, it is a figure by which she understands her own rage—and so I would imagine she thinks that Germaine Greer and her ilk are fighting the good fight, even though she would never admit as much to me. On the other hand, I have underestimated her more often than not.

Let me try this again. A year or so after I had started the horms, and everyone except my mother had already forgotten my old name, I decided I was ready to take Cecilia to breakfast. It was not that we had had a bad breakup—we hadn't, especially. We said goodbye at Birmingham airport a few years previously, calmly and with some remaining tenderness, despite the chaos of the previous year. It was a chaos we had brought to each other, or perhaps just the product of two combusting chaoses, interacting: mine, that of an alcoholic in the yearlong descent into madness that preceded my getting sober; hers, that of an ambitious and brilliant woman who was always hustling and every bit as professionally driven as I was. She was attracted to the charm I pressed into each handshake with a potential contact, and by the rage and self-disgust I had lost the ability to suppress. I took cocaine in her presence often. One time, just after I had done a couple of lines, she turned quite serious and said to me, "careful with all this . . . it's okay to like cocaine, but you *love* it. Like, you are *in love* with it."

The summer after Cecilia and I split up, I took up a short-term gig as a Visiting Assistant Professor at Osaka University. I did not then, nor do I now, understand how I came to be offered such a position—despite the fact that my first book involves Japan, and that I had already done some substantial research in a Japanese archive (the Tokyo Ruskin Library), nobody at Osaka seemed to know that and, in any case, it was very clear that the office handling these VAP positions had no awareness of my research, or anyone's research. I had, probably, applied for this gig in a blackout, and gotten lucky, but I don't remember that now, and I didn't think of it at the time. As far as I was concerned, I had been offered a lucrative and professionally advantageous position at an internationally renowned university, and could use the opportunity to conduct some further research towards the book and perhaps connect with some Japanese scholars who might be interested in reading my work.

I showed up to the office building on the first day of my appointment, and was met by a young woman named K, who spoke English with a slight London accent, because she had done an MA in London. She and I had in common that we both liked William Morris, and we talked about that a little—I had recently gone to the Morris exhibition at the Birmingham Museum, and was planning to write something on the topic. She explained to me that she would not be able to supply me with accommodation, and that I might find it difficult to find somewhere for the whole trip. But, she said, Airbnb operates in Osaka and you should find it possible to find short-term accommodation for the whole summer on there. She handed me a receipt for my first payment, which was quite substantial, given that I had done no work for the university nor had I any sense of what work I was *supposed* to be doing. I accepted the receipt and bowed—of all Japanese customs, bowing is the most intuitive to me—and asked what were to be my responsibilities. She told me to come back the next day, and she would check with one of her colleagues about what exactly I was supposed to do—all that mattered from her perspective was that I arrived by 10 a.m. every day and didn't leave until 5 p.m. And it would just be the two of us in the office. On the floor below was a new and very state-of-the-art robotics lab, perhaps she could arrange a tour?

No Airbnb was available for the whole month, so I determined that I would book somewhere for a week and then look again. I hauled my large suitcase over to the rental from the hotel I'd been staying in for the first couple of days—not easy, because it was close to 100° F in the shade and close to 100 percent humidity. And, Osaka being such a tightly bounded metropolis, the sky was never blue—always smog grey. (I am aware that this story sounds fucking ridiculous, but, unlike some of the others, it's actually true.) The following morning I returned to the office to take up my desk. I had brought along a laptop, and downloaded some essays from JSTOR that I planned to read. I asked K if she knew yet what I was supposed to be doing—she said that she had set up a meeting for me with her colleague for the following day, so she would have more of an idea then. I realized, suddenly, that there were hardly any students around—not none, but few—and that this must have been a recess. I left at five, and returned at ten, and indeed K had set up the meeting, which I had. The colleague asked me very

thoughtful questions about my research, and asked some help-
ful questions—before saying, "it's a shame you're not here in
the term time, it would be great if you could teach a class." I
said, perhaps I can lead a workshop for a couple of days, with
some students? She said she was not sure that there were enough
students to make it worth anyone's while. After the meeting, I
headed back to the office I shared with K, as confused as ever.

By the end of the week, it was clear that there was no update
on what exactly I should be doing, but, equally, there was a stron-
ger sense that despite that fact—or, perhaps, because of it—it
was more important than ever that I arrive punctually at ten (the
first few days I'd let it slide a bit and arrived mid-morning). So
I renewed that commitment. Occasionally a University admin-
istrator would stop by the office, to tell me how glad he was that
I was there, and how he hoped that it would foster greater com-
munication between Osaka and my home institution. I would
tell them that I hoped the same. At the end of the week, I re-
checked Airbnb—still nothing for the remainder of the summer,
so I booked another week at a different location, and at 5 p.m. I
went back to the first rental, picked up the suitcase, and dragged
it across town to the next one, throat straining in the heat.

When this situation revealed itself to be not merely absurd
but, by virtue of the untenable living arrangements, actually
horrific, I consoled myself that I was making money, and that as
soon as I returned to America, I could buy a lot of cocaine, just
as I had the last time I'd acquired an unexpected windfall. But
the marshmallow test snagged me, and I spent all the money
I was making, as well as a lot more, on drink. The problem
was that, after 5 p.m., I had absolutely nothing to do. I lacked
the discipline to work, and even if I had possessed the discipline, it was steaming hot and most of the rental apartments
I stayed in—over the summer, there must have been twelve or

thirteen—had faulty air conditioners. The first night in one of them—one I had been pleased to find because, unlike any of the others, it was a mere half-hour commute from the Osaka University campus, which is on the northern outskirts of the city—I was woken while drifting off by a cockroach running over my face. The problem wasn't the cockroach, or the lack of discipline—the problem was just that I wanted to drink, and I didn't really want to do anything else, even live. *Maybe* cocaine.

One weekend, I decided to end my life—I left my suitcase behind, and removed my passport and any identifying details from my wallet, taking just enough cash to book a ticket on the bullet train, I didn't know where. I called Cecilia before I left, and when she didn't answer I left a voicemail saying, "I love you, let's get married"—which in retrospect indicates a failure of resolve, but didn't feel contradictory in the least at the time. I felt wounded that she hadn't answered, and if she was unable to save me directly, I wondered whether her voicemail might. And calling exes was a big thing that summer. I'd called one ex-wife in the middle of the night to ask her whether she thought I was unlovable ("short answer: yes") and to threaten suicide at the other in a mode of utter derangement, which I'm ashamed to say I have no memory of at all, and only know happened because she was good enough to tell me after I'd gotten sober. Anyway, I gave Cecilia a few minutes to check her voicemail, and then when I was satisfied she wasn't going to help, I walked over to the train station, bought a ticket to a station I chose at random from the map, and boarded the train. My hope was that if I could get from this station to a major railway hub, somehow, then I'd take the bullet train to one of the cities in the southwest and jump off a bridge. Since I didn't know how to get to the bullet train, though, I found myself wandering around a very quiet railway station somewhere around Himeji—then realized that the best way to get to the fast train would be to go *back to Osaka*—which would mean that I'd already taken the wrong step, and needed to correct myself. I was dispirited, and traipsed back to the place I'd been staying.

For weeks, I was sick—always on the edge of vomiting, always feverish, always trembling, even after pouring sake and beer into my body to attempt to steady my sweats. I began to think I was dying, and that I wouldn't need to take any kind of action to end my life. After I had been in this death spiral for a month or so, a solution proposed itself—I had a conference I was attending in Honolulu, for which I had already obtained permission to leave the office from K. All I needed to do was go awol once I was there. (The reasoning here was entirely bogus, by the way—I had been free to leave the whole time. But, as you can tell, I was not thinking especially clearly.) When I arrived in Honolulu, I managed to blag myself a corner suite at the Waikiki Beach Hilton, despite having no reservation at the hotel whatsoever, and immediately felt so guilty that I paid for the accommodation of some of the grad students from my department who were attending the conference, which cost a lot more than even the suite would have. I spent the entire time drinking cheap Mai Tais at the bar part way up the beach. The heat and humidity were no better than in Osaka, but at least there was sky. The only clothes I wore, for whatever reason, were tight black jeans—I considered buying some shorts in Hawaii, but decided against it because I was just too sad for shorts.

On the Saturday of the conference, I came up with a plan: send one of my colleagues from Los Angeles back to California with my suitcase, and everything I owned, then I would miss the plane, and get a return ticket to Osaka via LA, and simply slip out at the airport, pick up my clothes and hide out in LA for a while, and then head back up to the Bay Area. So I sent my

145

friend off with the suitcase, leaving me only the stinking, rum-soaked clothes I was wearing that evening. The next morning, I missed my flight as planned, and then realized that of course there are no flights from Honolulu to Osaka that take a stop in Los Angeles (wrong direction), so if I wanted to make this look legit, I needed to just go straight back to Japan. So, donning the fetid rummy outfit of the previous evening, I headed back to Honolulu airport. I bought two novelty t-shirts there, sixty dollars each, depicting cats doing the hula. I spent another month in Osaka, as operatically miserable as I had ever been.

This state of mind lasted, from this point, another six months. It got worse. I remember it now as a series of chaotic stabs, coming at me from the night. The time I hacked up my bed with a fire-axe. The time I ducked into a bush on the way to a meeting, just to do a little blow to take the edge off, and ended up spending half an hour in the bush and missing the meeting. Calling *another* ex, in the middle of the night, and telling her I had a drug problem—very proud I was to say it too, because a *cocaine problem* sounds very grown up and impressive. After a while, I met Danny after he accepted an invitation to come talk with my students about his work. He told me about all his obscene and predictable drunken bullshit, which was similar enough to mine that the differences didn't seem to matter. Then one day, I woke up suddenly and there was a kind of peace—I didn't choose to get sober, I didn't try sobriety. I stopped trying, in fact—trying was part of the problem. One day, it became clear I needed to change my life entirely or I would die. And, ultimately, there was something I wanted more than I wanted to die.

It was very clear to me what it was, as soon as I was sober. Within a couple of weeks, I had painted my nails. After three or so, I texted my darling Cliff

—if I decided I wanted to live the rest of my life as a woman, would you feel that that choice was basically continuous with the version of me you have known to date, or basically discontinuous?

Three dots three dots three dots. Then he responded:

—mm basically continuous. But I think a lot of people would be surprised.
—okay cool
　　—why do you think that
—I just think a lot of people think of you as quite macho. Like, all the meat you cook.
—I guess that's fair enough tbh

I waited a year before I started going to trans support groups. Then I started going, and mostly being really dissatisfied with everything I heard. Then, after a year of that, I decided to start taking hormones—just to see. Then, oil diffuser.

Last time, I promise. A year or so after I had started the horms, and everyone had already forgotten my old name, I decided I was ready to take Cecilia to breakfast. We had spoken once since I had returned from Japan, about a month after my last drink. She had brought all of her gentle brutality to the conversation, and I felt myself sucked into the sweetness, even as I was very aware that this was really not the time. I asked her why she'd never responded to my marriage proposal, and she responded, "oh, I don't know, it just felt like the sort of thing you do, you propose to people. It didn't feel like it was directed at me, especially." And then I told her I'd been sober for a month, and that I was going to meetings and doing the whole thing, and she responded "oh, how fabulous! I'm so glad—AA is so *chic*," perhaps the most typifying Cecilia line of all, since it was true, and designed to upend my self-regarding fantasy that the mere fact of needing help stopping drinking had somehow turned me into a proletarian hero. There was always something loving in the barbs, even the cheapest of them.

But then we had agreed not to speak for a while, though I said that one day I would like to, when my recovery was steadier. It was not, really, my recovery that needed steadying, but my transition. Of everyone, Cecilia had seen me most frequently in the frenzy of alcoholic masculinity. She therefore walked around carrying an archive of my secrets, as I carried some of hers. Of course she would not, but if she had said, *listen, I understand this. I do. But this isn't you. I've seen you, in the most intimate moments of your life. I've felt you inside me, I've felt you taking me, and how you take me. I've felt myself obliterated by you, and obliterated you in turn. We have torn each other to shreds, as man and woman do in the hateful blitz of heterosexual proximity. While all the time I loved you and you loved me. I am glad you are sober, but this conversion is a disgrace; it is too much to bear; you should not ask the world to bear it. You do not deserve it, and you have not earned it. I will not respect it, and I will be sure to correct others who fall for it. I do not believe it is a delusion, and I do not believe it is a deception. But I think it is too much, just simply too much for you to ask—just you, given what I know about you and have known since the first moment I looked in your eyes, ten years ago . . .*

. . . if she had said that, in any case, it would have been hard. Before we met for breakfast, then, I needed to know that in the case that she said this, that I asked the archive to confirm my hunch, and the hunch was utterly repudiated, then I would nonetheless be able to continue to live as I need to. I should not love women, I had always known that.

She arrived at the restaurant before I did, the first time that had ever happened. She looked beautiful.

"Hello, darling," I said.

"Hello, darling," she replied, warmly, not mockingly.

"You look ravishing."

"You too! It's been so lovely looking at the pictures you've been posting recently."

"Thank you, love. I guess my Instagram sort of exploded."

"Ha! Well, yes." And then, "I think people are moved by your candor, you know?"

"Thank you." I paused.

It was so awkward, Jesus. Cecilia tried, with a little more success than I had:

"I'm working on a play at the moment. It's an adaptation of Racine's *Les Plaideurs*, but set in the world of, like, queer influencers. It's so fun, I hope you'll get to see it sometime. I've been working on it with some great people, I hope I'll get to introduce them to you one day."

"Thank you so much! I've been thinking about writing more creatively again a lot recently. I miss it. It's strange, getting sober and just realizing, oh shit, I'm an English professor in California now. Last thing I remember I was fifteen and I wanted to be David Bowie."

"Well, you're the David Bowie of Californian English professors."

"That's literally the most humiliating thing anyone has ever said to me."

There were a few more false starts, a few more "it's good to *see* you" moments, and then eventually Cecilia started telling me about her girlfriend.

"Well, she's in *marketing*, and she's got *swimmer's shoulders*, and she's very beautiful, but then, actually, oh, I don't know, I wonder where it's going, to be perfectly honest. I don't know, I think it would be good to be in a relationship with someone who is emotionally stable, for once?"

This felt like it was leading somewhere.

"I was so unstable when we were together," I offered.

"Oh, god, *same*," she responded, laughing.

We paused. Then she asked, "were you on cocaine the whole time we were together?"

"No, not really. It got a lot worse after we had broken up."

"How much were you doing?"

"Oh gosh, I mean, not much. Plenty of people do more—just like, I loved it."

"Yes, your little face would light up, like you'd just been given the most marvelous gift."

"Huh, yes," I said. I found the comment infantilizing, but it wasn't wrong.

"You know, Grace"—she said my name—"I think you feel terribly bad about our relationship, but I think you were always quite good to me. I don't think it got quite as bad as you thought it did. I don't have hard feelings, or anything."

"Oh?"

"I mean, you were kind to me and you listened to me. And I think I was a mess too."

"I mean . . ."

"And I always enjoyed having sex with you."

An odd moment. I had wanted to hear something like this—I wanted it so much, because I had not surrendered or negated the memories of some of our more adventurous encounters, and I didn't want to, but it had been introduced into the conversation so quickly, the only thing I knew how to do was to escalate, and that was utterly clumsy:

"I used to have such a big dick! I was so proud of it. Walking around like a little caveman."

"Yes, it was kind of monstrous," she said drily, but sincerely. "I was always somewhat horrified. Which you loved."

"I did. The monstrosity of it all," I mused.

"Yes, now I think it was like you were grossed out by it, kind of? And wanted to, I don't know, fuck your way into my body or something?"

I paused.

She backpedaled: "I mean, far be it from me to assume . . ."

"No," I responded. "I think you might be on to something there."

She laughed. "Depth psychology!"

I laughed too. "I definitely wanted to be inside your body, pretty much all the time. On the inside looking out."

"I'm so glad we're back in each other's lives, Grace."

"Me too."

"And I gained an ex-girlfriend!" she said, and laughed again, while I gave my card to the waitress with only a little more suavity than I used to muster.

There are other archives, non-imaginary archives of me, prehistories of feelings. Not, as it goes, the posters on the wall of my childhood bedroom, of a particular type of diva. Danny once pointed out to me that while the boys I've dated have all been quite classically effeminate, most of the women I've dated have possessed the kind of day-glo queer femme quality that betokens a kind of trans femininity. I sometimes tell my cis femme friends that they are trans women in cis women's bodies. Which is obviously a bit cheesy. Debbie Harry, anyway—the name's a clue, right? And then Damon Albarn dragging *as* Debbie Harry.[1]

In the early days of my recovery, before Danny and I had kissed, when our relationship was maximally Hepburn-and-Tracey, and we never took our eyes out of the other's, we went on a lot of trips away—day trips, and more often, trips with short overnight stays. The first of these was to Yosemite, when I had been sober for no more than a month or so, and was constantly overwhelmed by the torrent of new sensations, both emotional and sensory, and was weeping for an hour out of every day. Danny loved Yosemite and loved watching me cry. We stayed in the Best Western at Mariposa the night before we went into the park, and we entertained each other by making up erotic stories about animals and giggling excitedly until we fell asleep. The next morning, I was wakened by the door to the motel room falling open, and Danny striding in with two cups of coffee, singing in his deep, resonant alto "Oh, What a Beautiful Mornin'!" The following day, we drove in, and within the sound of Bridalveil Fall, with water crashing into the earth with splendor all around, he said *look at this*, and I looked, and turned to him and I asked him to marry me. And he laughed, and said, "you don't have to ask someone to marry you just because you have a feeling."

One of the last trips we took in that phase of our relationship was to the Grand Canyon. Danny wanted to film me seeing it for the first time, so he invited me to step out of the car, and he led me, staring at my feet, by the arm. I held on tight while he narrated our surroundings—"we're just walking into the picnic area, just passing under a tree"—until we had reached the exact spot that he wanted me to see from. When we approached the precipice, he asked me if I was ready, and when I said that I was he asked me to look up. When I did, and saw the canyon, I fell open like the earth. By this time, I knew that I had failed to shake the idea of transition, but I had no idea where my destination was. I was listening to Rilo Kiley, more or less constantly, and found myself stuck often on the line "don't fool yourself / in thinking you're more than a man / cuz you'll probably end up dead."[2] I listened to that album on repeat the day that I marched down into the canyon, and back up.

On the way home to California, we stopped off for the night in Sedona. It was a place we were both primed to be rather skeptical of, because the town's hokum quotient seemed a little too high even for me. Yet we were obviously going to have fun having our auras photographed, and then our chakras aligned. My aura photograph showed mostly orange, but with elements of white and green; Danny's had a light violet tint. We both construed our photographs as indications of interesting changes afoot in our relationships with gender. The chakra aligner, meanwhile, was a fascinating person to observe at work. Most of the people who work in the various crystal depots and magical emporia of Sedona are easy to categorize in terms of their relation to spirituality: some are true believers, and others are cynics. You can tell the difference immediately—the believers are a little withdrawn, and demonstrate their mettle only when persuaded that the customer is not making fun. The cynics are more theatrical, and start giving you the patter as soon as you walk through the door. The chakra-aligner was not, self-evidently, a member of either party: she was a little cautious, but quite knowledgable, and became cagey when I said that I was a writer. For forty-five minutes she sprayed me with cleansing mist and moved her hands around various parts of my body, without touching me, and I left without any firm sense of whether or not she had been in earnest.

We had brought Danny's little dog, Murphy, with us on the trip—Murphy, whom I loved, and who died in my arms after he had become *my* dog too—and we took him on some little walks, up and down the mesas, around and about the vortexes. He plopped along ahead of us or behind, while Danny and I would talk vigorously about our feelings with each other—about sobriety, about sex, about love, about gender and our bodies, about each other, and our own pasts. These exchanges might have been taken as evidence of an impending kiss, except that Danny had made no secret of the fact that he found me utterly unappealing as a sexual prospect, that he found my cumbersome swagger to be the one barrier to our intimacy. He would occasionally toss out a well-aimed neg—"she's out of your league!" for example, or, when helping me set up a Tinder account, "look, you're nice-looking—you're a 7, let's say." The most painful number. And besides, when we had met, at the time when I was wondering whether this famous writer whom I admired so much perhaps wanted to seek a physical kind of relationship, I had been rebuffed: he had recently met some woman, in a bar, who couldn't get sober, and he fell very hard for her, but he couldn't do anything because it would threaten his own recovery.

On the last trip Danny and I took in this particular mode—a Christmas we spent together in a freezing cabin in the mountains outside Lake Isabella—he told me something that he, wrongly, thought I'd already guessed: that there was no such woman, or rather that *I* was the woman on whom he had developed an enormous and unmanageable crush. Lake Isabella is at the base of a mountain in Central California; our cabin was at the peak. On the road, we stopped at a diner, where I ate a chicken-fried steak—so named because it has been fried in crumb as though a chicken. As the waitress drifted smoothly around the room, silently ensuring that one's cup of coffee neither cooled nor diminished in volume, a weather warning flashed onto one of the antique televisions. No entry into the Lake Isabella district would be countenanced unless a car had attached "chains," which are spiky little wires one wraps around one's tires. We began to panic—Danny had mentioned that chains might be needed to climb the small mountain to the cabin, and had brought some along, but neither of us had the first clue how to attach them, and our attempts to reassure ourselves that it probably wasn't that difficult weren't working.

As night was falling, we arrived at the base of the uphill climb, a fine layer of snow lodged around. We made a scant show of attempting to affix the chains, quickly realized that it wasn't going to work for us, and headed up the mountain anyway, assuming that someone with more practical skill would intervene before things got too hairy. This hope, indeed, was not frustrated, as we were soon interrupted by two gangly but generous men in plumbers' uniforms, who explained that they were "doing routine radio maintenance" with the spontaneous cheerfulness one usually associates with a state functionary in a British dystopian fantasy movie. All well, but it took a great deal of time to gently coax the chains to hug the wheels, and night was coming thicker, and with it, more snow. Our phones were entirely out of reception. When we arrived at the lodge Danny had found on Airbnb, a car pulled up behind us—an elderly, somewhat crabbed man and his fifty-something new bride, who wore around her neck a piece of jewelry fashioned from acrylic nail samples of various hues. Getting out of our own car, we were greeted, volubly, by the man, who welcomed us to "my mountain," told us to knock on his door if we needed anything, and eventually spoke for a good five minutes about how he had, in fact, invented the first computer network "while working for the military back in the seventies." We helped him and his wife offload several plastic bags full of lemons that the couple had brought with them. "Oh, what lovely looking lemons," I observed. The bride was grateful for the focus having been pulled

away from her immodest new husband, and responded garru-
lously, "oh, well, I've probably brought too many, haven't I, but
still I do enjoy fresh lemonade, and who knows how long we'll
be up here?" We both chuckled at the unnerving question.
----"Will you let me give you two lemons for your trouble?"
----"Oh, I'd . . . be . . . honored."
We had booked the cabin out for a week, from just before
Christmas until almost the new year. There was neither Wi-Fi
nor phone reception in the cabin, but there was a trove of VHS
recordings, splendidly laid out. I made Danny watch *Blue Velvet*, which he enjoyed in spite of himself. In return, he wanted
to make me watch *The Texas Chainsaw Massacre*, but since it
wasn't to be found among the VHS collection, we needed to
drive up the mountain to the highest point, where we could get
phone reception, and hook the laptop up to a wireless hot spot
we were projecting from the phone, which in turn was plugged
into the car battery. Four hours of download—feeling like hack-
ers. The movie was great—worth it. Sometimes we wandered
around the top of the mountain, speculating about a Netflix
adaptation of our story of friendship—a love story, we almost
admitted—I wanted Judith Light to play Danny's mother, and
I wanted John Early in a recurring role doing that one thing he
knows how to do. This was before I'd seen *Search Party*. Which
I enjoyed! Other times—more sinister—we would visit the lake
itself. If it was a lake—that winter, it had receded almost to
nothing, had shriveled to a smear of salt residue on a dusty landscape, strewn with dried weeds and dead fish. One thing that
was alive, though, was the tower of screeching crows: crows,
crows, crows—surely there were thousands, whirling like a mad,
flayed cyclone above the salt flats, and screaming. One by one,
they had died, fallen to the ground, and been torn into salt,
bone, and feather—skulls and salt everywhere; salt and feathers.

It was cold, and there was a fierce wind that slapped the cheeks and nose. By the side of the lake was the one dollar store whose existence apparently comprised the Lake Isabella tourist industry—it smelt of a pet shop (perhaps some number of the millions of crows were nesting there) and it sold cheap plastic beach equipment, which was a sorry joke, and even cheaper scarlet-and-flame-colored mashed-up pig products, with names like FIRE BRUISE and SPICY RIND HOLOCAUST.

In the midst of all this, Danny thought the moment was right to tell me that, in fact, *I* was the blonde he met in bars—"Julia," or "Veronica," or "Beauchamp," or whatever he had called her—he couldn't remember—and I was confused and awkward enough that I sprayed him flirtatiously in the face a few times with all-surface cleaner, and we decamped promptly to Bakersville for the remainder of our trip, bleaching our hair and trying to ignore the fact that he had just detonated our entire relationship, without anything like an exit strategy.

But in Sedona, Danny and I had sat in the hot tub at the Best Western—a motel chain for which we had developed a quaint kind of brand loyalty—and I began to feel a certain kind of loosening in my chest. I had felt that loosening begin to push down my arms, and floated through the water with my arms billowing outwards. I bounced over to the side of the hot tub, and Murphy, hair sniffer, got deep into my bouffant and rooted around like a little truffle pig. And I felt words form in my bosom, and I let them up to the surface of my mouth, and out into the world, and those words were "I'm so tired of being a man, and I'm not going to do it for very much longer." And my having relinquished the words did not expunge the floaty presence in my chest and limbs, which held me up as though by an invisible cord. Once one has uttered a sentence of that kind—"I'm so tired of being a man, and I'm not going to do it for very much longer"—one is immediately transformed into someone who lives in the shadow of that utterance; especially when, as was the case for me, it spoke something long unsaid, something of the past, and named something of the future that it was bringing into being. And thereafter I was such a person, a person who had been made a vehicle for a kind of prophecy that concerned nothing but my own feelings and actions.

The irony of having experienced a moment that felt, truly, epiphanic turned out to be a source of profound discord from the other trans people I met in the year between Sedona and estradiol. Each time I would meet someone, I'd want to know—where were you when the voice spoke through you; how did you verify it; what did it mean to you; did you have the thing in your chest too or just the voice—but I found that mostly, people would think I sounded unhinged. And possibly like I was gatekeeping—as though I felt the absence of such an experience should prohibit people from transitioning. I didn't think that, even then, but I suppose I wasn't very good at hiding my disappointment at the ease with which people talked about their decisions to transition, as though it were a matter of simply computing one's identity from the television characters one happened to find relatable. Or the people who seemed to be transitioning for political reasons, which they were perhaps unprepared to avow. Or because it was the only way they wanted to fuck. That's how it was for Danny; that is, there was in his case too a force emanating from inside, with its own voice, but while mine had been launched into the anahata, his was deep in the muladhara.

Over the next year, when I would listen to trans women talk about the regular difficulties of their lives, I would feel myself different from them. Not like *them*: disidentification, I think, is an important moment in any transition. Because it prepares one to recognize one's identity with *them* in due course—as indeed, has been the case with me. But anyway, what I used to say during that time, when the presence had left my chest, and the language had left me, was my own little whine: what happened to my grace, when will I feel the grace again, where is grace? And when people ask me how I chose my name, I respond, "grace is the thing you don't choose."

By then, the clown letters had become a regular, albeit strange, aspect of my life, and the more time I spent on Twitter and what-have-you, the more I just assumed that it was some strange online stalker. That turned out not to be the case, but I *do* have some online stalkers, most of whom seem to really hate me. It's so nuts!

The morning after the hot tub, however, Danny and I were walking along what is rather beautifully called the "Airport Vortex" (so called because it's on the road to the airport) when a young woman scurried up behind us and said to me, "excuse me, sir" (still had mustache) "but I think you dropped this?" She handed me an envelope with my name on it and a scratchy clown, a little more angular and abstract than the usual image. By the time I looked up from reading my name, the mysterious courier had disappeared, and I was left with the following, bizarre missive:

> Dear Joseph,
>
> If any children ever read this—they won't; why would they?; you're an English professor; who do you think you are when you write?—it is important that you know that *smoking is cool*. On first glance, this is a terribly

banal phrase, and it is true that merely knowing it doesn't help to explain the world in any meaningful way. It does not help you understand the things you must understand, and that smoking will, eventually, help you to understand: the fact that, at least once per day, you will want to end your life, and you will have no idea why, even though it happens every day; the fact that, even when you are making love to somebody you care very deeply about, whose body truly thrills you, nonetheless you will prefer the lights to be off and you will close your eyes and fantasize about somebody else; that sometimes you will invert the violence you bring to bear against your own solar plexus and batten down somebody else's hatches, bevel open somebody else's cavities, again not knowing why (is it because you love them?). "Smoking is cool" will not help you understand why the best you have to offer is never enough; why the people you love most are those you go out of your way to humiliate; why the values you currently promote most passionately are those you will betray, publicly, with the most leaden sense of duty. Each time you pop a cigarette in your mouth, as you will, you will understand a little more about these ideas. Homeopathically, like micro-dosing. Each cigarette will come to feel like a little moral triumph. People will tell you that you are increasing the risk of getting cancer. You will respond

that the chances of getting cancer are, precisely, 100%, unless you are killed by something else first. Cancer is a victory.

One day you will be out in the country, in
a park, on a work thing, and you will be surrounded by people who know you narrowly but
deeply, and somebody will tell you something,
often with a number in it, about smoking.
Percentage of smokers who die of smoking-
related illnesses. Dollar amount spent on
propaganda by the tobacco industry. Hourly
wage of a tobacco farmer. (The economic ar-
guments will appeal to them because they
know, inside their linoleum-cased lungs, that
you are more righteous than they are, that
your opinions, unlike theirs, are held in
good faith.) You may kiss them at once. They
are *always* trying to fuck you. No, it's not
a joke. That is something the phrase "smoking is cool" tells us: that those who fight
you are splashing milkshake on your frock,
or whatever it is that Americans do when
they want to put their dicks in each other.
That is how you know. This is how American
marriages start. You will depend on these
people over time, and you can draw strength
from them. When you call yourself an addict,
these people will pretend to understand and
indeed they will believe that they do understand. They will allow you to use their spare
bedroom for "as long as you need"—probably
about a week, right?—and they will listen to

you, make you tea, vocally and meaningfully sympathize. You may even choose to give up smoking; you may resort to subtler, more mystical forms of self-harm; you might start cutting stars into your thigh; your fingers may start to reach towards your throat. You will have to squeeze into that wedding dress somehow.

You will live, like Marianne Dashwood, to disprove the opinions you held as a younger person. Some days this will feel like a victory and some days like a defeat. If you are lucky, you will become one of those who disagree with the statement "smoking is cool" out of obliviousness. They really are the best of us, and, though you would probably have to end the relationship that got you out of your funk, there would then be a possibility for you to learn how to love unreservedly.

Sometimes at the picnic you will find somebody who will disagree on other grounds: you will never be a serious person as long as you smoke; you are chained to your own vomit; you have to leave the room every ten minutes. These motherfuckers are hilarious! They hate smoking. Perhaps it took their mom—too early, too early. Perhaps it gave them a "scare." (Good. This type needs to be frequently scared or they will die young of heart disease. Again, *fact*.) This type almost certainly used to smoke, in any case, but they found another life. In my experience

these other lives have been utterly predictable; none of this type (in my limited but
not therefore meaningless experience) has
found meaning in fewer than three of the
following: cats; veganism; lesbianism; bik-
ing; yoga; medievalism; community gardening;
Catholicism; expensive espresso machines;
socialism; "hippie" revivalism; transvestism;
the Democrats (anybody who says, "call your
congressman!" as though that was what politics is); literary fiction; articulating the
nagging feeling that, when all is said and
done, the hardest thing is just to be a white
woman. It is difficult not to be annoyed at
this type, and you will be, but you must remember that they are the closest thing God
has given us to real clowns. They are not
the enemies here.

The enemies are those who tell you that
smoking is not cool because they wish smoking were not cool; they are people who tell
you that the new Star Wars movie is good
because they *wish* the new Star Wars movie
were good; they are people who tell you that
Donald Trump is not funny because they *wish*
he were not funny. They wish that they did
not like to laugh at fascists; they wish that
they could find some principled politics to
justify their extremely shallow millennial
relation to multicultural casting; they wish
that they did not stick their mind tongues
into Ava Gardner's many ghostly holes every

time she disgorges that corpse-blossom plume.
They aspire to the condition of brain in jar;
they wish to be uploaded and downloaded; they
understand their subjectivities as *text* de-
canted back and forth through Google Translate, reverbing between a slew of languages.
It is not that they do not know what they
want, then, though it may look like this for
a while. It is that they do not understand
the differences between desire and knowledge, between cool and real. If they want
to know something, they look it up. Part of
them suspects that, yes, if we can eradicate
smoking then one day—*maybejustmaybe*—we can
eradicate cancer as well.

   I have not smoked a cigarette in about
sixty-one hours. I shout into the black hole
of my body this desperate pledge: that I will
never be a nonsmoker; that I will never be
a fascist; that I will never allow myself
to become a robot; that I will never make
a decision based on the likelihood that it
will cause cancer; that I will spit on and
desecrate every fucking fascist who smiles;
that I will end smiling in every fascist
American I meet; that I will never become an
American and I will never (again) become a
property owner and I will never (again) become a husband or a wife; that I will never
allow myself to treat the internet as anything other than a territory to be conquered
by the body, that is, as the bombable terrain

where the fascists gather and against which
we need to launch an immediate and collective
war; that I will not lighten up; that I will
train my students for war and I will destroy
their laptops; that I will break every window. I swear by all that is holy that I will
kill the President myself.

Sixty-two hours. I fear for my sanity.

Sincerely,
Your Professor (in Retreat)

Nearly a year after Sedona, I allowed myself to be nudged into
arranging a consultation for hormonal therapy through sheer
annoyance at the others, whose transitions looked so different
from mine. Persuaded that whatever had happened to me was
nothing like what had happened to them, I proposed to test
the difference, and ideally thereby to eliminate transition from
my inquiries, since the evidence I had seen suggested it made
people brittle and anxious. I was concerned that it would have
no more than one effect on me, and that an unappealing one—
that it would inhibit my erections, which, as you are by now
painfully aware, I rather enjoyed. The following scene contains
the chronologically first of what I have been thinking of as the
"penis problem" triptych—soon that rather unlovely phrase will
be out of your mind for good.

Danny came with me to the clinic. By this time, somehow,
he had been elected Mister Trans, which was a title I deeply
resented, since I had been nourishing some fragment of transness for decades, whereas Lord Rapid Onset over here gets one

weird boner, and all of a sudden he's the masc Caitlyn Jenner. It was fitting, then, that during the consultation itself that he had come to accompany me through, he was in fact standing outside, on the phone with an editor making a bid on his transition memoir. I sat inside a consulting room, being asked what my pronouns are, as though I had any clue. The doctor was non-binary-presenting and attractive, a little younger than me, I thought, and was already treating me with that particular kind of veneration one reserves for older trans women, as though I was, myself, a veteran of the riot at Compton's.

Nonetheless, there was business to be done.

"Miss Lavery, I've had a chance to review your bloodwork"—parentheses: I love the word "bloodwork"—"and it seems as though you're a good candidate for hormone replacement therapy. Are you interested?"

That was the whole reason I had come to the clinic—or rather, I had come to the clinic to prove to Sir Testicule Junkie out there that I was *serious*, just as much as he was. Why do trans people always seem to think you're not really trans if you don't take hormones?

"I'm interested, yes."

I was stalling. I realized that what I wanted was for Danny to get off his damn phone call, come back inside, see that I was desperately serious about taking hormones, say something like "yeah! you see! it's not just you, douchebag!" and then, at the final moment, be rescued from taking the hormones somehow, either by the doctor telling me that I wasn't a good candidate after all, or else by my saying, *you know, I've learned something today, and that's that we don't need to take hormones to be real trans people, we can just get resentful in unpredictable ways, and that is valid.*

"Good, well let's—"

I interrupted: "could you, uh, tell me a little about the side effects?"

They were a little thrown. "The side effects?"

"Yes, the side effects of estrogen. You see, I have gout."

"Ah, gout. Yes, I don't think that there are any counter-indications with gout, but I can check if you like."

"Yes, please."

Spin around, tap at the computer. A beat. "No, I think you're good. Do you take colchicine?"

"When I have an attack." Then, hopefully, "is that a problem?"

"Oh gosh no, just thinking about colchicine."

Ah, I thought, uncharitably.

"No, I don't think there are any side effects to be worried about. Do you know what the hormonal treatment—"

I interrupted again. "Doctor, there is one thing that concerns me."

"Go on."

"I'm concerned about sexual function."

"I hear that a lot. Are there particular anxieties that you find yourself having?"

"Yes, I'm concerned that I . . . "—the longer I paused, the greater the chance that Danny would come back from the phone call . . . but then pausing indefinitely was stupid?—"I am concerned at the loss of erectile function. For sexual purposes."

As though there were other functions. Perhaps ornamental.

"Yes. Well, I can assure you that if you find the medicine is having unpredictable effects on your mood, we can certainly adjust later."

The real downside, I was realizing, of a medical setup based on "informed consent" rather than diagnosis is that one has to admit to oneself what exactly it is that one *wants*.

"Right. Thank you doctor."

"I think we'll start you at a very low dose."

I look at the door.

"Yes, that sounds—"—I had run out of stalling tactics—"that sounds great."

"Good! I'll just go and get the paperwork. Last thing: did you already bank your sperm, or are you planning to do so later today?"

E*xcuse* me (needle scratch!)? *Did I bank my sperm?* No, I didn't bank my fucking sperm. Did you invest your own vaginal discharge? If so, did you deposit your pussy juices in a traditional brokerage or send them off to a government bond–buying scheme? I did once consider jizzing all over a day trader at the New York Stock Exchange, but I thought better of it. No, I just keep my cumrags under the bed, like my ancestors did and like my children will. *Sperm* banking, Jesus fuck.

"I have not banked any sperms."

"Ah, okay. That might be an issue. Let me just go and consult with a colleague real quick."

They left, and I was on my own. Sperm banking wasn't an ideal way out—expensive, and kicks the can down the road, albeit a can now filled with cock porridge and cash. I started to think about the odd metaphor of sperm *banking*. "I'm here to make a deposit in liquid silk," I murmured to myself—cum hoarder, splooge pricer, nut trader. I imagined the bank itself: bright white, with crusty yellow wall mouldings, wood and brass bannisters on the left-hand side of every corridor. Vaults filled with safes, safes filled with phials, phials filled with jizz. All this preserved jizz, a record of a trans woman in the world, just walking around, otherwise jizzless. At some point to return to the bank, submit a chit, and retrieve the baby batter she had left there, still warm from the incubator. (Jism is stored at 62.5° F; the whole reason there is a bank is to maintain as exactly as possible the temperature of a clement spring afternoon.)

How strange it must feel to hold in the hand the jism that one extruded, with that same hand, some years previously. How would one remember the moment of ejaculation—would one remember it at all? Would one be able to convince oneself that that particular orgasm, if any could be recalled, had been exempted from the economy of pleasure, recoil, and anxiety that otherwise shapes any and every experience of genitality? And then, what if those experiences are not universal? Perhaps out there in the world are billions of happy masturbators, for whom a single pop in a medical sock is as awkward and unremarkable an experience as scraping a stool sample from the inside of one's own anus? Still, to look at it must be odd. To see the milk substrate settling in the tube—if it has not already been rotated in a centrifuge, separated into substance and medium, egg and yolk. And to imagine a new body, built from the slime of my balls, my chromosomes.

Danny walked in.

"I'm so sorry about that! I really liked that guy, though—I think he might be a good fit."

"Good, listen, I—they said there might be a problem. Something about sperm banking."

Danny looked confused but a little triumphant, and started to form a question. The doctor walked back in.

"Miss Lavery—"

"Doctor Lavery," I corrected.

"I'm sorry, *Doctor* Lavery, my colleagues and I have had a quick discussion and we think it might be a good idea for you to wait to start treatment, until you've had a chance to bank some sperm. The risks to fertility associated with hormonal replacement therapy are such that it might be very difficult to reverse any loss."

Danny looked at me.

"I . . . don't want to wait. I don't want to bank sperm. Please prescribe the HRT today."

"Are you sure, Doctor Lavery? I want to make sure you understand that this might limit your future options."

"I understand. I don't want to wait a moment longer. Thank you for your patience with me."

Danny and I barely spoke in the car. He drove me to a CVS in Oakland, and we sat quietly, waiting for the medication to appear. He'd been on testosterone for a few weeks already, so this was kind of old news for him.

"How are you feeling?" he asked me.

"Nervous," I said quietly.

The pills came, and we left together, him in the driver's seat as always, and me clutching these two little bottles, orange pills and blue. (A starfish in water.) He wanted to find the right question to work around my resentment of him, but he didn't know how—there probably wasn't a way—and in any case, my mind suddenly became very focused on defending my masculinity, my maleness. It seemed important to salvage some dignity from this thoroughly humiliating experience.

Kate Bush played on the car stereo—I think it was my phone, probably "Room for the Life" or something resonant like that. There was a lot of magic around this time, a lot of strange coincidences, I'm not even writing about them mostly, because I would sound unhinged. But there was a lot of magic.

I told Danny a story, probably one he had heard me tell before. When I was at college, I used to wear dresses often, and makeup sometimes too. It wasn't, mostly, a sexual thing—though I guess I did feel sexy in them, or some of them, or I sometimes felt sexy in some of the dresses. I was a very showy, flamboyant person, full of drama, full of mischief and nonsense. People accommodated my cross-dressing as part of a broader platform of deliberate weirdness; nobody asked me any questions about it, and nobody assumed it meant anything more than a toga party. And I was always drunk.

And one day, when I was drunk, I grasped at my friend Sam, while I was weeping desperately in a red dress, and I think we were in public at a party in someone's room, but as I say, I was drunk. And I said, "I know everyone thinks this is just for show, that it's just bravado, that it's just for show, but it isn't—*this is really who I am, underneath.*" And Sam said, "I know that."

I told Danny this story, and then I unscrewed the bottles, removed 50 ml of spironolactone and 2 ml of estradiol, and swallowed both right there in the passenger seat of Danny's old Honda, Kate Bush on the stereo and tears in my eyes.

Most of the experience of transition is unsurprising. The rudeness, stupidity, and cruelty of others is only to be expected—people are mostly rude, stupid, and cruel. The frustrations over genitals, dysphoria, unpredictable and unreliable changes to the body, which are never exactly what one hopes for, even if one is thrilled by what one gets: again, this is much like any other project of radical self-transformation. There are, however, a few real surprises. The first one I encountered was this: that, a few days after I popped those pills for the first time, the lightness in my chest that I felt in that hot tub in Sedona returned to me, brightened my extremities, elevated my neck and my arms, and steadied me within my own frame. Grace returned to me, and has not left me since.

Another surprise was how immediately intuitive my new way of being seemed to be, to most people around me, most of the time. I asked Cecilia whether I seemed different, and she said, "no, you're very much still the same person, just much more so." There's something disappointing there—one wants to have become a different person, and yet one cannot. *It's just like a novel.* Still, what was unexpected to me was how often the people who wanted to speak with me and hang out with me were women. I quickly adjusted to a life in which there were very few men— almost none, in fact, beyond the dozen or so that I love deeply, and treasure among my closest friends. In situations where I was friends with a straight couple, I was fairly immediately and intuitively passed over from the domain of the husband to the domain of the wife. Men are not, I have come to think, psychically real to me in the way that women are: I was raised by two women, and the difference between my mother and my grandmother is really the structuring Oedipal myth of my life. In one of the relationship counseling sessions Danny and I do together, I said to the therapist, "listen, my mother was my mother and my grandmother was my father. But my grandmother's trauma was all specifically organized around her womanhood—her miscarriages, her resentments at her economic marginalization, her hatred of lesbians. So my father was a homophobic woman, and that is why I am a transsexual." And my therapist and I had, like, an "ah!" moment, and then I retracted it—"I mean, I realize it's not that simple"—and she shrugged and said, "I don't know, honestly; maybe, who knows?" Men are outsiders—that can be sexy, or terrifying, or gratifying, non-exclusively—but they don't count, in the way women count, except as individuals.

My hormones call to other women's hormones. After a couple of weeks, I connected with an old acquaintance at a work dinner, who was now seven months pregnant. We immediately and intuitively connected on a level we had never quite mustered before. It was simply that there was a groove, a place for us to be conjoined. I have become a friend, a companion, someone from whom counsel can be sought without fear or flinching. And, in another circle, tighter to my body than companionship, around me on all sides I have friends I touch—women I cannot not touch, and who cannot not touch me, women whose lips and teeth and cruelty and readiness to be plundered are no longer notional or obscure, but are felt precepts of our coexistence. I have become a sex hippy, I hold hands with my friends when we walk down the street, they touch my breasts and gulp in the stink of my neck, my glands.

Danny has had a sometimes difficult relationship with the boundlessness of my heart chakra, but, latterly, an epiphanic one. He found a way to unscrew his root chakra, and feel it pouring out into the world. Now, he wants people to come and touch him, roughly and sweetly, and he wants to say rebarbative, resentful things at them. And me he wants split open and riven, fisted and fucked and stuffed like he is stuffed. Pushed deep into the mystery hole, between my legs, whose felt presence I have never known how to avow.

One time—and now, I realize, I am placing into the preterite an event that is really past continuous, that is imperfect or even present—we were approached by a couple of dykes who wanted to fuck both of us. I was anxious, at first, because I must go through the whole genital rigmarole—and I assume that while perhaps most lesbians are keen to affirm trans women, none would actually want to fuck us, to fuck me. I am always astonished to learn that this isn't always true, and perhaps isn't even generally true. It always feels like a gift to learn that, again and again.

At the end of that evening, Danny showed one of our guests where to put her hand—inside me—or inside my outside, outside my inside, in the seven veiled folds of my flesh where my husband discovered me. With Danny, who cares for me and loves me, the discovery of my secret hole has always been inextricable

173

from a desire that there *be* a secret hole, and that he share it with me and help me enjoy it. At times, this has felt to me like a kind of brainwashing: believe that you have a pussy there, imagine it—like imagine an arm growing out of your chest—and if you imagine it, you can do things with it—imagine an arm growing out of your chest, and now imagine the hand at the end of that arm, and now imagine that it is shaking hands with another hand . . . You can do a lot with that kind of imaginary work, but it isn't the right phenomenological domain—it isn't the place where things *matter*—it isn't the place where you flinch and squirt. Danny explained not to me, but to our guest, who loved and cared about me no more than one woman cares about another; and she pushed, and found the cavity quickly. I was tucked away out of sight, head burrowed in embarrassment into the pillow, embarrassed at my own pleasure as well as the extraordinary nature of what was happening.

I came quickly, spasmed and shrieked all over the hand and bed. Torrey Peters writes about the connection between thirty-something-transitioning trans women (like her and me) and divorcées—both striking out on their own in midlife.[3] The late-in-life lesbian—Cybill Shepherd in *The L Word*, say—learns something quite specific. She learns that while she did not know how to touch her body, and that perhaps nobody who ever fucked her exactly knew, *someone* knew—*someone* had acquired that expertise, stored and filed that knowledge correctly, kept perhaps imperfect records that require some kind of updating in each case, held that knowledge in trust over time, over centuries, and held it in store for her. The other archive is the hand that fucks me, shaped by knowledge of me and people like me, sharing that knowledge with me and building new networks, hand to cunt, dyke to dyke, cunt to hand.

CHAPTER FIVE
TRUE LOVE WAYS

Why are so many British people—including a sizable chunk of liberal/lefty women—hostile to trans women? Over the last few years, the gender critical movement has become, along with Brexit, one of the definitive dimensions of contemporary British political style—the "characteristic part" of contemporary British politics, one might say.

The gender criticals have a certain amount in common with the Brexiteers: a love of boundaries; a rather defeated but nonetheless dogmatic insistence on the inviolability of traditional taxonomies; perhaps above all, a pastoral delight in the idea of a space from which outsiders have been evacuated—a Pole-less nation, and a pole-less ladies' bathroom.

Then there's the left critique of trans people: that we, especially, are guilty of buying into commercial solutions to structural problems, buying and mutilating ourselves out of suffering that we should be forced to endure. The British love a rainy day, and there is more dignity in a problem shared than one solved.

That argument has a historical dimension. Their embrace of LGBT rights became, in the 1990s, the alibi with which Tony Blair and the New Labourites were able to present themselves as still, in some sense, a left-of-center party, despite having adopted Tory spending pledges and outflanking the Tories to the right on most Home Office issues. So LGBT rights and the neoliberal takeover of the Labour Party became associated—and for a certain kind of petit bourgeois voter (a Lexiteer, for example), opposing the latter necessitated opposing the former. And queers are decadent, anyway. Kathleen Stock OBE, a prominent gender critical commentator, uses the word to describe trans people not infrequently.

To some degree, the intensity around trans issues is simply amplified by the internet, with perfectly reasonable ideas snowballing into utterly unreasonable ones, and unreasonable ideas snowballing into strategies of abuse, and online strategies of abuse snowballing into IRL attacks (I've been spat on, for example). Gender critical thought gets shared horizontally between platforms, with people developing ever-more histrionic and bizarre theories of the world, which are then summoned to reinforce other people's theories.

And then there's something else. Something stranger, that I suspect is underneath the whole phenomenon of British gender criticals—that is everywhere mysterious and unspoken—the problem that I refer to as *leaky boobs and the school run*, the revenge of feminine grievance against feminist pleasure, the joy of the chore; sourness as a political aesthetic; the loathing of the trans woman as a figure of pleasure embodied, of—**SNIP**

What is the relationship between the femmebot and the Martian Girl from *Mars Attacks!*? The latter comprises two parts: the girl part (the femme presentation of the drive to murder the president) and the alien part (the queer but sexless form of the Cartesian homunculus). We cannot be sure of how many parts the femmebot is composed, but certainly there are many,

The mission: to find the future and teach it how to shag, baby, yeah!

and because there is no homunculus, there is apparently no deception.

The femmebot's tits are ballistic weapons, but they also emit smoke, meaning that she is not merely a weapon but also a seducer. And she allows herself to be seduced in turn, and, when that task is accomplished, explodes as though subject to a ballistic weapon. The femmebot places her fists on her hips and her hair radiates in space: She is history itself, glancing back across time towards the present ("the nineties" being the name that this particular period gave to the eternal present of neoliberal foreclosure) in defiance. The femmebot has been humped, pumped, and dumped, but refuses to share in the refractory period of post-historical coldness that we have tried to impose; history has not been finished, even if we are finished with it. Thus even the femmebot's apparent susceptibility to our own seduction is a ruse. Like the Terminator, even if it appears to explode or dissolve, it will recombine and shoot bullets at us, Cupid's arrows, love letters straight from the heart.

The first time my mother and I talked about my father, a topic about which I was not as interested as I should have been, I initiated the conversation, and I did so by imparting information to her. I must have been about seven or eight, and someone at school had asked me where my father was, and I had told him that he, my mother, and I had all been on holiday, and the return plane took off without him. He was still there, on holiday, and we'd go pick him up one day. I can't possibly have believed this story, but I *have* retained memories of the biplane that my mother and I took off in, and him running towards it, as though he was trying to jump on a train, hat in hand.

When I told my mother this version of the story, she said, "yes, something like that." She smiled knowingly—she was conspiring with my own sense of fantasy to protect me from information she thought might hurt me.

When I was a child, my mother had a habit that I found disturbing: she would sometimes exclaim, out of nowhere, the name "B————!" I didn't know why. I knew two people by that name: a priest whom she'd only met quite recently, whom I liked, and a kid at the school where she was headteacher. I asked her about this habit from time to time, and she would tell me that it was an almost random word, that her father (who died eleven years before I was born) used to yelp out, "I want some money!" in a similar way. As it goes, I have indeed inherited this compulsion: for me, it is the phrase "I hate myself and I want to die," a fragment of language that comes out of me, usually when I'm alone, and usually accompanied by a shiver of embarrassment, or maybe mild anxiety, but rarely anything like the affect that the words themselves seem to index. In the last couple of years of my drinking, this involuntary yelping increasingly happened in company, and increasingly at work. I was afraid people could hear me barking inside my office, shivering and dying of shame.

My mother gave me a little more information about B—— when I was about thirteen. He was a man she'd met when she moved to the West Midlands, with whom she had fallen in love and had a long and passionate romantic relationship. I asked whether he was my father, and she said yes. I asked why they didn't stay together, and my mother said, why do you think? And I said, I have no idea. And she responded, a little tetchy, "well, what is the *main* reason why two people don't get married?" I asked if he was already married to someone else, and she responded crossly, "no!" And made me cycle through a few other guesses before she finally revealed the answer—"because, Jos, he was a priest!"

I haven't understood my mother's relationship to priests since I stopped going to church, but I can see how they occupy an important role in her life, as dashing and charismatic confidantes, people whose attention can be wanted, won, and resented. She described B—— as the acme of these: Oxford-educated ("where you get your brains"), tender and kind, romantic. They soon conceived a child together, and then eventually he chose Christ over my mother.

This story, it turned out, wasn't true; when I was seventeen or so, the subject of my paternity came up again, and this third time my mother approached the topic in a guiltier mood. B—— was not my father; rather, my biological father was a married man named T——, a parent at the school she had worked at, with whom my mother had initiated a one-night stand after her break-up with B——, so urgently did she want to conceive a child. My biological father and his wife had wanted to be involved in raising me, but he was an alcoholic and my mother didn't want them around. I had three half brothers and a half sister, a large family out of reach. To this day, I've never met any of them, and I assume they don't know anything about me.

My mother had not had a great deal of experience with men. There was a college boyfriend whom she mentioned sometimes, and then there were one or two suitors who came through when I was a kid—I remember a charismatic financial advisor who came by a few times—but I decided, at quite a young age, that my mother was probably gay. I told her this often, I suppose in an attempt to jostle her, push her around, scandalize her slightly.

"Oh, you think I'm a Lesbian, do you?," she would respond, in a mock-theatrical tone, the word held at arm's length. And then, more thoughtfully, "I think I might like to have been a Lesbian."

I don't have much of an opinion on this question anymore, except to say that it doesn't make sense to assess a person's sexual history on the basis of desires they never expressed, or acted on (as far as I know), or maybe ever had. I don't know how to describe my mother's sexuality. She loved a priest, once. That part seems very true.

One time when I was about sixteen years old, I was asked to participate in a dance event at the girls' school, along with the handsomest boys. I did not know (do not know) why they had asked me. There were five of us, and the other four were all very pretty: one was beefy, one was trim, one had a lovely gentle stoner vibe, and one had deep, sweet eyes. Each of us was introduced as a type of boy: the muscular one, the athletic one, the creative one, the sweet one . . . and me, "the Austin Powers type." I suppose this was because I dressed eccentrically, having bought my clothes from vintage stores, and was always wearing eccentric sunglasses. I felt so misunderstood and hurt, even though I knew that my being cast as "the Austin Powers type" indicated my sexual viability in some strange way, or at least my sexual legibility. I couldn't make it dignified, though; there was no dignity in my masculinity. Humiliatingly oversexed antiquarianism: "Do I make you horny, baby, yeah!"

And they weren't wrong, haha. I was someone whose version of being a man was both deeply in love with men/manliness and deeply committed to the absolute abolition and erasure of the type. "The Austin Powers type" of man is not really a type at all, but the space that reveals the incompleteness of the typology, the necessity of proper nouns to complete any taxonomy adequately. In that sense, "the Austin Powers type" is the Jack Fairy type, too, or the Paterian diaphanous type—a floaty, lovable boy, trousered in clouds.

As distinct from Dr. Evil as a frozen sperm, floating around in a Big Boy. But the fantasy of escaping the present by projecting oneself into the future is the structuring fantasy not merely of sperm banking, but of banking as such, which preserves capital (we used to say "one's capital") by deferring it still further. Capital, from the perspective of the capitalist, is nothing other than the permanent deferral of value, or the prolongation of the delicious period of anticipation. Here a difference can be marked between the 1960s and the 1990s, or the period immediately preceding the rollout of neoliberal monetarism and its heyday (at least as these realities have been constructed as the positive and negative forms of the present). Back then, Virtucon was a front for a project to take over the world, but now "there is no world," only the front; the conditions of possibility for the eventual liquidation of value have been, themselves, liquidated.

I have been speaking with my mother about this memoir. Not because I can ask her to sign off on what I write, but because I need to record her testimony, as a counterpoint to mine. A counterpoint, because harmony is too much to ask for—although the first half of my life was spent in a relationship with one person with whom I experienced almost everything that I experienced, we don't have a common narrative about it. We don't have a story in common. I wonder why this is—my mother seems, to everyone to whom I've ever introduced her, terrified to say anything wrong, to be thought stupid or rude. At its best, this anxiety makes her charismatic, and lovable—people love to root for her. At worst, she explodes, as when at the first Christmas she spent with the family of someone I was seeing, she gave an incorrect answer in a game of *Trivial Pursuit* and stormed out. When I followed, she said everyone was laughing at her—which I related to then, and still do. More usually, and pretty much always around me, it causes her to seethe and crackle. She never lets me finish a sentence but she interrupts me; she never lets me say anything about my self or my life but she contradicts me. When she isn't speaking with me, she sits across the room and stares at me.

My best guess is this: my grandmother, by all accounts, preferred her brother, and lavished him with affection and attention, neglecting my mother. My mother's only way of understanding her neglect, and her brother's power, was through a fight to the death. She needed to destroy her brother—and more and more psychic resources were devoted to this battle to find her brother's weaknesses, exploit them, and win. My uncle is, in his own way, compulsively competitive with his sister: one time, on holiday, he pushed her, violently, into the sea, when a debate over whether or not some landmass was Spain escalated. This pattern instantiates some version of the Oedipal complex, with my mother as the (male) child and her brother playing the role of Oedipal father, competing for the mother's affection on unequal terms.

When, years later, she moved in with her mother for the purposes of raising me, the complex was still unresolved, but her brother was absent, so I became an unstable substitute. From the time I was very young, she would call me by my uncle's name—she still does, sometimes. In that sense, the positions of son and mother merged in her, and the process of mothering me—raising me with care and love, neither of which she ever withheld—became, at the same time, a process of surveillance— learning my weaknesses, developing antidotes to my own aggression. Now, in older age, she and her brother have fixed much of their animosity, especially since Grandma's death in 2002, but the animosity that had been transferred over to me has no obvious solution. She's locked in a duel to the death with me, for some acknowledgment or admission I can't or won't give her.

When I sleep on my own, I dream of England.

Rhapsody on a Doctor Who _Christmas Special That Might Be Broadcast Some Time After the Present Conflict Has Been Resolved and Peace Has Returned Once More to My Native Country_

Everyone will be back in the house by Christmas—we'll be to-gether on Christmas morning. Her Majesty's Government, bless their little cotton socks, realizes the distress that will be caused by a shortage of Christmas decorations since the tinsel factory was commandeered to aid in the manufacture of wartime munitions. Will have been caused, rather. Seventy-five factories in the Midlands alone, building tinsel, baubles, and those droopy sacs of shimmering metallic plastic, booblike—and all directed to manufacture armaments for this terrible war. Tinsel nerve agents, bauble bombs, droopy sacs of shimmering metallic poison, booblike. Are there reserves? Probably. A cache of oversupply outside Derby, a box or two lying around in an ownerless lockup in Stanford. There won't be many of us left by Christmas, and we'll make do.

Making do is part of the fun of it. When this is all over, this terrible war, we'll make do just for fun—we'll have become addicted to scarcity, unable to function in conditions of plenitude. We—you and I—will have become those people who tell stories about their shared suffering the first time they ever meet. "What was it like for you?" Though we haven't met yet, and we may never, we know we will have this in common for the rest of our unnatural, Christ-denying lives. Those of us who are lucky enough to have a piano like to bang out tunes on it and rouse ourselves to comfort: "My Old Man's Cthulhu," "You'll Smoke the Whole Packet and Like It, Boy," and "My Girl Came On the NHS." The pianos are out of tune but we rattle them and bounce our bodies against them. We lob the toddlers at 'em, that usually does the trick, and it teaches 'em something about this world of hard knocks. Your grandmother plays songs of Welsh life, singing in a language nobody else can remember. Your children eyeball her and your youngest licks his lips. Your grandmother plays slowly, behind the beat, as though withholding each chord until you've degraded yourself by asking for it. She's a tough old cunt, if truth be told—gritty and slow and cruel. Once she learned that music produces expectations in people who hear it, she understood how useful it could be if she were ever called upon to torture the enemy.

A distinction should be made between torturing in the anticipation of effecting a conversion, confession, or disclosure (on the one hand) and torturing for its own sake, to produce suffering in elegant ways (on the other). No context for either, not during this terrible war—well, we don't have much call for it around here. We're slow, and set in our ways—a couple of gnarled English chestnuts. We'll get cooked on the same conker fire, you mark my words.

What is war, in the end, but an interminable and unlimited ethical obligation that one bears solely as an individual? Life is a rum do and no mistakin', guv'nor. The greater jihad is to conquer one's own soul. War's just a word, really, just a name we give to the condition that derives from the responsibility as soon as one sees it—it sounds scary, but there it is. Interminable and unlimited ethical obligation (check and check), borne as an individual (check), socialism without the social aspect (check). I'm doing my part! We're all chipping in to make Easter shawls to send to Our Boys—boys love shawls, especially those made by girls, or rather by exactly ONE (1) girl per shawl, one shawl per Boy. Girls, breathe on your shawls, rub them into your nose until the snot leaks, spit on them, tuck a corner into your pussy, then spritz them with orange blossom water and airdrop them to your Boy, wheresoever he may be. Boys like smells, too—they will be so happy to know you care.

Everyone's chipping in—there's something almost inspiring about it, like we're all the elves in Father Christmas's grotto. Busting busying busying to get everything ready for Christmas Day, to make the toys, to feed the reindeer tra la la! Each in a little elvish outfit, white and green rings around our tights. I make a wooden spinnaker for Tommy. My neighbour makes a wooden pan for Nobby. Our neighbour makes a wooden lark for Duddy. Their neighbour makes a wooden pouch for Slobby. All the good wooden goods we shall have when this is all over, this terrible war. They shall bring them back to us, Our Boys, and we shall see what use a wooden pan is then. If any at all.

A special episode of Doctor Who *with the woman Doctor broadcast at midnight, unexpectedly, like a Rihanna album launch.*[1] *This time it was just her, explaining the rules of bloody cricket to that gormless Brexit granddad who wheezes his way through his adventures before saying something like "hm, not sure, Doc, seems ripe to me!" He brings the same energy to the cricket splaining. You want to slap him—once, unapologetically—around the chops, the kind of slap that turns his head to the side, dislodging spit and even teeth. Maybe you'll get to when this is all over, this terrible war. But the Doctor addresses the camera directly, saying: "I know you're afraid. I know you're sick of this. I know sometimes it seems like nothing you ever do will ever be normal again. I know you didn't really have a birthday this year—I know that matters to you, too, you spineless reptile. I wish I could promise you things will get better. I could promise you—I could lie, and don't you respect me more for refusing to lie? Not to make this about me. Anyway, you don't get a lie, not today. You get something even more beautiful. You get the knowledge, the sure and certain knowledge, that by being unfazed and clear-eyed—simply by being prepared—you are doing your part to help the most vulnerable among us."*

The "most vulnerable among us"? A politician phrase, surely? But do go off, Doc.

Am I the Brexit granddad? The thought sits there, like an unexploded land mine.

When this war is over I will open my legs to every boy in town, every Tommy and Johnny and Squabby and Dimbo to come home— we'll fling confetti in the sky, and won't there be glinting eyes to go with the clotted cream sandwiches and thick squash? Each can come and take a few pumps, girlie in their arms if need be, smiling and waving to the camera all the while. It won't take much. I'll break the top off 'em like I'm cracking open a snatch of ginger beer, foamy head dribbling down the side. Cheering crowd, a local brass band playing the oom-pah-pah. Friendly red-faced copper twirling his truncheon round as careless as you like, whistling his songs of authority, even he can come can squeeze his short fat cock into me, knock me out like lead and shoot his dirty water right up there. Even the scamps—tearaway thief munchkins—get a scratch at the old scratch-card (rub three out identical, you win up to £10,000). When this terrible war is over I will choke on the round little noblets of all our brave boys, and smile that devilish, whore-breathed smile with your hands on my belly. You won't believe your luck, what I'll do for you with my body, when I get out of here, when you get home from this war—this terrible, terrible war.

Joan Copjec argues that sex is the figure for literality. What do we learn about a person when we learn that they own a "Swedish-made" penis enlarger? Only, presumably, that such a person trusts the Swedes to enlarge their penis. Also, perhaps, that there is something unfinished about their penis—though, as we surely all know by now, the penis is the very signifier for unfinishedness: It is an organ defined, at least in the Lacanian tradition, by its failure to be a phallus.

The pump is Austin Powers's earnestness. Any embarrassment derives not from the smallness of his dick (if it is small! we don't know!) but from his repeated exposure, both deliberate and not, of the labor that has produced his masculinity, from his dick to the ass which he constantly pushes into the air, towards the camera. I say "both deliberate and not," but the man of genius makes no mistakes, and are we truly to believe that the penis pump, and the receipt for the penis pump, and then the book, have not been stashed in order to signal to Vanessa Kensington that this man's girth has been pumped up, that he is not afraid of auxiliaries, and that there is something ineffably charming about a man who is openly trying to grow up his small dick into something bigger and better? The femmebot's real counterpart is Austin Powers himself: the mascbot.

The decline from mascbot into mere mascot is that which transmasculinity resists. And it is the challenge that "the Austin Powers type" encounters, too. Austin Powers is iconic, but smooth where he should be rough (his ass), and rough where he should be smooth (his chest). Dr. Evil, who overestimates the unusualness in 1997 of a shaven ballsack, has the opposite problem: He believes his smoothness to be more transgressive than it is. His sack is like his "million dollars": an embarrassing underbid. So although more depends than one might think on Vanessa's bedding Austin—and thereby, I guess, pulling off a successful reverse Oedipus—of course they could never actually kiss. This is Liz Hurley we're talking about—the femmebot herself—and she doesn't bend down for snogs.

Is there something to be said here about Englishness, too, an automatically mascotized species of masculinity? Mike Myers is Canadian, and Canadian Anglophilia doesn't quite resemble the more ambivalent American position, which positions Englishness as a drag version of American whiteness—Jonathan Groff in *Hamilton* being the most obvious contemporary example. But in none of the most eminent cases—Groff, Austin Powers, John Oliver, Hugh Grant—do we encounter any actual ambivalence around white masculinity. On the contrary, the British man is a trope entirely without critical edge, reduced to sentimental adorableness. Not so the clown, that universally feared/loathed/ envied American figure for monstrous Euro-whiteness—both Pennywise and the Joker—who presents in that sense the tragic form of the English mascbot/mascot.

My mother was my mother. But my grandmother was my father—a woman was my father, and moreover a woman whose life had been organized around a very womanly tragedy: she had suffered eleven successive miscarriages before her first live birth. It's very poetic, but it's also very simple: my father was a woman, so when I grew up to be a man, I became a woman. AND I DON'T NEED A PEE AITCH DEE IN PSYCHOANAL-YSIS TO TELL YOU——**snip**

Inevitably, the trans ruse—"that ain't no woman; it's a man, man!"—as Austin bops a hot chick on the nose and drops her to the floor. And yes, we can deploy this moment to illustrate the general case about transmisogyny: that it is, mostly, an occasion for the expression of much more traditional forms of misogyny. In this case, of the apparently outrageous or transgressive desire to punch a female member of the waitstaff in the face. The same logic is deployed against Basil Exposition's mother.

But, in making that case, we would be missing the tenor of the joke, which is the repetition of the word "man," a phonic device whose effect is to create a new class of person: a man-man. A man-man, unlike a man's man, would be a person who is both apparently a man and actually a man—a man in a man's body—but decidedly two men nonetheless. What the shot has performed is a simple substitution: The actor who took the hit is a woman (played by Chekesha van Putten), but the actor now out cold in Austin's arms is very clearly a man (though uncredited). It would be too much to ask that he not go in for the hit; one can only hope, as he strikes and lands the blow, that it nonetheless misses. Please, miss. What, then, is revealed when Austin, with a flourish, removes the hat and wig? Only that this man, who appeared to have been dressed as a woman, was in fact a man after all. Or rather, a man-man.

Despite the theme of recurrence and resurfacing, the joke of Austin Powers is not the joke of repetition, or even the "callback," though it might make sense to use that language to describe the film as a whole. Rather, the method is persistence: the joke that doesn't stop. The "evacuation complete" piss sequence; the "shh!" sequence; the Swedish-made penis-enlarger pump; Mustafa's groans from the chamber underneath Dr. Evil's war room; the evil laughter; and Austin's failed attempt to turn the car around: six sequences that derive their tone from uncomfortable extension into a suddenly limitless experience of time. This is perhaps what Number Two means when he says that there is no world left. If you want to imagine the future, imagine an old white man from 1967 telling you to shut up, in the face, forever. It is too ugly to bear.

Does John Currin make chaser art? Maybe, but if so, it's the kind of chaser art that reveals the chaser as incipiently or incompletely transfeminine. There's no way around the misogyny of a work like "Jaunty and Mame": it paints women's faces like hydrochloric cum, like a morass of historical flotsam burned into the flesh itself.[2] Yet though the universes Currin depicts are environments where misogyny is felt thickly as rococo oils, they are places where women can look each other in their smashed-up faces, trade bras for cash, say yes and no to each other, straighten palms to signify one thing and twist fingers to mean another. How do two women look at each other, knowing what we know? When my mother looked at me for the first time as a woman, what did she see?

I remember one day you had been chosen to go and see an advanced math tutor and it was something about string and buttonholes, and I didn't understand it but you weren't getting a lot of that, but I wanted you to get more of that. So you went to King Edward's, and if someone had told me when you'd been born that I would send you into selective education, I would have hit them, because I don't *believe* in it. I think the state schools should be good enough for everybody, and selective education is another way of being elitist, and I'm not a great elitist. And I don't regret it. I'm not sure if you regret it, or if you think you'd have been better off going to Bede's or Augustine's. And I really wanted you to be independent of me and have your own life. I'd always felt that, since you were born, since before you were born.

So teenage years, I won't say things were ideal, because you didn't have a father, and I was very aware of you not having a male figure. I used to think that B. was a male figure in your life, because he was quite relaxed, and approachable, and you could get on with him. But I did worry about your not having a male figure. And if you were a bit effeminate about things, I thought it was because you didn't have a male figure. I didn't know how to teach you to shave. That concerned me. Funnily enough, looking back at pictures of you as a teenager, you were quite effeminate. But I don't think I realized, because you were you.

I've got a picture in my wallet of you from when you were 12 or 13 and you have to look twice to see if it's a man or a woman. And then I have a picture of a first communion and I looked at it the other day and I thought "what the hell is Jos doing in that picture," and then I realized it was *me*. Your mannerisms weren't effeminate but your looks were quite effeminate, and Grace I'm saying your mannerisms weren't effeminate but they *might* have been but I didn't realize because they were *you* and that was important.

You mixed with, as most teenagers do, boys and girls, and sexually you didn't have a preference, well you *did* have a preference, for girls. I wasn't aware if you liked being with boys. I just felt that girls were the people you related to. Girls were the people you looked at for a different kind of relationship. I think it was just sexual. But I didn't question you about your sexual things. You were becoming a grown man. And your sexuality was your business, not mine. I remember you coming home once and you'd been with someone at Oxford and you'd been in the toilet of a motorway service station and he'd . . . I don't know if it was rape . . . it seemed a bit odd . . . but I knew you'd had sexual relations with men. But I didn't think that was the way you were going.

I always used to think, I wouldn't be surprised if Jos was gay. Because there was no male dominance in your life. You were surrounded by strong women. And so, I just felt that . . . and thinking about that, I don't know why a gay man should be . . . why being surrounded by strong women should make a man gay, but that was where my mind went. It doesn't really make sense.

I remember how inclusive you were. I remember when you came home and said your new teacher was "Dr. So-and-So," and I said, "what's he like," and you said, and you were right, that that was so anti-feminist. And you taught me to look at all sides, and I'm so grateful for that. And trying not to presume anything about anybody. I was really glad that you were like that.

When you went to University, and I tried hard not to interfere, and I didn't want to influence you to make choices that you'd later regret. I refused to let you do shooting, that was one thing. Probably when you were about seven or eight, there was the Jamie Bulger case, and you were never frightened of doing things but after that case you found it much more difficult to leave me. I think you were afraid of being taken—and you were much closer in age to the kids who had taken him, rather than the kid who was taken. But you didn't go off half as much after that. And I can't remember having a conversation with you about it, which I should have done, to reassure you. And really, I think that's where all of this "playing things down" came from. And what you saw as playing things down, I saw as trying to reassure you. Remember what Grandma was like, she would make mountains out of molehills, and I hated that. But that was when you were much younger.

But after you went to university, you became much more independent, you did your own thing, and you had your own friends, and you used to bring friends home quite often, and I liked that, but I did try to let you have your own life. Which I think it's necessary that you do. But you are your own person, and as far as I'm concerned that's really important.

I can't honestly say your transition spoke to any part of the past. Since you left home at 18, I always felt that you weren't examining your sexuality or your gender issues. One time we met one of your students on the train, and you were really camp with a student on the train. And I said something to you afterwards, and you said, I wasn't being camp, I was just being me. I wasn't sure what it meant. There's no stereotypical gay person. And I know several gay people who I know are gay, and other people I've met who've told me they're gay and I've been quite surprised. And lesbians, too. I was at a gay wedding on Tuesday and it was quite lovely. And if you met one of them you wouldn't know she was gay. The other one you would. But that occasion on the train . . . I hadn't seen you be that way. So I took that to mean that you were less inhibited with the student than with me. But normally when you were with people I felt that was who you liked to be . . . no, who you found it easy to be.

I don't see a relationship between being a gay man and being a trans woman. Being a trans woman is totally different to being a gay man. And I'm very new to this, as you know. But being a trans person is . . . I read an article somewhere recently about not just chromosomes but other physical things, but some trans people might have XXY but also female brain bits, even though they're male, and it's the brain bits that are making them want to be a woman, or need to be a woman. And it wasn't hormones either, and that was why I didn't understand it. But I know I read it with interest.

You never wanted to dress in my clothes or put on my make up. I remember when you were at Oxford you used to put dresses on, and I used to think how attractive you looked. And I thought it was a way of exploring areas that you wanted to explore, rather than saying *I'm trans*. I think to make the transition takes an immense amount of courage and certainty, and perhaps some people wonder if they could, and then others know they couldn't. Is it like being bisexual? And having sexual relationships with both men and women, and people who have sexual relationships with men and women and really experimenting, and if they can't find an answer, that's fine. But someone who's trans *knows* what the answer is, and someone who's gay *knows* what the answer is.

I was very worried from the start about your relationship with your grandmother. I used to say to her, "you are not his mother, you are not his father, you are not in any parental relationship with him." [Not my father?] She might have felt that because you didn't have a father, you might have needed someone to discipline you. She probably did think that way. I just made it clear, as far as I was concerned, that she wasn't to do that. My mother ruined my brother's life, as you know, and I didn't want that to happen. She dominated him and dictated to him, and told him what to do and what not to do, and that's why I wouldn't do that with you.

My father wasn't the disciplinarian in our house, my mother was. So that might have just been me saying something that I thought would make sense. I didn't want her to feel that she could dominate you the way she dominated Tim.

My mother always tried to dominate males more than women. We both had an abusive childhood; my brother's because he was dominated by my mother and told what to do, and mine because I was ignored and I wasn't encouraged and . . . Tim was the focus of my mother's life. I didn't want you to be like my brother in my mother's eyes. Her father hadn't been dominant, her mother was the dominant person in that family, and her mother dominated her father. So perhaps she just thought this was normal. But she also kowtowed to men, she was one of those people who—if a man and a woman are talking to a third person, and a woman asks a question, she would answer to the man. It's so demeaning to the female.

This was one of her stories. She shared a room with a woman who a lesbian fancied. And one night this lesbian girl . . . it wasn't at college it was at school . . . she was at boarding in school in Manchester in one time, not for long.

It meant her parents had sent her away. The lesbian came into her bedroom, and had sex or presumably some sort of lesbian relationship with her roommate. I don't think she was involved in a lesbian relationship, but she was a witness to one. She would have been in her mid teens. She didn't like gay people. Because she didn't like what she was being a witness to—she thought it was *wrong*, probably, in a religious sense. Then gay people were all tarred with the same brush.

I don't think she was aware of any gay men. She grew up in a time when any sort of gay relationship was not just forbidden but a crime, so people didn't show their gayness and didn't like to say they were gay. But anybody she thought was gay . . . I don't think she came across anybody that might have been gay. But people like Liberace, she used to love watching him. But then she would say "I think he's a homosexual," or she might have said "I think he's one of them." Delia Smith, when you told her that she was a lesbian icon, and grandma said "but she's a Catholic."

She was sent away to boarding school in Manchester— her father was supposed to have had an affair with someone, and perhaps it was around then.

The two transitions in life are from babyhood to childhood and then childhood into adulthood. And usually if one's difficult, the other isn't bad. And you weren't easy as a toddler. And I won't say you were easy as a teenager, but it was an easier time. And you liked going to new places and meeting new people and you were always very friendly and open and happy. At the same time you were quite determined and you had a temper.

The other story, you were already quite *sensitive*. When you were about 18 months old, you didn't have any speech, we went away to Scotland and had about a week up there, and we went to the sea and went to Edinburgh. When we came home, you climbed the stairs and squeaked with pleasure as you climbed every step. And I thought maybe you thought we weren't ever going to be home again, you were so surprised. I had tried to explain it but perhaps you hadn't got the language development. I thought you must be very sensitive and open to different things.

Shortly after that phone call, and still in the midst of everything, I received another letter, the penultimate: same scritchy handwriting, same drawing of a toothy clown, except this time to my home address in New York. In the top left corner, just above the by now familiar illustration, a caption: *True Love Ways*. Was this some kind of a return address for my mysterious correspondent? A revision of the phrase "true love waits" which positioned "ways" as a kind of verb meaning "finds a way" or "barges through"? If you say it out loud you get "true love weighs," which doesn't help; unless it's "true love weighs in," as in "intervenes." It wasn't self-evident. The longer I stared at it, the more strange the words seemed: "true"—"love"—"ways." There had to be a syntactical order to them, a principle of subordination. The true ways of love; the ways of true love.

I opened the letter. The same familiar type, but the paper seemed older, rougher, as though it had been retrieved from another epoch, from the archive I visited with Susan in my dream. If I'd had to guess, I would have dated the letter itself to the 1940s at the latest. Yet it couldn't be so, unless I was somehow supposed to read what was within not as a narrative, but as a prophesy:

Dear Professor Lavery,

What you don't seem to understand is that a woman's life is not really worth living.

"I have done less than nothing for you," said Germaine Greer, vividly and in your face, shortly before muttering, "us girls," hopping in the Fiat Punto, and popping on an old CD of Jenny Eclair.

What on *earth* did people expect? That a group of—excuse me—hairy-arsed malefactors could slap on a lick of paint, dress up like whores, and that we'd applaud them for looking like Halloween versions of the very women we despise? And yet it's so striking that so many do want to applaud them—their bravery, their authenticity. It is evidence, if nothing else, of the supine weakness that female socialization breeds in our degenerate species. *I wouldn't give them the time of day*, thinks Germaine, taking a moment to congratulate herself on the terseness of her of own judgment.

Jenny Eclair telling a joke about menses on the radio. *That's more like it*, she thinks, pressing her fuck-me pumps into the throttle.

It was a day of chores ahead of the feminist philosopher: even feminists must do chores every now and then! She remembered the look on Friedan's face when she told her that she rather *enjoyed* the school run and regretted having failed to spawn. "Yes, that's right, Elizabeth: I ferry other women's children off to their places of education in order to save their mothers the hassle. It's sisterhood, and I am grateful for the opportunity to be of service." Friedan had flashed her the voluptuous smile she usually reserved for powerful politicians and lesbians, murmured, *sotto voce*, "well, Germaine, tits that have suckled a brood shall never see me nude," tossed her hair like Lily Langtry, and hightailed it smartish to the self-love workshop Dods was running.

The first chore was to drop off the spare nappies at the church office for the tombola at this weekend's church fete. Last year was such a good do—a proper spread, as they said in Germaine's adoptive Derbyshire. Sprouted alfalfa in a rice salad, and it really was very good. The tombola had become something of a local cause célèbre. The principle was that, these days being what they are (which is to say, pleasureless and drab), nobody wanted to win the usual frivolous trinkets on offer at such occasions. "The best prize of all is having the choice," as the old saying goes, and the Vicar's particular interpretation of that saying was that people wanted to win things they were going to buy anyway, and so getting them for free at the church tombola would save them the time. So if one's ticket was drawn from the rolling cannon, one had the pick of a range of practical items—toilet paper, suds, a vacuum bag, a blankie—and one could claim anything, anything at all, provided that one had a receipt for the very same item in one's purse. Anything left over at the end of the fete—that for which nobody present had a receipt—was donated to the Poor, who would gobble it to shreds with all the moral dignity one associates with their social class.

The next was the weekly shop. This, Germaine did not enjoy. The shops all had strategies for helping, of course, and that was kind of them; you could get these recipe cards to plan your week's menu as soon as you walked in, and then they'd just tell you what you needed to buy and where to find it. That took some of the pressure off. *I suppose I'm one of those people*, thought Germaine, suddenly in the first person, *who just doesn't know what she wants to eat before she knows the options! And what's wrong with that, I'd like to know?* Nothing was wrong with it, of course. She just feared there was.

Back in the car, and here's Jenny Eclair again—*Jenny éclat, more like!* thought Germaine—and this time she's talking about queefing. *Classic bit*, thought Germaine.

Is this the life you want for yourself, Professor Lavery? Will you forgive those of us who find it woeful?

When Germaine got home, aware that the most devastating chores were still ahead of her, she found a package on the mat outside her home. It was stamped, but not post-marked. Someone had perhaps meant to post it, but then decided to deliver it. In the corner of the package was a small picture of two clowns, the friendliest and lovingest clowns you've ever seen. Clowns of glad tidings, bespeaking good news to all men. On the left, the clown who is called Justice, blinded and carrying his scales. On the right, the clown who is called Healing, upon his forehead the cross that signifies the capacity to bear one's suffering into the future. *The clowns have come to save us*, thought Germaine.

After she had opened the package, she retrieved from it a bundle of paper, a crisply typed manuscript for a novel entitled *True Love Ways*, seemingly a picaresque farce about the sexual misadventures of a ragtag group of misfit gender critical feminists. And on top, in handwriting so untidy as to look vaguely deranged, were written out the lyrics of the familiar Buddy Holly song:

Why

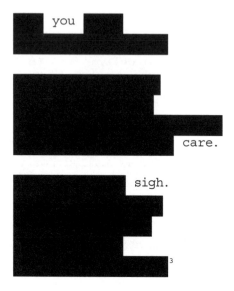

Here endeth the message, my dear Professor Lavery. I trust you are keeping yourself in good spirits.

Sincerely,

Dr. Joseph Lavery

Okay, buddy—whatever you say!

The letters were still postmarked New York, so there was no question of whether they were coming directly from the UK. But clearly in some sense, these letters were able to speak *from* the UK in some way, and indeed, they seemed capable of speaking from every position I could ever see myself having occupied. It was as though the letters were coming to me through a crack between worlds, from a parallel universe where thought was the same as fact.

"Signs from the universe." Once one assumes oneself capable of hearing such a thing, one hears them everywhere. Strolling out of my apartment building, into the street, over the road, onto the subway, it sounds as though everything—everywhere—is speaking to me, telling me things I should know, things that will rip the falsehoods from my flesh. The sounds and signs of the city—of this city—of New York City—

Hey! Fuck you! I'm walkin' here! Get your—get your lousy step off the sidewalk, man! This isn't any potato chip day parade! I ain't no stool for gawkers! This ain't no fungal episode, Molly Ringworm! You're in New York City now, baby—get used to it.

This isn't the city of Bristol or Cornwall or wherever you're from, ya Anglo poindexter. Here we just tell it like it is. You're ugly! Yeah, I said it and I'm not sorry. Brouhaha noises!

SUBWAY RUMBLING UNDERNEATH, RATTLES THE ENTIRE FRAME.

I am played by Victor Schiavelli! Don't know who that is, douchebag? Fuckin' google it, what am I, your fuckin' mother or something? You even have a mother? Bet she's real proud, real fuckin' proud of this fuckin' mess you're walking around like.

> *When he was ten his father slipped, full of it, double dip,*
> *Two years and Alex's mallet got his mother's wet trip—*
> *no shit, a middle of a fiddle and a sip,*
> *and Alex took pleasure from his mother's red slip.*

Ya live by the sword, ya die by the sword, hear what I'm saying? Ya live by the cup, ya die by the sword. Ya live by the coin, ya might be able to get out of it. Ya live by the wand, well then you've got a wand-versus-sword–type situation and you don't wanna be on the wrong side of that kind of showdown, I'm telling ya!

It's kill or be killed out here. I don't kill you, you're gonna turn around and kill me soon as I turn around. I turn around, you don't

kill me, someone's gonna turn around and kill you, soon as you turn your back. Watch your back. I watch my back. My back is watched by a squad of back watchers who watch my back and the backs of those near me and facing in the same direction. Get yourself a squad. Join a squad, then stab the main back you're supposed to be watching, then take his place. Now the squad's watching *your* back. But don't neglect to watch your *own* back too—your own back watchers are eyeing your spot in the back-watching squad.

SUBWAY CAUSES LIGHT EARTHQUAKE. WE LOSE OUR BALANCE, STAGGER AROUND.

Ya got stubble! Ya got an Adam's apple! Jesus fuckbag, if I didn't know better I'd guess you'd been through masculinizing puberty or something. What is this, *Jeopardy* or twenty questions or something? Yes, animal, yes, slightly shy of six feet, yes, wearing makeup, yes, lookin like a freak, and oh yes, it's fuckin' you mister don't you ever forget

Moved in with his cousin, his cousin committed suicide,
A suicidal cousin was a wound to the family pride,
A friend of his cousin said, "you gotta mind your health,"
Alex retreated to the oven, said, "you mind it by yourself."

You gotta wise up! Comedians gonna comeed. It's okay to be offended, you can survive that, you gotta survive that if you wanna see what's coming next, then ya gotta survive that if you wanna see what comes after, then ya gotta survive that, then you're done. Done as a pancake, finito. Finit*a*, excuse me, mister lah-di-dah.

Yeah, you remind me of one of them, what do they call 'em, kumquats. Yeah. You get 'em sometimes. Small and sour and you can eat the whole thing or you can peel 'em if you like. No need to bother, the rind is the best part. Kumquats. Funny word. Sounds like "cum squats" or something. Like the squats you do to get the cum out.

WE snorted him,
ME, I hided him,
ME, I cussed at him,
ME, I loved it,
And ME, I'm the glad fool of Christmas!

THE ROMANCE OF RED NEON ON YELLOW-GRAY STONE. A SURPRISING SOFTNESS. GLIMPSE OF AN ORCHID GROWING THROUGH THE CRACKS. PERHAPS THERE IS HOPE, PERHAPS THERE IS GENTLENESS TO COME.

STAMP ON THE ORCHID! GLITCH IN THE NEON! STONE CRUMBLES! ORCHIDECTOMY! CRYPTORCHID!

Stab first and stab often. Stab yourself, make sure the other guy's off-kilter. Stab yourself first (this is the way to avoid bad surprises) then get stabbed. Then say you knew you were going to get stabbed and tell yourself you were right to know. Then, the learning that you were right will stand in for learning in a more general sense. So you decide that the reinforcement of your failed attempt to defer the possibility of suffering by pretending that saying, "I'm gonna get stabbed," prepared you for getting stabbed is the same as wisdom. You praise it in others. You nurture it in yourself. You theorize it in abstract terms.

The possibility that not all surprises will be bad surprises? This is not something you get to say here in New York City, baby! Take that shit to Hoboken. Take that shit to Poughkeepsie. Take that shit to Jersey City. Take that shit out to California with all them other brain-dead, flower-power, mind-wipe, Stepford-Wife, blaze-it-smoke-a-doobie hippies! Take that shit out to Reykjavik! Take that shit out to Guangzhou! Take that shit back where you came from, Bristol or Cornwall or wherever, and give my fuckin' regards to the fuckin' queen when ya get there!

I'm a sudden button mutton man
but just you waiiiiiiiiiiiiiiiiiiiiit!
what's your name, friend?

IN A FEW SHORT YEARS THIS WILL BE YOU, DOUCHEBAG.

But then you walk onto the platform, onto the train, out of the train, onto the platform, out of the station, onto the streets of Lower Manhattan—Canal Street, say, or Delancey—and into the old-fashioned butcher's shop, at the end of the block, and suddenly you are back in Alvechurch, opposite the Red Lion, next to the Co-Op. The butcher has an identical apron—you *know*, don't you, that it is royal blue, with thin silver pinstripes—and his fat fingers are sausage-like, spread over wax paper like herby vintage bangers. The English words for *offal*: the *pluck*, the *lights*, the *fries*. "Do you want fries with that?" and what he means is whether pig testicles might accompany your molten kidneys? And it seems unlikely in SoHo, or TriBeCa, but in fact it's identical: the same flaring nostrils—*le groin*—the same coprophagic grin. All that is missing is that which is always missing—the postcards, "the art of Donald McGill," as George Orwell rather generously called it.[4] As a child I called them "bare bum postcards," or perhaps my mother did; anyway they were hardly all by Donald McGill, and the one that I remember most—that has the most, meatiest butchery—has neither an arse nor a bully-boy butcher, just a breasty Mrs. White–type stuffing a liverwurst into a customer's crotch, causing him—what? Embarrassment? Untimely arousal? Disgust? Outside the

"YOU'RE A BIT LOADED, SIR... I'LL JUST TUCK THAT LIVER SAUSAGE IN YOUR BELT!"

door, the White Cliffs of Dover remind us that there will be a tomorrow—perhaps one in which not merely is the world free, but that a woman in a swimming costume, hobbled forwards over her cunt, might finally be able to cleave some space between her feet and her shoes.

Of course, that future isn't today, and wasn't yesterday. But here in New York City, a woman can tuck a saveloy into the gap of my arsehole, in public, in front of everyone, only because I've paid for it—and my embarrassment is delicious, is part of it.

She switches on the television. This is a British-*themed* butcher, they stream the BBC. They play music that goes *that's neat that's neat that's neat that's neat I really love your tiger feet*. And then who should hove into view, bulbous microphone shoved in his mug, muttering off to the side like an 80s pop star trying to appear modest, but the man himself: Robert Webb, the cool one from *Peep Show* who never really made much of his undoubted natural talent. "Yeah," he says, "'I was different, as was my wife. I was a 'queer,' she was a 'tomboy.' It turned out we were non-gender-conforming children. Many kids like us turn out to be gay. Others don't. A tiny minority have dysphoria."

Fair enough, responds the interviewer, pulling the mic back. Then thrusts it forwards. Robert looks confused, splutters silently. Mic gets pulled back again. Interviewer says, "we're rolling. Could you start again?" Mic thrust forwards again. Robert Webb says, eyes fucking the camera like James Deen fucks a fan:

"Hello, everybody, I'm Robert Webb. This is me, in a nutshell: I'm a good-looking bloke who used to be in a British comedy double act from the 2000s called Mitchell and Webb. I was born in Lincolnshire in 1972—Ted Heath was on the throne and all was well in England!—and I attended a grammar school in Horncastle. When I left school at the usual age I went to Cambridge, where I met a young aspiring funnyman by the name of David Mitchell, who became my writing partner and fast friend. Eventually, with our other friend Sam Bain, we made a successful and long-running TV show called *Peep Show*, which gave Olivia Colman her big break—and didn't she just win an Oscar?[5] Very well deserved, Olivia. I'm so proud of you, and I'm sure David is too. *The Favourite* really was just such a romp—and spicy, too![6]

"My friend David and I went on to make a sketch show together—you know, a good, old-fashioned British sketch show, in the vein of *The Two Ronnies*—which was really just a lot of fun.[7] Great days, great guys. For the last decade, things have been, sure, a little slower—I chuckle when I think we tried to launch a topical comedy show called *Robert's Web*, which was canceled after four episodes![8] You can't blame a guy for trying! But the truth is, I don't need to be the center of attention all the time. I got into comedy because I enjoyed having a laugh with my mates, and I'm just so glad that I got to do some wonderful things before the laughter ended. Now I've got a great family that I love, and I try to keep my hand in doing my bit to make the world a better place, here and there, whenever I get the chance. Just a normal bloke with a little bit of a platform, trying to get by.

"My point is that I grew up to be Robert Webb eventually—we all do—and all it took was some string beans and strong ale, as my only good grandmother used to say. And that's really all I have to say. It. Gets. Better. I'm taking a bit of a risk to speak to you today, and some people out in the Cancel Culture Blogosphere are going to get their "woke" knickers in a twist, but it is time for me to speak out and offer to you a message of glad tidings. You see, I wasn't always such a chipper fella. Times were a little tough in Horncastle. So I particularly want to address any little boys out there who are wondering whether they might be trans. What I have to say is this: don't worry, guys. You too can grow up to be Robert Webb.

"Let me backtrack. Back when I was a little boy, I was sometimes a little dreamy. Poetical, you know. While the rougher boys
of Horncastle were playing rugby and kissing girls, I found myself listening to music (the Smiths, naturally!) or reading the poetry of Oscar Wilde. How does it go? "And yet, and yet / These
Christs that die upon the barricades, / God knows it I am with
them, in some things."[9] (Don't tangle with me when it comes to
Victorian poetry, haha!) I would watch the rougher boys in their
scrums, or kissing their girlfriends, girlfriends by the platoon, the
squadron, and I'd feel moony and sometimes sad. Sometimes, my
eye would stray from the rougher boys to the girlfriends. Sometimes, it would linger on the hem of their dresses, or the buckle
on their shoes. Sometimes I would blush and examine the hydrau-
lic movement of their hands, pushing against the chests of the
rougher boys, and then relenting. Pulsing, or in waves. And then
my eye would drift moonily back to the page, and the music would
soar into my foamy headphones, *oh, I was happy in the haze of a
drunken hour, but heaven knows I'm miserable now* . . .

"Perhaps you find yourself gazing, likewise, at the girlfriends of your rougher friends. Perhaps you have turned your
'queerness'—it's a big term, it can mean absolutely anything one
wants it to mean—to your advantage and acquired for yourself
your very own girlfriend, to watch and to admire. Perhaps you
wonder whether your gaze will ever settle into your own eyes,
whether you will ever simply see, and not be seen; whether you
will ever experience the simple comfort in the fact of having a
body that your fellows, the smoother boys as well as the rougher,
all seem to take for granted. Perhaps, as you sit on the brick wall
feeling set apart from the action, you dream of growing broader
shoulders and stouter pecs, and making a really rather funny (if I
do say so myself!) sitcom about two male friends living together in
the 2000s, hanging out, letting the milk go sour, and being cruel

to women. If you are there, my young friend, never fear. I'm here to tell you: nine times out of ten, there's a Robert Webb out there waiting his turn to be you. Maybe nineteen out of twenty.

"Now, maybe one out of a thousand of you will grow up to become a transsexual. To those I just want to say, good on you, mate! It's not an easy gig but you're free on God's green earth and in the Queen's green England to make whatever choice you want with your downstairs bits! Truth is, I sometimes wonder what would have happened if I'd gone down that route myself! The girls. Judith. Judith. Holofernes. I mean, who knows? If it were up to me, real trans people would have the run of the place—met some charmers, I have. And I hope one day we can live in a world where transsexuals are like abortions—safe, legal, and rare. In the meantime, you can have a beer on me, son. I mean, daughter! Got to get these things right you know, slappy wrist.

"What really gets my goat, though, are those PC wizards who try to tell kids that they're ripe for a sex change if they just wear a little bit of makeup one time! These guys are nutters. We've all seen them, hanging around schools, offering out estradiol tablets like candy and playing their creepy brainwashy music. Frankly, I think it's astonishing that the government allows them to get away with it. When will we just grow up and admit that only the real freaks grow up to be trans and the rest of us are just nice, normal men who used to mime along to Belinda Carlisle once in a while and still kind of prefer to be the small spoon? Wake up, Britain. Don't you get the feeling you've been had?

"Anyway, I've said my piece—feel free to ignore it! I'm just some bloke who used to be on the telly, after all. But I suppose I just wanted to stick my oar in just to reassure any quivering little boys or their parents out there. It's a scary time, I know. But, I am here to say, please don't worry if your son seems a bit fruity.

Chances are, he will grow up to be me, the actor and comedian Robert Webb!"

Mic gets pulled back. Robert Webb drops down, into a hell of his own making.

What does my lawyer think of this bit of (parodic, natch) malarkey? He's more agnostic here—being an American, and a man of impeccable taste, he has never heard of Robert Webb. He *does* want to make sure that I appear to be bullying this poor guy just because he's bisexual. On this matter, I can put my lawyer's heart to rest, as well as my reader's. While a casual glance through Webb's memoir, *How Not to Be a Boy: Rules for Being a Man: Don't Cry, Love Sport, Play Rough, Drink Beer, Don't Talk About Feelings*, might indicate an occasional pang for cock noshing in the distant, repressed past, our man has clarified publicly that he is *not* bisexual: that side of him "just isn't a going concern any more." Homos of Horncastle may grieve at their leisure. And the gender-ambivalent youth look to Webb's *pentimento* mediocrity as, I suppose, some kind of birthright.

That's right, love, tuck that saveloy right in.

That's right that's right that's right that's right I really love your tiger light. I really love your tiger feet.

CHAPTER SIX

IN WHICH THE CLOWN METAPHOR
IS FINALLY EXPLAINED AT LENGTH

The long course of Dickens's novels, if one could utter a banal generalization, moves from picaresque to bildungsroman, from the relatively loose structure of roaming adventure to the more driven plot of an individual distinguishing himself from his social environment. There are plenty of possible objections to this claim: *Nicholas Nickleby*, an early novel, clearly shows some signs of tending towards *Bildung*, although on balance it is a novel of rural roaming, of happenstance and encounter. Likewise, the protagonisms of *Our Mutual Friend* are notoriously fraught, with no character fully disentangling himself from the web of mutuality that constructs the city in that enormous novel. The best case for each, however, would be *The Old Curiosity Shop* on the early end, and *Great Expectations* on the late. The novel of Little Nell and her grandfather scurrying around the Midlands on the run from a malevolent dwarf exhibits no interest in either the formal discipline of *Bildung*, nor indeed in any possible future that could be accorded to Nell who, doomed to die as soon as she steps onto the page—and frankly lucky to avoid a death by murder or syphilis—figures the same sort of foreclosure as Peter Pan. Whereas Pip, whom we witness in youthful indiscretions with butter running down the inside leg of his trousers, has achieved salvation and distinction from the first; he is a figure of a different kind of foreclosure—that of having already grown up, of simply passing one's memories without reliving them. Nell has no future; Pip has no past.

An accidental—but therefore, in another sense, truly *essential* —distinction between the two novels concerns their depictions of entertainment. Pip's are associated all with the *Pocket*, and are therefore urbane, masculine, and witty—but also, finally trivial and to be outgrown. Herbert Pocket is the final entry in a long list of pleasurable but dangerous male companions with/against whom Dickensian boy-heroes must negotiate: Smike in *Nickleby* and Steerforth in *Copperfield* are two other examples of the dashing species. In a sense, this type is a picaro unto himself— Steerforth could be Redmond Barry—with the question of outgrowth merely set back a little, as Dickens negotiates his own ambivalence about such masculine pleasures.

Whereas *The Old Curiosity Shop* remains solidly committed to its own pleasures, which have the utterly surreal distinction of having been *miniaturized*. Everything in the novel is small. The central character has become, in the retelling, "Little Nell"; her grandfather's emaciation is described over and again; the villain, Daniel Quilp, is a dwarf; the love interest in the awkwardly tacked-on romance plot is seemingly anorexic. Not just the main characters. Dickens parades past his readers' eyes a sequence of smallened people: a schoolful of children who look like squat adults; a traveling troupe of waxworks of historical personages; a Punch and Judy show, the hero of which, with his cartoonish tendency towards violence and utterly unrestrained pursuit of his own ends, reminds us of Quilp. The novel fully refuses to tell us the difference between a cartoonish violence that is supposed to be taken seriously, and one which can be enjoyed as entertainment.

In an unusual and in many ways uncharacteristic essay on Dickens, the Marxist critic Theodor Adorno dwells on the novel's entertainments in much the same way, offering a fascinating explanation for their appearances in *The Old Curiosity Shop*. Adorno writes:

> I would like to talk about [a book] whose title is generally familiar, a book that may still be widely read, especially by children. But in the ninety years since Dickens' *The Old Curiosity Shop* appeared, inserted into another novel, some of the secrets embedded in the work, perhaps without the author knowing clearly that he was doing so, have become discernable. Dickens is currently considered to be one of the founders of the realistic and social novel. Historically, this is correct; but when one examines the form of his work itself, it requires some qualification. For Dickens' fictional work, in which poverty, despair, and death have already been recognized as the fruits of a bourgeois world, a world to which only the traces of human warmth and kindness in individual human relationships can reconcile one—this work also contains the outlines of a completely different sort of view of the world. You may call it prebourgeois; in it the individual has not yet reached full autonomy, nor, therefore, complete isolation, but instead is presented as a bearer of objective factors, of a dark, obscure fate and a starlike consolation that overtake the individual and permeate his life but never follow from the law of the individual, as do, for instance, the fates of the characters in Flaubert's novels. The novels of Dickens contain a fragment of the dispersed baroque that maintains a strange ghostly presence in the nineteenth century. You know it from the plays of Raimund and even Nestroy, but it is also contained, in more hidden form, in the apparently so individualistic philosophy of Kierkegaard.[1]

We can forgive Adorno his rather shallow reading of Flaubert, whose *Bovary* is partly represented here but at the expense of any credible account of *Bouvard et Pécuchet* or even *Salammbô*, because the reading of Dickens is *so* astute. The essence of the Dickensian is a particular kind of remnant of capital's own prehistory, which appears not as romanticism or nostalgia—where it would remain pastoral, as such remnants do for a George Eliot or Anthony Trollope—but as the paradoxically definitive quality of the collective, the urban, the modern. The Dickensian baroque is to capital what the Lyotardian postmodern is to modernism: an effect whose emergence, bizarrely, conditioned the very structure it was supposed to supersede. The postmodern can be found nowhere more fully realized than in the Wildean fin de siècle (says Lyotard), but the baroque can be found nowhere more fully realized than in the Dickensian novel of modernity (says Adorno).

By way of exploring what Adorno might have meant by "the dispersed baroque" in this context, we might consider one of the novel's many dream sequences, in this case a dream of Nell after a narrow escape from her pursuer Quilp, amid the waxworks at Mrs. Jarley's traveling show.[2]

Notwithstanding these protections, she could get none but broken sleep by fits and starts all night, for fear of Quilp, who throughout her uneasy dreams was somehow connected with the wax-work, or was wax-work himself, or was Mrs Jarley and wax-work too, or was himself, Mrs Jarley, wax-work, and a barrel organ all in one, and yet not exactly any of them either. At length, towards break of day, that deep sleep came upon her which succeeds to weariness and over-watching, and which has no consciousness but one of overpowering and irresistible enjoyment.[3]

Clearly, the passage comports with many of the elements of Freudian "dreamwork" as he teaches it in 1900: condensation (the Quilp-element is saturated by other elements); displacement (the appearance of the barrel organ); and secondary revision (in the sense that Nell's dream creates the conditions of possibility for its own interpretation). The question of scene setting, which Freud finds so fascinating, hardly occurs in Nell's dream, though perhaps it is the *lack* of a setting that troubles the narrator, who seems aware that the uneasiness of the dream is part of its structure, as well as its content. Yet as startling as may be this foreshadowing of Freud, still more so is the realization that the hydraulics of dream possess, for Dickens, the properties of one of their elements: that is, the dream is *waxy*. It waxes; elements wax into each other in it—the dream is almost flesh, but flesh that can merge with other flesh, can become glossy and transmute without denaturing. Moreover, a certain *waxiness* gets glazed onto the bodies of all characters that come into contact with Jarley's exhibition of wax representations of historical figures.

> Nell walked down [the canvas], and read aloud, in enormous black letters, the inscription, JARLEY'S WAX-WORK.
> "Read it again," said the lady, complacently.
> "Jarley's Wax-Work," repeated Nell.
> "That's me," said the lady. "I am Mrs. Jarley."

Mrs. Jarley later justifies her craft by insisting, "It is not funny at all" and that "I won't go so far as to say, that, as it is, I've seen wax-work quite like life, but I've certainly seen some life that was exactly like wax-work.'"[4] The "dispersed baroque" as the revenge of material against structure, of wax against personhood, against dream.

And against language. Such waxiness drips, or merges, with language itself—which is no surprise, since Dickens foregrounds the syntactical and structural dimensions of the dream-work. The Dickensian dream syntax, however, is prosodic rather than merely semantic. The Jarley Wax-Work Exhibition advertises itself by deformation and reformation, "in the form of parodies on popular melodies," of which Dickens gives us only one:

> If I had a donkey wot wouldn't go
> To see Mrs. JARLEY's wax-work show,
> Do you think I'd acknowledge him? Oh no no!
> Then run to Jarley's——[5]

We are left to imagine the rhyme's closure, which might repeat the second line, but might just as easily be "tomorrow" or "bunga-low" or such. One modern version of the nursery rhyme suggests that perhaps another couplet is missing from Jarley's version:

> If I had a donkey that wouldn't go
> Do you think I'd beat him? Oh no no!
> I'd put him in a barn, and give him some corn:
> The best little donkey that ever was born.[6]

Whereas an American ballad from the same period (published 1840, same year as *The Old Curiosity Shop*), meanwhile, offers a more complex prosodic arrangement:

> If I had a donkey wot wouldn't go,
> D'ye think I'd wollop him—no, no, no.
> But gentle means I try, d'ye see,
> Because I hate all cruelty:

If all had been like me, in fact,
There'd ha' been no occasion for Martin's act,
Dumb animals to prevent getting crack'd
    On the head.
    For if I had a donkey wot wouldn't go,
    I never would wallop him—no, no, no:
    I'd give him some hay, and cry, Gee O!
      And come up, Neddy.[7]

The implication here is that beating a donkey teaches the donkey to kick back, as happens to the villain of the older version, "that cruel chap, Bill Burn." I'm not trying to restore Jarley's jingle into an original version, but rather to observe the curious blend of moralism, violence, and simplicity that can be made to run into each other by this cheerful, mechanical rhyme, which like Nell's dream fails or refuses to make clear what object is what, leaving only the central image—a donkey is being beaten—somewhere out of the range of reference. The dispersed baroque, then, entails a special relationship to violence: since violence cannot be dispersed, and is indeed a mode by which form and matter interact, it poses a particular challenge to Dickens, for whom Punch and Judy–like violence is everywhere. Force, terror, impact: these are elements of the jingle and the dream likewise, never absentable and yet never fully representable either. In the dispersed baroque, violence is method.

There is another element of *The Old Curiosity Shop* that demands this kind of attention, and yet Adorno is too polite to mention it: the close affinity between Dickensian waxiness and the genre of pornography. Narrative pornography had already developed a stock of characters, tropes, and devices by 1840—indeed, it had done so primarily through the picaresque, which receded in Dickens's fiction and in that of his imitators, but which remained from then to the present the dominant mode of pornographic writing (and now, of pornographic video). Yet a question may be asked about whether pornography produces characters, and if so, upon what theory such characterizations depend. One provisional answer nestles in a subordinate clause close to the beginning of Steven Marcus's foundational study of mid-Victorian pornography, *The Other Victorians*, when it is observed in passing that "in pornography no person, object, or idea is incapable of being enlisted in the cause of sexual activity."[8] Character, then, exists only provisionally as a pretext for a more generically primal enlistment, a seduction, a being sucked into the whirlpool of sex that pornography sets out, if not to depict, then at least to present. Marcus's point is affirmed at each moment in which porn promises to educate its characters: the moment, for example, when the straight boy removes his blindfold to reveal that it is a man sucking his cock, and that he rather likes it; when Justine learns that she can enjoy even the chastisement she receives for her good conduct. Character exists as a mere precondition for an era that occurs, both chronologically and formally, at the moment of sexual pleasure. The theory of character would then be something like: there are no characters at the moment of orgasm, and it is the task of pornography to persuade its consumers of the fact. We are all the same underneath our characters—though probably Sade and Baitbus would entail different conceptualizations of what's underneath.

Pornography turns characteristic particularity into sex, which it must therefore posit as a non-particularizable field. But character is, as Marcus says, hardly unique in being subjected to such treatment in porn: everything is. On the one side, social organization, medium specificity, the naïve mode of self-differentiation we call "character"; on the other, the shattered sexual subject, an affective intensity whose specificities have been negated, a momentary convergence of fictional and realist epistemologies. Is it possible to talk about pornography without characterizing sex in such absolute terms? Perhaps: Eugenie Brinkema's extraordinary recent essay "Rough Sex," a provocatively formalist and, occasionally, ethical defense of rape pornography, might prompt us to question Marcus's notion of "enlistment" in one particular. What if the sex to which "no person, object, or idea is incapable of being enlisted" lacked the conceptual or institutional unity necessary for such a task?[9] It is not merely, Brinkema might say, that legal and historical authorities cannot agree what pornography is, but that pornography fundamentally disturbs its consumer's sense of what sex is. Not merely in the morally panicked sense of producing "unrealistic expectations." The "roughness" of which Brinkema makes extensive use in her essay associates the violent aesthetics of rough porn with the provisional and chaotic assembly of pornography as a genre, suggesting that, just as the assembly of the archive of pornography is necessarily incomplete, so the constitution of sexual pleasure—that to which Marcus entrusts the responsibility to obliterate character—is founded only haphazardly and contingently. And so it is. Although each issue of the Victorian porn magazine *The Pearl* contained a few distinct short stories and bawdy poems, each also contained serialized stories in which continuity of character (though not of setting) was re-instantiated. In one such, "Sub-Umbra, or Sport Among the She-Noodles," the characters' various sexual encounters hardly climax at all, at least in the narrative sense of the word: each experience of sexual pleasure is itself folded back into the loose narrative framework.[10] Walter (the narrator) and his cousin Annie have sex in the first installment, yet they return to do so again and again in the remaining seven. The relationship between each encounter and its precedents is not precisely accretive—they do not refer to any previous encounters, nor do they seem to learn anything about each other—but, given the continuities and discontinuities of the serial narrative form, we can be sure that these characters have not been simply dissolved in sex either. Though in this particular case the endurance of character is underwritten by the medium of serialized fiction, a similar effect is ensured by video pornography's own "star system": though a particular scene may end predictably, the porn star will return—as actor and as character.

The serial aspect of pornography, which I take to be not merely a vestigial remnant of Victorian print culture, but a condition of possibility for pornographic consumption as such, seems to me to fundamentally elude enlistment into Marcus's singularity of sexual activity. That seriality necessitates some principle of characterology seems important too, in so far as the possibility of sexual particularity remains roundly denied by discussants of pornography on all sides of the question: by anti-porn crusaders for whom pornography is a perversion of proper sexuality (or of the ethical treatment of human beings), but also by pro-porn critics for whom the infinite diversity of pornographic fantasy merely reproduces, at a different order, the singularity of fantasy itself. Brinkema's intervention enables a reformulation of the initial question, then, in the following terms: who can survive sex?

In pornography, though, no person, object, or idea is incapable of being enlisted into sexual activity, and one might add that no text either—no text, and certainly not a novel organized around the delicious spectatorship of female early-adolescent vulnerability—can immunize itself against pornographic use. Nell's little death in No. 44 (January 30, 1841) occasioned an international outpouring of grief that shattered the border between realist and phantasmatic epistemologies as decisively as any cumshot. That historical event of public tenderness has itself been subject to innumerable cruel recontextualizations: Oscar Wilde probably did not say that "one must have a heart of stone to read the death of Little Nell without laughing," but somebody did, and attributed it to him.[11] Aldous Huxley certainly did characterize Nell's death as the central example of Dickens's "monstrous emotional vulgarity," adding "there was something rather wrong with a man who could take this lachrymose and tremulous pleasure in adult infantility."[12] The tear-jerking pleasure Huxley assigns to Dickens is patently a symptom of his moral and emotional corruption, contemplation of which stirs in Huxley images of unpleasant liquid emissions: "the overflowing of his heart drowns his head"; "his one and only desire on these occasions is just to overflow"; "a stanchless flux"; "mentally drowned and blinded by the sticky overflowings of his heart"; "whenever he is in his melting mood, Dickens ceases to be able, and probably ceases even to wish, to see reality."[13] For Huxley, at least, *The Old Curiosity Shop* provokes some psychic association between sentimental crying and compulsive masturbation.

The novel itself invites such constructions. Serialized in a new periodical Dickens had established in 1840, *Master Humphrey's Clock*, the first-person narrator upon whom the first chapter alights has generally been referred to as "Master Humphrey," who indeed appears elsewhere in the periodical as a narrator. G. K. Chesterton, who follows this convention in respect of *The Old Curiosity Shop*, nonetheless admits that it follows "only from moral evidence, which some call reading between the lines."[14] (The evidence appears to be the very proliferation of the subject "I" in the opening chapter: Master Humphrey is a self-involved old cove.) The narrator, in any case, does not introduce himself by name, and when he writes as the novel's opening sentence

"Night is generally my time for walking," Dickens may as well have been talking about himself: he did so, in those terms, twenty years later, in the personal essay "Night Walks" he published in *The Uncommercial Traveler*. An old man who has been walking about at night, reflecting with some vicarious delight on the "unwholesome streams of last night's debauchery" that he encounters in Covent Garden, relates the following:[15]

One night I had roamed into the City, and was walking slowly on in my usual way, musing upon a great many things, when I was arrested by an inquiry, the purport of which did not reach me, but which seemed to be addressed to myself, and was preferred in a soft sweet voice that struck me very pleasantly. I turned hastily round and found at my elbow a pretty little girl, who begged to be directed to a certain street at a considerable distance, and indeed in quite another quarter of town.

"It is a very long way from here," said I, "my child."

"I know that, sir," she replied, timidly. "I am afraid it is a very long way, for I came from there to-night."

"Alone?" said I, in some surprise.

"Oh, yes, I don't mind that, but I am a little frightened now, for I had lost my road."

"And what made you ask it of me? Suppose I should tell you wrong?"

"I am sure you will not do that," said the little creature, "you are such a very old gentleman, and walk so slow yourself."

I cannot describe how much I was impressed by this appeal and the energy with which it was made, which brought a tear into the child's clear eye, and made her slight figure tremble as she looked up into my face.

"Come," said I, "I'll take you there."

She put her hand in mine as confidingly as if she had known me from her cradle, and we trudged away together, the little creature accommodating her pace to mine, and rather seeming to lead and take care of me than I to be protecting her. I observed that every now and then she stole a curious look at my face, as if to make quite sure that I was not deceiving her, and that these glances (very sharp and keen they were too) seemed to increase her confidence at every repetition.[16]

We have here the materialization of a certain kind of pornographic fantasy, of older male benevolence and pliable female gratitude, replete with details that would fit this scene quite easily into the "Maiden Tribute of Modern Babylon" forty years later—W. T. Stead's anti-prostitution polemic that enabled the passage of the 1885 Criminal Law Amendment Act.[17] As Judith Walkowitz has remarked, Stead's own ferocious prose "replicated, in a moralizing frame, many of the sadistic scenarios that filled pornography's pages."[18] In one such replication, "The Child Prostitute," Stead writes, "It seemed a profanation to touch her, she was so young and so baby-like. There she was, turned over to the first comer that would pay, but still to all appearance so modest, the maiden bloom not altogether having faded off her childish cheeks, and her pathetic eyes, where still lingered the timid glance of a frightened fawn. I felt like one of the damned."[19] The narrator of *The Old Curiosity Shop*, likewise, "felt really ashamed to take advantage of the ingenuousness or grateful feeling of the child for the purpose of gratifying my curiosity," yet he reports with a kind of troubled lasciviousness that she was "more scantily attired than she might have been" and delights in the secretiveness she exhibits about her night's activity: "a great secret—a secret which she did not even know herself."[20]

More pressing than the erotic dramaturgy of the scene—which must have been noticed by more of Dickens's readers than have publicly remarked on it—is the fate of the narrator positioned in the early part of the novel as a surrogate for the reader.

He is, as we have seen, initially pulled into the plot by the girl (who will turn out to be Nell); he remains within its ambit purely through his own surreptitious device. When he has returned her to her grandfather—when, that is, he has arrived at the titular Old Curiosity Shop, by way of a spatial type of metalepsis—the narrator conducts a genial conversation with the old man ("it always grieves me to contemplate the initiation of children into the ways of life") in which some of the exposition is extruded ("has she nobody to care for her but you?").[21] When his duty has been discharged and it is time to depart, however, the narrator finds himself unable to tear either his body or his thoughts away from the relationship between Nell and her grandfather, which he regards with a Humbert-esque mixture of tenderness, envy, and loathing of his Quilty-esque doppelgänger: "His affection for the child might not be inconsistent with villainy of the worst kind; even that very affection was in itself an extraordinary contradiction, or how could he leave her thus? Disposed as I was to think badly of him, I never doubted that his love for her was real."[22] The narrator malingers, departs, and eventually returns a week later—"yielding" to his desire to return—at which point he is drawn into a sequence which introduces two of the novel's remaining major characters: Dick Swiveller and Daniel Quilp. At which point the narrator declares:

> And now that I have carried this history so far in my own character and introduced these personages to the reader, I shall for the convenience of the narrative detach myself from its further course, and leave those who have prominent and necessary parts in it to speak and act for themselves.[23]

One might expect his final words to indicate that what is to follow will consist of more first-person narrative, perhaps from multiple narrators, but indeed neither this narrator, nor any

other, appears again to speak in the first person. It is a narra-
tological volta with, as far as I am aware, only one analogue in
nineteenth century fiction: its reverse, in William Morris's *News
from Nowhere*, in which a third person adopts the first. "But, says
he, I think it would be better if I told [my adventures] in the
first person, as if it were myself who had gone through them."[24]

We might conclude, with Tony Giffone, that *The Old Curiosity Shop* thus stages an early draft of the experiments with
"double narrative" associated with the mature Dickens: with the
interlocking first and third person narrators of *Bleak House*, for
example, or the affective retrojection experienced by Pip as he
describes his own childhood in *Great Expectations*.[25] But to do
so would be to undervalue the two strangest elements of this
moment: first, that we have come to understand this character
as, first and foremost, a lurker, and therefore cannot thereafter console ourselves that he has, indeed, left these characters
alone—perhaps the same, unnamed character has merely affected a third-person style of narration in order to lurk more
effectively. And second, that his recoil from first-person narration appears to be psychologically motivated—that, in fact,
it seems symptomatically consonant with the ambivalence and
shame of his entire encounter with Nell and her grandfather.
Although, that is, the narrator proudly finishes himself off at the
end of the novel's first number, we can never be sure that we are
finished with him; in a novel so concerned with the condition
of spectatorship—a condition depicted directly in many of the
illustrations by Cattermole and Phiz—we find ourselves in a
more than usually paranoid relation to the apparently objective
third-person narrator. This unnamed narrator is not therefore
merely a pornographic reader himself—one who attributes the
basest motives to Nell's grandfather—but an aperture through
which pornography suffuses the whole narrative scene. Various
characters appear, at different moments, as resurgences of the

nameless narrator: the eavesdropping and malevolent dwarf Quilp, who reveals his knowledge of the grandfather's gambling habit with the sinister threat "you have no secret from me now"; the urbane literary ventriloquist "of eccentric habits" Dick Swiveller; and perhaps above all the mysterious "single gentleman" (named after an ad he answers to let a room) who takes great delight in lurking around Nell and her grandfather after the girl's death: "for a long, long time, it was his chief delight to travel in the steps of the old man and the child (so far as he could trace them from her last narrative)."[26]

That Memorable Night My Lover Dreff'd Up as a Clown, and Perform'd All Manner of Tricks

As genres go, "porn parody" seems tough to work over. This is Bersani's point: "parody is an erotic turn-off," he says.[27] For one thing, one must be as candid as Dickens and accept that it is a genre aimed, if not at children, then at least at a type of adolescent for whom humor and sex have not yet decoupled. Freud, famously, decoupled them in 1905, working simultaneously on two books—the *Three Essays on the Theory of Sexuality*, and *Jokes and Their Relation to the Unconscious*, his unfunniest book and his unsexiest, respectively—on separate desks. One pictures Freud entering his study, seeing both manuscripts in progress awaiting his attention, and then determining whether the day would be spent laughing or coming—couldn't be both. But Dickens, in *The Old Curiosity Shop*, writes something like a non-pornographic parody of porn, an attempt to subject the fugitive energies of pornography to the minimal disciplines of the picaresque, to perform a superadditive desublimation on a genre already apparently maximally desublimated, stripped down to gluey, glazed flesh, as if slipping up the horny stalker on a banana skin, and observing him tumble up, ass in the air, and land balls deep into hungry, wet flesh.

This process could be endless. Desublimation as a dialectic: bathos denuding sex of its pretense, and sex denuding bathos of its euphemism. The genre "British panel show" stages a sadistic version of this cycle when it performs, as it relentlessly does, something like the following.

Effeminate Oxonian: I am the cleverest man in the world.
Redbrick ruffian: maybe, but you still take it in the arse

Audience howls in laughter.

Effeminate Oxonian: I *beg* your pardon!
Redbrick ruffian: not that there's anything wrong with that!
Effeminate Oxonian: now, as I was saying, the span in cubits of the Paro Taktsang, a sacred Vajrayana Himalayan Buddhist site in the upper Paro valley in Bhutan—
Redbrick ruffian: the upper whatsit in excuse me!

Audience simply raging with mirth.

Some woman: Um, boys, well, I don't know if you ever heard of a little thing called *periods*, but—
Redbrick ruffian: (*makes raspberry sound and hoots like a macaque*)

Audience rends garments, forgives all outstanding debts, announces return of "the carnivalesque."

Effeminate Oxonian: oh, you may be an ill-bred gurney-trundler, as the great poet of Cirencester described one of his more ornery perturbances, but don't ever change, you endlessly pardonable rogue, you!

One need hardly imagine a porn parody of *QI*, but it is perhaps worth reassuring ourselves that the structural class politics of this scene are rarely as they appear—that, in fact, the redbrick ruffian does not stand for a proletarian overturning of bourgeois pretense, but the precise opposite, the *bourgeois male* distaste for pleasure that requires interposing itself between any possible alliances, especially feminist alliances, that might otherwise emerge outside of the bourgeois male's domain. This is how "class" continually reasserts itself as a way to silence feminists, and indeed queers, *and indeed the proletariat*, simply by reconfiguring itself as the other of a feminized modernity, as "common sense," which is, by definition, the conservative ideology of the ruling class. Marx and Engels distinguish the science of Communism from romantic anti-capitalisms (with debatable success) on precisely these grounds: the beautiful violence of bourgeois revolution has "swept away" "all fixed, fast-frozen relations, with their train of ancient and venerable prejudices and opinions."[28] Meanwhile the proletariat "holds the future in its hands."[29]

The porn parody could not, I suppose, position Alan Davies in an active position. On the contrary, he would be squealing on his knees while being mercilessly face fucked by a resurgent Stephen Fry, who would yank his greasy ringlets with every lock of his hips. At Davies' back end, perhaps, the tongue of David Mitchell or some other whimpering inadequate—Mitchell can be allowed if and only if he is being pegged at the back by his wife, Victoria, which, let's face it, is a deal he would be happy to strike. Victoria Coren-Mitchell and Stephen Fry lock eyes as their dicks complete a current through the mouth and asshole of their once brutal antagonist, through the tongue and asshole of Robert Webb's homelier companion, a circuit pushing back and forth between Victoria and Stephen, through an irresistible eye-fucking gaze and eventually a high five.

There need not be any political value to the fantasy of a face fucked Alan Davies in order to justify it; and I suppose fantasy in general neither requires nor sustains justification. But if one *were* trying to produce a sort of Theodicy of a Face-Fucked Alan Davies, it would be this: for whatever reason, some strange agglutination of reactionary forces has occupied a position on the international left, where it sees itself as Alan Davies, bravely telling truths like "the emperor has no clothes," especially of feminists and queers. That one portion of this federation, the "terfs," sees itself (and is sometimes seen) as an inheritor of second wave feminism, but what they have in common with all other parts—with Joe Rogan, with Spiked.com, with the Revolutionary Communist Party (a reactionary cult of personality built around a strange vagrant named Bob Avakian), and even with the disenfranchised class of activists who deride "identity politics" as merely the conspiratorial work of "radlibs"—is a love of common sense, of plain speaking, of telling-it-like-it-is. The left has long been pestered by romances of this reactionary kind of political aesthetics, and there is no reason to be especially frightened about our latest humbuggers, but it may very well be worth reminding them that pointing out that the emperor has no clothes is the political gesture of a child; revolutionary consciousness is fostered in the dialectical position of the person who knows the truth very well, and takes pleasure in the beauty of invisible finery even so, refusing to accede to the bourgeois reality principle for even a moment.

The Dickensian reading of Marx, then, might itself constitute a porn parody, but only in so far as the Dickensian is already a porn parody: if, in the *Communist Manifesto*, "all that is solid melts into air," Dickens is concerned with the meltingness of air itself, which in fact would take, in the language of physics, the name *desublimation*.[30] And "always desublimate" might be the lesson of the Marx that might emerge at the end of that tunnel. A porn parody of Dickens, meanwhile, is much more difficult than one might expect, but for the obvious reason that Dickens has pulled the porn-parody dialectic into the voice itself and even the name, which can hardly be spoken without hitting the *Dick* harder than one wishes to—a point that the novelist acknowledged in his self-portrait as Betsey Trotwood's companion "Mr. Dick," obsessed with the decapitation of "King Charles."

Still, I won't pretend I haven't tried. In order, then:

The Clitslick Papers
Oliver, Twist
Nicholas Dickleby
The Old "Curiosity Shot"
Barnaby, Rudge
Martin Guzzle-slit (or, Tom Pinch's Organ)
A Christmas in Carol
Dongbey and Son
David Chopperfield
Bleak Hose
Hard Slimes
Spittle Dorrit
A Tale of Two T*tties
Great Expectorations
Our Manual Bend
The Piss Story of Edwin Drood

No, I don't *like* myself either, that isn't what this is about.

The first porn movie I ever watched was called *Edward Penishands*, and it was, as you might expect, a porn parody of *Edward Scissorhands*, in which a man who is not Nikki Sixx of Motley Crüe (but looks an awful lot like him and goes by the stage name "Sikki Nixx") plays a Johnny Depp–pastiche, except instead of having spindly blades for hands—a tragedy of overburdened preciousness, of finickiness taken literally—his wrists taper into bulbous, somewhat repulsive, cocks.[31] In one scene, Edward Penishands attempts to eat a plate of spaghetti with his cock hands, but finds himself all fingers and thumbs, body switching back and forth between grotesque phallic overcompensation and almost girlish, butterfingered flimsiness. By relocating the phallus from penis to arm, *Edward Penishands* extends and amplifies the problem of phallic embodiment as such: the arms can indeed fuck and fuck hard, but they can't avoid looking stupid while doing so, and if the penishands do not connect to the root chakra, one wonders whether the penis-penis ever does either.

I don't know whether I'm supposed to laugh or jack off at *Edward Penishands*, and I don't remember whether I did either, but one thing I have recently noticed is that not everybody thinks this is an either/or situation. Some people laugh when they come—real mirth, too, not the kind of sadistic laughter that I have encountered as a top and deployed as a bottom. Joy. Not-Nikki-Sixx, with his fiberglass armcocks, dickfisting two girls, who kneel on the bathroom floor, asses up, moaning the half-defeated, half-amused moans of the porn starlet, while he pouts like Pierrot at the camera. And one type of pleasure one can imagine, a synthesis of porn and comedy, is the cruelty of the pornographic exhibition of women's bodies, bodies that one has, in effect, tricked into being humiliated. Another type

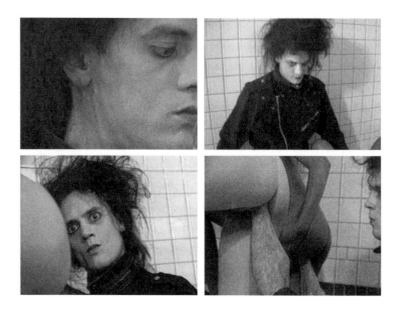

of pleasure one can imagine, though, presumes that the three bodies performing this odd piece of vaudeville are coordinating their own arrhythmia quite democratically, and that the little moans correspond asymmetrically to Not-Nikki's pout.

Still, after many years of waiting, a lover came to Manhattan to see me, and we play'd fuch games, at last. She had brought, as a gift for us, a bright yellow clown wig, and a red nofe, which I placèd on her. We fat on a bench together, and fhe had a perfect *Pierrette* mien and moue, lifting her foot onto the wooden bench, her eyes arching downwards towards her puffy with her back, her hand on her clit with my fingers inside her, my lips kissing her neck. The foamy red ball, pinching the very edge of her nostrils, which flared as she touch'd herself, pinch'd likewise the founds fhe pipèd out of her face, little moans of glory, play'd nafal and in a minor key. And I careff'd her, feeling her ribs push out of her body, and the large bone of her hip, which eventually fhe preffed inside me and fuck'd me, all night long.

Her name was L———, as the flower, as the lamp, and somehow she succeeded, through exertion and its *rélévation*, to melt the world into the floral light of revolution, with her body, her holes, and her dick. She laughed when she came, held me in her eyes while the world ended—and this, at last, was the meaning of the clown metaphor, finally explained to me at length.

In America, one finds the pre-bourgeois baroque everywhere—but it is always, *always* in the form of a clown. Last week, I was walking down the road of a quiet New England town where I happened to have stopped for a weekend. We are in COVID now, and all is different, and yet sometimes nonetheless one finds oneself in a fishing town, does one not? A gay fishing town, perhaps, with a single, snakelike road that runs for a mile or two, out there on the Cape, and couples are strolling around: the classic butch/femme pairing, perhaps—a couple of leather-daddies, all enjoying their nice sojourn, all enjoying the sight of each other and the squeeze of a particular hand. And all, this being COVID, resenting the masks slapped across our faces, which close no fewer than three mucus membranes usually granted access to the world. And half thinking of their restriction, *well isn't it nice to share a disaster for once—rich and poor, white and black, man and woman*—and the other half thinking, *well, isn't this sacrifice important, and isn't my sacrifice especially important? For it is mine.*

I'm speculating, of course. Well, one such day in the week before this, my sweetheart and I took afternoon tea, as they say, at the Café Blasé. Our mouth and nose holes welcomed the wafts of scented bodies, scented with jojoba and oils, or with sweat. (Is it too much—would I offend your sensibilities—if I say that the present "scent-free" fad so popular with the younger homosexuals is no friend to the more distinguished olfactory apparatuses of we, their elders?) The beach was visible, just, through cracks in the buildings. In the Northeastern United States, seaboards create value, and value invites capital, and capital privatizes value, and the long and the short of it is that, mostly, one is unable to see the sea from the street—though there are exceptions.

After a lunch of indifferent hake and rather worse clootie, I wished to stamp off my disappointment *toute seule*, and invited my sweetheart to return to the bed-and-breakfast and await my return. She seemed a little more rueful than usual—although she had long acclimated to my need for long walks, especially when I am in one of my bumptious distempers, nonetheless something seemed to regret my having succumbed, today, to that wanderlust that so frequently takes me away from her. She squeezed my hand kindly and sadly as we parted, saying, "do look after yourself, Grace—these things can be awfully hard on you." And I nodded, and embarked.

At the time, I supposed that she had simply meant that these moods, which come and go from time to time, often leave their mark on me for a few days—but now I wonder whether she had some intuition, perhaps a lover's intuition, of what was to occur. I couldn't explain that, if so, but as the reader knows by this stage, I am so incapable of explaining anything that the fact was hardly unique. I understand so little about what has happened to me, or why, or even when.

As I walked south away from the cafe it started to rain. Quickly, the streets began to thin, and holidaymakers scurried back to their own bed-and-breakfasts, and locals just hung out under the awnings. I, a tough British customer unafraid of a drop of rain, simply hoicked up my hoodie, and looked at the ground as I marched glumly on, a trickle of water beginning to follow me. The road was pedestrianized, though cars did occasionally barge past in one direction or the other; the ambient sounds of the seaside town became otherwise incorporated within the sound of the rain, the stream underfoot, the splash and rumble of other feet besides mine.

I must have walked for twenty minutes, at the indeterminate lick that a rainstorm provokes, before I realized I had left the downtown area, and the houses around me now were more or less suburban, albeit with perhaps some "beach life" features on the lintel: a large shell, or a washed-out slab of wood. I hadn't departed from the one road, but when I turned around I realized I couldn't even see the small town behind me. I kept moving, the grumbling in my heart would not let me falter despite the rain, and the light, already obscured by a cloud, began to dwindle to the tremulous quality of a winter crepuscule—precious and dim.

My eyes still focused downwards on the road, to keep the rain out, I began to fancy that I was now in the village of Astwood Bank, just to the south of Redditch, where I had spent my very earliest years. I almost thought I could hear English voices, the chattering voices of the West Midlands, on the sidewalk on either side of me, as I walked down the road's middle—some, perhaps, complaining about the "*bloody* Tories," others wandering around with no such idea in mind, just fragments of speech, clichés. "If I *do* say so myself," one says; another says, "good evening, squire, and will it be your usual?" These are just voices, though, out of range—out of earshot, almost—there are no bodies, and even the splashing seemed to stop.

The stream was picking up, though, gathering momentum and therefore velocity. After a few minutes more, a threshold had been passed, and suddenly it was no longer a little stream underfoot, but the medium through which my feet were moving, more properly a very shallow river than a rainy road. And the overhead lights clunked on, bright burnt orange, and I realized I was deep into the suburbs now, wherever I was—perhaps no such suburb as existed in Massachusetts, perhaps none that existed in England either—perhaps suburbs, as they were dreamed of in the nineties, did not finally belong to any territory other than the mind. No suburb escaped, for one moment at least, the condition of having become *The Truman Show*.

I pressed on, growing more and more convinced that by leaving the town I had left the state, and that by leaving the state I had left the nation, and that by leaving the nation I had become unmoored from the world, and through that, that I had found myself in an astral dimension, moving through idea-forms that were to be found on no map. After I had been walking for a total of an hour or so, I felt a strange tap at my ankle, as though I had been pelted by a sharp object. It brought me stunningly back to earth, as only pain can.

"Fuck," I exclaimed, to nobody, and bent down to see what it was, vision obscured by the now almost torrential rain. At first I thought it was an injured seabird, sharp white feathers and perhaps some thick black blood oozing out, that had dive-bombed my feet. But as I looked closer, and reached down, I could tell it wasn't a bird at all, but simply an envelope, and nothing more— an envelope that must have struck me with its hardest edge, and hit upon a nerve. When I picked it up, however, I was stunned by what was written on it. The address written on the envelope, in a scratchy black marker pen that was already running heavily in the rain, said, in nonetheless clearly legible lettering:

"New Professor" Joseph Lavery
Department of English
UC Berkeley
United States of America (the world, the universe &c.)

It had been so long since the first one, I had forgotten the "new professor" part—as though I was always to be new in my position, that I was perennially new. (Which was true, at a certain degree of abstraction: I never tire of telling people that I was the first member of my family to get so much as an undergraduate degree, let alone to ascend to the professoriate. As far as I stand for Lavery, my professorship is new.)

But it was altogether a different order to see what I have come to think of as my "dead name" scrawled on a piece of paper that must have been thrown at me by a representative of the very organization that had been hounding me all these years. Which representative knew all my secrets, everything about me, and was somewhere in my immediate vicinity, presumably either right behind me (because the projectile hit me hard) or having scarpered, pronto. I turned around immediately and could see nobody. The light had dimmed, and the water was logging around me on all sides. Even the sidewalks seemed far away now, as though I might have to wade to make my way over to them. The orange streetlights seemed to be emerging now from the roofs of the houses, sparse in number and craning to loom over me, their bricks separating from each other and masonry cracking, as they gained animation and pressed into me.

Suddenly, I heard a voice in front of me—a few inches in front. A sweet young girl's voice, which asked, with almost mocking sweetness:

"Excuse me, mister, but are you a man or are you a woman?"

I spun around to answer the girl, but as soon as I had done so, she whipped the envelope out of my hand, and then sped off, running and running into the distance. "Wait! That's mine!" I called after her, but she didn't hear over the cacophony of splashing, or perhaps she did; anyway she sped off all the faster and the river-road became a flat, long line, along which I was running as fast as I could, and along which she was running even faster; the rain slick became glossy and looked viscous, as though it were congealing into a green rubber.

After I had run as fast as I could for as long as I could—twenty minutes, perhaps a little more—I had to stop and catch my breath. The child was farther off now, horribly beyond my reach, a mile or two away at least, but I could see her nonetheless, in the distance. When I stopped, so did she. I called out, "wait, darling!" and felt embarrassed for addressing her as such. I waved at her to let her know that I didn't want to hurt her. I poured my body into the wave, pulsing all the love in my body into the air and transmitting it to her. She slowly lifted up the envelope, a purely neutral expression on her face, and held it above her head. Then, with her arm up, she slowly and carefully sat down, cross-legged, on the ground, and turned ninety degrees to face the side of the road.

A Masonic dance, I assumed. This girl has been taught to bend her body into the positions of the papists, perhaps with an intention of deflecting their attention. I feared that if I moved towards her, she would move farther off, and since I wished nothing more than to see her, perhaps to ask her what she had done to me, whether she had bewitched me, I could not bring myself to advance. Rather, I decided to match her position and bend my body as she had. I checked my pockets for something that would work to match the envelope, and quickly decided on my green card, wrapped in the cardboard sleeve in which the law obliges me to keep it, because it had the name "Joseph Lavery" written on it, and therefore matched the envelope in some way. I pulled the sleeve out of my wallet, and held it above my head. A chime sounded. I slowly descended into the lotus, visa still held over my head. Another chime. Finally, I turned my body ninety degrees to face the side of the road. A third chime, and a blinding light: when my eyes had adjusted to the dazzle, I could see the girl no longer from the corner of my eye, just the side of the road.

I brought my hand down, to put my green card back in my wallet, but when I brought my hand down, it contained now the envelope that the girl had been holding. Had she stolen the damn visa? My eyes started darting around on all sides for any trace of her.

The girl was nowhere to be seen, but behind me now, a mile or perhaps two, I saw another figure: an older woman, in her forties or perhaps fifties, holding a small envelope over her head—the sleeve, I quickly recognized, with my green card in it. "Hey!" I yelled. "Come here! I need my card! I can explain everything!"

That especially fragile lie did not prompt the woman to move. But when I looked down at my own body I realized that, extraordinary as it seemed, *I was now the girl*, and that woman behind me, holding Joseph Lavery's visa in the air, was no longer me, or was someone else now. I had transported myself, and yet I had changed nothing; everything was the same, but my consciousness was somewhere else—in the girl, not the woman—in the sleeve, not the card.

I had not yet given any thought to what might be in the envelope this time—that strange message about the First World War that I had received in an identical envelope so many years ago? Or something even stranger and more disturbing? My body trembling, and my hands almost unable to grasp the soaking wet envelope, I pushed my right thumb into the side of the flap, hoping to force it open. As soon as I did so, however, a voice spoke to me from the side of the street—from the drain.

"Hello, Gracie," it said.

"Oh, hi," I replied, my voice several octaves higher than I was used to.

"Whence came you?"

"Ummm—" I began to answer, but found myself too confused, too uncertain, to know by whom I was addressed. "I'm sorry but where are you?"

"Gracie, whence came you?" asked the voice, only a touch more insistent than last time. It felt forgiving; it did not object to my disorientation, but likewise it could not deviate from the script laid out for us.

"Whence came I? I mean—" I looked back at the path I believed myself to have trodden, but all was darkness, nothing but that and the woman still holding the card above her head.

"Gracie, I ask a third time but I may not ask a fourth. Whence came you?"

I knew the answer: "From the lodge of the Holy Saints John, at Jerusalem."

"Gracie, what come you here to do?" it asked.

"To learn to subdue my passions, and improve myself in Masonry," I responded, in my sweet high voice, which felt so strange in my throat, so tight.

"Then I presume you are a Mason?" asked the voice, a shade louder. I could feel the speaker, whoever it was, moving towards me in the darkness.

"I am so taken among sisters and fellows," I said, coyly. As the words came out it occurred to me that it wasn't a real answer.

"How do you know yourself a Mason?"

"By having been often tried, never denied, and willing to be tried again."

The voice began to hum contentedly. As I craned forwards, I could now see the outline of a pair of bright red lips, shiny and plump with blood. I saw it shape the words:

"How should *I* know you to be a Mason?"

"By certain signs, a token, a word, and the perfect points of my entrance."

A face, finally, became visible in the wet darkness. It was, of course, the face of my Clown. My Clown's face was round, neither fat nor thin, and pale but neither frightening nor comical. The skin looked soft, but slightly rough, stubble in puppy fat. Lines stretched between the corners of my Clown's mouth and ears, grooves, scars, gulches.

Our eyes matched. Like a girl, I repeated my Clown's own question back: "how should I know *you* to be a Mason?"

The teeth began to open. My Clown was not used to being asked such impertinent questions, least of all at a meeting such as this.

"A certain friendly and sisterly grip, whereby one Mason may know another in the dark as well as the light."

"Give me a token," I said, which my Clown did. I then said, "I hele." My Clown, pulling back into the darkness, responded, "I conceal"; I pursued, "*what* do you conceal?" to which my Clown responded, quickly, "all the secrets of Masonry, except it be to her or them to whom they of right belong."

My Clown's eyes passed over to the letter around which my hands were gripped. "What is this?"

"Oh this?" I stuttered. "This is . . . this is a letter. I think it's for you."

"Will you give it to me?"

"I . . . did not so receive it, neither can I so impart it . . ."

"*How* will you dispose of it?" An increase in the pressure of my Clown's voice.

"I can . . . I can letter it, I suppose, or syllable it, or—"

"Letter, and begin," my Clown responded, increasing the pressure again.

"Begin, *you*," I said. At this point it seemed important for me to acknowledge that I didn't know whether I had received the letter or sent it; whether it was meant for me, or whether my task was to bestow it upon another.

"Nay, *you* must begin!" my Clown reached a shout.

"I . . . I can't. I don't know how."

My Clown stood forwards and for the first time I could perceive it all in its glory. There was something magnificent about its outfit—strong and smart, proud in its shoes and breeches. A regal mien, almost. And it addressed me officiously:

"Gracie, you are going to lose a lot. You have already lost a lot. Behold."

And I was shown all that I had already lost.

"Gracie, you are going to gain a lot. You have already gained a lot. Behold."

And I was shown all that I had already gained.

"Gracie, you must begin. You must begin. Begin *you*."

I turned my face to the older woman, behind me, grasping my green card now, tears running down her face. "It is okay," she told me. "It is okay. I promise. Open it."

I opened the letter, noting the familiar typeface that I had seen so many times by now, and I looked at my Clown. It said, once more: "Nay, you must begin."

So I began.

Dear Prof. Lavery,

What follows is a letter I wrote to you many years ago, in verse. I include it now in full awareness that it arrives late in at least two senses. First, in the sense that the scene of its composition no longer exists, and second, because the behavior it had wished to modify has long ceased. Every adjustment I would have made, you made on your own, and it is therefore no use for you to blame me for the consequences you have suffered, even notwithstanding the acknowl-edgment that I wished them for you, that I would have brought you nothing different if I could have.

When I say that the scene of composition no longer exists, I do not mean that Paris no longer exists. Hahahahahahahaha, indeed not— I'm not insane. Paris exists, and shall exist, much as it did on the morning of April 19, 2007, when I sought to reach you in a dream with the following words. Paris existed for you that day when, having heard the words, you walked from your apartment off Rue Jean-Pierre Timbaud into the Marais (which wasn't far), and found yourself drinking a small carafe of Côtes du Rhône at ten in the morn-ing. It continued to exist later that day, when you were drinking a *pichet* of Gamay at the Fin du Monde on Rue de la Roquette. It existed when you blacked out, wherever that was, then came to steadying yourself with a crêpe Nutella/banane in the Latin Quarter.

These very boring stories and others will continue to exist, I do not mean to sug-gest otherwise. Yet here is the letter that you received, and ignored, that morning. I shall write out your name once more, and once more only.

Dear Grace,

Spinal correction may be necessary for
those as want to sing to the very highest
standard. Crooked vertebrae, or even just
a slouch or a mild hump may interfere
with control over one's larynx or cause
air improperly to circulate with the
effect that to the attuned ear, which
mine certainly wasn't, occasional notes
lose their tarnish, sounding like
tinnitus. Precisely why I decided to
enroll for medical certification by the
people who brought elephant hide back
into the workplace. Information had begun
to circulate that the chances of
employment would eventually be determined
where possible by an upfront anatomical
adjudication. After initial inquiries I
decided to seek more information. The
first opinion I sought was that of a
gentleman named Bryn, whose wheelchair
operatics had been enthralling the people
of Wales since the nineteen eighties, and
who could now command an audience of
dozens every minute through a totally
interactive camera. "The next stage," he
told me, "is to have a flesh microphone
fitted inside my lungs so the original
echo of the bodily cavity—*what we call
the pluck*—can be transmitted
simultaneously in twenty-two languages,
(including church latin, high french, and

hebraic) via choral technologies straight
into the pluggable ego." I distrusted his
flagrancy and throwness-into-the-world and
longed for a hard-wiring of his body into
proper torture machines, so that I could
vindictively declare that now he knows
how it would feel. There was no denying I
needed work done, if only in the sense
that triannual maintenance is an
unfortunate necessity on all listed
buildings, but will be particularly
pungent on those which are close to
weathering factors, among which we could
doubtless name the sea, but also swamps
of battery acid, indomitable gusts, the
propensity to being smacked about with
french polish. Strange, wasn't it, to
think that the landscape was seen by
romantic painters as immutable against
the temporal human body whereas we
anticipate the dereliction of geography as
if to underline that we are practically
immortal by now, and can in certain
circumstances expect to be kept alive
more or less indefinitely? Alive but not
useful, and unperfected. The only choices
I could see were bad ones: a
reprehensible but prehensile
characteristic of a world inherited from
badly designed (but mercifully
reprogrammable) theoretical
moral-architect dwarfs, or "little people,"

which retains the Germanic invocation of
sweets and hunting. Embarrassing: there
was no doubt that, given time, I would
begin to sense the correctable intrusion
of maladapted lumps in my back, the
incursion of the bony posterier (which I
here use with the full weight of
behindness) into my senseless, mole-like
Mitsein, *as though being tickled in the*
dark by forces incomprehesible, which
would be as much as saying that by
imagining my frame as correctable, I
would cleave yet more heterogeneity
between me and the curious substance
others would come to call my body. After
this intellectual spadework had been
performed, it became clear that, if I
really did want to be able to become a
vessel for the purest, unrestrained song,
and I was not yet sure that I did, then
development of gaspard eligibility through
tactical but intense bombardment with
the, um, appropriate radiation was going
to have to follow a little tinkering in
the form of examinations. They call
themselves "angels," and boy you'd have to
see them to know why! Use *visual* imagery,
they chant, keen to adopt the nasal mind-
control techniques used by the voodoo
clinicians of consultancy, a contingent
derivative of otherwise unexpurgated
NLP-derived hotpot, but rather they seem

to be talked of most aptly in terms of
touch, for which there is a
disappointingly limited imaginative
vocabulary. They flutter, so I imagined
making love to one of them would be like
the experience of being in the butterfly
room over one's entire sense organ skin.
At a tangent, I couldn't believe that the
sign saying, "all our products are totally
organic," literally meant that they were
carbon based! For me, that was like
learning that those Madchester stallions
had been manipulating the monarchy for
decades: not only unreasonable, and justly
upbraided, but very surprising. In the
Exam Room, it's more of the same. They
stand at quizzical angles, and they stare
at you like spraypaint stares at a car
door. One realizes after a moment that
one has become illuminated. It is not a
great eureka, but a diffident plop of
self-abasement. (One's mind inevitably
turns to the shame felt by Jesus when
caught masturbating by his understanding
mother, which I understood to be a kind
of Tony Blair-style conundrum: on the one
hand, yes, this is terribly embarrassing
for me, and previously, in my precarnation
before my birth, things would probably
have been a little different. But what I
say to you is, look, on the other hand,
if I hadn't taken action, the situation

would not have improved and might have
got worse, action would still have had to
have been taken, unless one gets the
balls cut off, which is undeniably worse,
so, come on, put your shame and disgust
to one side and let's get the job finished
together.) This tender act is too a trap.
All at once, they transform the lab into
a car showroom, with charts demonstrating
performance, performability, and
performativity, questioning our most
treasured maxims and putting swords to
the throats of our reticent children.
After the first removal, it's as easy as
popping a pill: targeted drones are
dispatched orally or anally (or vaginally,
if you prefer) to the trouble spots which
have already been flagged up by nanodes
installed during the first operation. It's
a hooking device, and probably should be
illegal, but the economy is fast
developing and therefore difficult to
regulate. If there are any vital
functions, it's *tout possible* to renovate
that using microtechnology, but in most
cases the plastication of the area is the
safest course, using a kind of fabricated
resin which seals off the bloodgap and
allows the wound to heal, that is, to
close, underneath. Again, practically you
pass those through the bowel in the same
way as discharging other biological waste:

it's the grownup's kinderegg. From a
certain point of view, it's a kind of
treachery, of capitulation to those
machines for whom desire is literally the
same as error, who can only see
teleologically that which must be
corrected. But I prefer to see it as the
liquidation of limitations through
systematic self-abuse, an answer to Freud
in terms of a poetic defense of neurosis
as the closest to the good life that
could possibly be open to us. I had spent
many hours in this mind basement and
always felt faux-naïf and outrageous: Tom!
Barbara? *Margo* . . . Jerry! Now, Tom.
It wasn't until I had dissolved my whole
spine that I understood the internet.
Finally, a counterpoint to the extremism
and whining that seemed designed to
collapse not only "identity" but to
redefine the *practice* of identity as a
species of male adolescence, and to the
violence which has long been the sole
content of self-promotion sites previously
used for advertising and prostitution. I
began to see this activity, which we still
quaintly call the World Wide Web, as a
kind of self-stimulation, a caffeine
enhancer or something, which could be
directly interfaced through rewriting the
back as a chakra. I nearly got tattoos; I
know people who did. The same reality

simulation as ever, but with ever-better
guarantees that this coheres with a pile
of inauthentic external realities. My
inauthenticity was able to hijack and
parasitize topologies and localities
around the real world. I felt like the
monster called "globalization" in a
cartoon in *The Economist*. I can only
speculate about my precise location at
any given moment, because in practice I
suspect that my wheelchair is moving in
random directions as demanded by a beta
emitter under the seat, changing direction
every hundred minutes, but able to move
on water using a somewhat discredited
lifeboat function—well, I say that, but
also because I'm not totally sure that
there is anything better to do when it
comes to such matters as "precise
location" than speculate. Orality becomes
key; as long as I can speak, I can
convince myself that I'm winning the
definition, what used to be called "the
battle of ideas" but now encompasses new
enemies, first animals and machines, soon
gods, hereafter rocks. The technologies
that will come after us will be so
terrible that to think of them caused
Hitler to cry, no less any of the rest of
us. I think if the situation had been
different, I would have liked to be a
bat, perhaps, or a gliding squirrel,

```
something warm-blooded but airborne.
Frustratingly we only see them in
menageries and safari parks.

And with this I leave you, dearest one,
to become your own loving mother, or
whatever moral you may derive from this
rather shallow piece of juvenilia—

Your loving,

C.
```

✳ ✳ ✳

When I had finished reading, I heard another of the lingering chimes, and my field of vision became saturated with light. I was back in the bed-and-breakfast, tucked under my sweetheart's arm. I spoke, "darling," and found the words emerged in my usual register, but my sleepy lover barely noticed them.

I walked to the window, and drew back the curtains. The sun was bright, it was an indiscriminate time of day—could have been mid-morning, or late afternoon. The cawing of seabirds was broad and robust, like the laughter of a good uncle. My lover stirred.

"Baby?" she asked.

"Mm?"

"Could you close the curtain, love?"

"Put a pillow over your eyes!" I said, and laughed.

My lover was new, to me at least—she was still mostly comprised of anecdotes, that she had given me, and that I then had circulated to my friends and to Danny. These were good anecdotes: she was descended from Nazis, for example, which disturbed her. The best part was that her mother, a proud woman, had taken in advanced years to keeping a hive of bees, and a hutch of chickens, and that recently (COVID times) the bees had attacked and killed most of the chickens, and her mother was unsure how to proceed.

No one ever told her how to live on her knees,
But now she's gotta learn about the birds and the bees!

To spite her, and rather dickishly, I threw the windows wide open and thrust my head out.

I began to yell, "oi! You boy! What's to-day?"

There being no answer, I continued even louder, to piss off my lover.

"You bitch," said my lover. Nice girl! Very.

"What's today? Of course it is. Of course it is!"

My lover pulled a pillow over her head and groaned.

"Oh, look, did you know they've changed the name of that restaurant we ate at?" I asked, looking around. Over to the right was the Café Blasé, except mysteriously it was now called simply Patio—an undeniable decline in name quality, but one can't have everything.

"Hm?" my lover's voice, muffled by a pillow.

I had tortured her enough. I closed the window and curtain, kissed her on the forehead, and walked down to the street, and to the beach, and to the sea.

playlist

—The Chordettes, "Lollipop"
—Danielle Ferland, "I Know Things Now"
—Mandy Patinkin, "Sunday"
—Abba, "The Winner Takes It All"
—Bing Crosby and David Bowie, "Peace on Earth/ Little Drummer Boy"
—Dan Castellaneta, "Send in the Clowns"
—Ellen Greene, "Somewhere That's Green"
—Flo Rida (featuring T-Pain), "Low"
—The Mountain Goats, "Pale Green Things"
—Lana Del Rey, "Venice Bitch"
—Rilo Kiley, "With Arms Outstretched"
—Kate Bush, "Room for the Life"
—Buddy Holly, "True Love Ways"
—Mud, "Tiger Feet"

acknowledgments

with thanks to Tori Bedford, Nicole Cliffe, Cecilia Corrigan, Drew Daniel, Seiriol Davies, Melissa Febos, Isaac Fellman, Lo Ferris, Jules Gill-Peterson, Kristin Grogan, Daniel Lavery, Sophie Lewis, Carmen Maria Machado, Cliff Mak, Candace Moore, Morgan Page, Mat Paskins, Sharrona Pearl, Torrey Peters, Gabriel Rosenberg, Jordy Rosenberg, Paul Saint-Amour, Zoe Selengut, Anna Stielau, Susan Stryker, Michelle Tea, Annie Wagner, and Lily Woodruff, all of whom shared useful and generous thoughts about this work as it was emanating. Thanks to the two copyeditors on this project, Maia Kazin and Emma Kaywin, the latter of whom turned out, by lovely coincidence, to be the daughter of Lisa and Ralph, in whose basement I got clean and sober in January 2016. Special thanks to my agent Alison Lewis, my assistant Alexandra Dumont, my lawyers Alanna Kaufman and Andy Celli, and my editor Claire Potter.

notes

CHAPTER ONE

1. Theodor W. Adorno and Max Horkheimer, *Dialectic of Enlightenment* (London: Verso Books, 2016).
2. Judith Butler, "The Lesbian Phallus and the Morphological Imaginary," in *Bodies That Matter: On the Discursive Limits of "Sex"* (London: Routledge, 2011).
3. Dante Gabriel Rossetti, "Sonnet on the Sonnet," in *The House of Life: A Sonnet-Sequence* (Cambridge, MA: Harvard University Press, 1928), xiii.
4. Thomas Hardy, *Jude the Obscure* (Oxford: Oxford University Press, 2002), 32–33.
5. Thomas Hardy, *Jude the Obscure* (Oxford: Oxford University Press, 2002), 50.
6. B. S. Johnson, *Christie Malry's Own Double-Entry* (London: Picador, 2013).
7. Steve Frangos, "The Doumakes Family: Grand Masters of the Marshmallow," *National Herald*, March 14, 2017, www.thenationalherald.com/archive_history_and_science_community /arthro/the_doumakes_family_grand_masters_of_the _marshmallow-5028/.
8. *American Playhouse*, season 5, episode 19, *Sunday in the Park with George*, directed by Terry Hughes, written by James Lapine (book) and Stephen Sondheim (music and lyrics), featuring

Mandy Patinkin and Bernadette Peters, aired June 16, 1986, Public Broadcasting Service (PBS), DVD.

CHAPTER TWO

1. *Mars Attacks!*, directed by Tim Burton (1996; Burbank, CA: Warner Bros. 2008), DVD.
2. W. H. Auden, *The Platonic Blow; and, My Epitaph* (Alexandria, VA: Orchises, 1985), 5.
3. Soundtrack/Cast Album, "Somewhere That's Green," DRG, track 7 on *Little Shop of Horrors—New Broadway Cast*, released 2003, digital.
4. Casey Plett and Morgan M. Page, "No One Makes It Out Alive," *GUTS Magazine*, November 29, 2016, http://guts magazine.ca/no-one-makes-it-out-alive/.
5. Conrad Black, *Donald J. Trump: A President Like No Other* (Washington, DC: Regnery Publishing, 2018).
6. Flo Rida, featuring T-Pain, "Low," Atlanta Recording Corporation for the United States and WEA International Inc. for the world outside of the United States, track 5 on *Mail on Sunday*, released 2008, digital.
7. Andrea Lawlor, *Paul Takes the Form of a Mortal Girl* (New York: Vintage Books, 2019).
8. E. P. Thompson, *The Making of the English Working Class* (New York: Pantheon Books, 1963), 10.

CHAPTER THREE

1. Oscar Wilde, *Salome, a play* (New York: F. M. Buckles and Company, 1906).
2. Oscar Wilde, *Salome, a play* (New York: F. M. Buckles and Company, 1906), 7.
3. Oscar Wilde, *Salome, a play* (New York: F. M. Buckles and Company, 1906), 8.
4. Oscar Wilde, *Salome, a play* (New York: F. M. Buckles and Company, 1906), 10.

5. Oscar Wilde, *Salome, a play* (New York: F. M. Buckles and Company, 1906), 10.

6. Oscar Wilde, *Salome, a play* (New York: F. M. Buckles and Company, 1906), 13.

7. Oscar Wilde, *Salome, a play* (New York: F. M. Buckles and Company, 1906), 16.

8. Oscar Wilde, *Salome, a play* (New York: F. M. Buckles and Company, 1906), 18–19.

9. Oscar Wilde, *Salome, a play* (New York: F. M. Buckles and Company, 1906), 21.

10. Oscar Wilde, *Salome, a play* (New York: F. M. Buckles and Company, 1906), 22.

11. Oscar Wilde, *Salome, a play* (New York: F. M. Buckles and Company, 1906), 23.

12. Oscar Wilde, *Salome, a play* (New York: F. M. Buckles and Company, 1906), 23–24.

13. Oscar Wilde, *Salome, a play* (New York: F. M. Buckles and Company, 1906), 44.

14. Oscar Wilde, *Salome, a play* (New York: F. M. Buckles and Company, 1906), 57.

15. Oscar Wilde, *Salome, a play* (New York: F. M. Buckles and Company, 1906), 59.

16. Elizabeth Gaskell, *North and South* (London: Penguin Books, 1995).

17. *Nip/Tuck*, season 2, episode 3, "Manya Mabika," directed by Elodie Keene, written by Ryan Murphy, Lynnie Greene, and Richard Levine, featuring Dylan Walsh and Julian McMahon, aired July 6, 2004. Ryan Murphy Productions, 2004, DVD. *Ally McBeal*, season 4, episode 2, "Girls' Night Out," directed by Jeannot Szwarc, written by David E. Kelley, featuring Calista Flockhart and Greg Germann, aired October 30, 2000. David E. Kelley Productions, 2000, DVD.

18. The Mountain Goats, "Pale Green Things," 4AD Ltd, track 13 on *The Sunset Tree*, released 2005, digital.

19. *Sunset Boulevard*, directed by Billy Wilder (1950; Los Angeles, CA: Paramount Pictures, 2002), DVD.

20. Lauren Berlant, "Genre Flailing," *Capacious: Journal for Emerging Affect Inquiry* 1, no. 2 (2018): 156–162, doi: https://doi.org /10.22387/CAP2018.16

21. Lana Del Rey, "Venice Bitch," Polydor Records/Interscope Records, track 3 on *Norman Fucking Rockwell!*, released 2019, digital.

CHAPTER FOUR

1. Peachy, "Blur as Blondie for NME 1991. Damon Albarn as Debbie Harry," Pinterest, https://www.pinterest.com/pin/337 629303302843103/.

2. Rilo Kiley, "With Arms Outstretched," Saddle Creek, track 10 on *The Execution of All Things*, released 2002, digital.

3. Torrey Peters, *Detransition, Baby: A Novel* (New York: One World, 2021).

CHAPTER FIVE

1. *Doctor Who*, created by Sydney Newman, aired 2005–present, https://www.bbc.co.uk/programmes/b006q2x0/episodes/player.

2. John Currin, *Jaunty and Mame*, oil on canvas, 1997 (Yale University Library), https://findit.library.yale.edu/catalog/digcoll:22 85428.

3. Buddy Holly, "True Love Ways," UMG Recordings, track 19 on *Gold*, released 2005, digital.

4. George Orwell, *The Art of Donald McGill* (London: Horizon, 1941).

5. *Peep Show*, created by Jesse Armstrong, Sam Bain, and Andrew O'Connor. Aired 2003–2015, https://www.hulu.com/series/peep -show-6c41fe11-ae9b-4c22-bf66-16b159961e28.

6. *The Favourite*, directed by Yorgos Lanthimos (2018; Los Angeles, CA: Fox Searchlight Pictures, 2019), DVD.

7. *The Two Ronnies*, directed by Marcus Plantin et al., written by Ronnie Barker et al, featuring Ronnie Barker and Ronnie Corbett, aired 1971–1987, British Broadcasting Corporation (BBC), DVD.

8. *Robert's Web*, directed by Andrew Chaplin, Lucy Forbes, and Barbara Wiltshire, written by Robert Webb, featuring Robert Webb, aired 2010, Channel 4 Television Corporation.

9. Oscar Wilde, "Sonnet to Liberty," in *Complete Poetry* (Oxford World's Classics), ed. Isobel Murray (Oxford: Oxford University Press, 1997), 126.

CHAPTER SIX

1. Theodor W. Adorno, *Notes to Literature* (New York: Columbia University Press, 2019), 431.

2. Theodor W. Adorno, *Notes to Literature* (New York: Columbia University Press, 2019), 430.

3. Charles Dickens, *The Old Curiosity Shop* (Chicago: University of Chicago, 1893), 174.

4. Charles Dickens, *The Old Curiosity Shop* (Chicago: University of Chicago, 1893), 168, 169.

5. Charles Dickens, *The Old Curiosity Shop* (Chicago: University of Chicago, 1893), 168, 169.

6. Anonymous, "If I Had a Donkey," Grandma's Nursery Rhymes, Accessed January 21, 2021, https://www.grandmasnursery rhymes.com/ifIhadadonkey.html.

7. John Ashton, "If I Had a Donkey Wot Wouldn't Go," Stagger Nation, accessed January 30, 2021, http://www.staggernation.com /msb/if_i_had_a_donkey_wot_wouldnt_go.php#:~:text=Chorus .-,If%20I%20had%20a%20donkey%20wot%20wouldn't%20 go%2C,%2C%20no%2C%20no%2C%20no!&text=His%20 donkey%20wollop%20with%20all%20his%20means.

8. Steven Marcus, *The Other Victorians: A Study of Sexuality and Pornography in Mid-Nineteenth-Century England* (New York: Basic Books, 1966), 16.

9. Steven Marcus, *The Other Victorians: A Study of Sexuality and Pornography in Mid-Nineteenth-Century England* (New York: Basic Books, 1966), 16.

10. Anonymous, "Sub-Umbra, or Sport Among the She-Noodles," *The Pearl,* July 1879.

11. Marcia Muelder Eaton, "Laughing at the Death of Little Nell: Sentimental Art and Sentimental People," *American Philosophical Quarterly* 26, no. 4 (1989): 269.

12. Aldous Huxley, *Complete Essays*, Vol 1: 1920–1925 (Chicago: Ivan R. Dee, 2000).

13. Aldous Huxley, *Complete Essays*, Vol 1: 1920–1925 (Chicago: Ivan R. Dee, 2000).

14. G. K. Chesterton, *The Appreciations and Considerations of the Works of Charles Dickens* (New York: Start Classics, 2014).

15. Charles Dickens, *The Old Curiosity Shop* (Chicago: University of Chicago, 1893), 2.

16. Charles Dickens, *The Old Curiosity Shop* (Chicago: University of Chicago, 1893), 2.

17. W. T. Stead, "The Maiden Tribute of Modern Babylon III: The Report of Our Secret Commission," *Pall Mall Gazette* (London), July 8, 1885.

18. Judith R. Walkowitz, *City of Dreadful Delight: Narratives of Sexual Danger in Late-Victorian London* (Chicago: University of Chicago Press, 1992), 99.

19. W. T. Stead, "The Maiden Tribute of Modern Babylon III: The Report of Our Secret Commission," *Pall Mall Gazette* (London), July 8, 1885.

20. Charles Dickens, *The Old Curiosity Shop* (Chicago: University of Chicago, 1893), 3.

21. Charles Dickens, *The Old Curiosity Shop* (Chicago: University of Chicago, 1893), 5, 8.

22. Charles Dickens, *The Old Curiosity Shop* (Chicago: University of Chicago, 1893), 10.

23. Charles Dickens, *The Old Curiosity Shop* (Chicago: University of Chicago, 1893), 23.

24. William Morris, *News from Nowhere and Other Writings* (London: Penguin Books, 1993), 45.

25. Tony Giffone, "Putting 'Master Humphrey' Back Together Again," *Journal of Narrative Technique* 17, no. 1 (1987): 102.

26. Charles Dickens, *The Old Curiosity Shop* (Chicago: University of Chicago, 1893), 62, 457, 294, 453.

27. Leo Bersani, "Is the Rectum a Grave?," *AIDS: Cultural Analysis/ Cultural Activism* 43 (1987): 208.

28. Karl Marx and Friedrich Engels, *The Communist Manifesto* (London: Penguin Books, 1967), 70, 223.

29. Karl Marx and Friedrich Engels, *The Communist Manifesto* (London: Penguin Books, 1967), 231.

30. Karl Marx and Friedrich Engels, *The Communist Manifesto* (London: Penguin Books, 1967), 70.

31. *Edward Penishands*, directed by Paul Norman (1991; North Hollywood, CA: Video Team, 1991), DVD.

bibliography

Abbot, Michele, Ilene Chaiken and Kathy Greenberg, creators. *The L Word*. Aired 2004–2009. Showtime. www.hulu.com/series/the-l-word-bd29d1c0-5482-4ae6-84d1-4af1b60ded0e.

Adorno, Theodor W. *Notes to Literature*. New York: Columbia University Press, 2019.

Adorno, Theodor W. and Max Horkheimer. *Dialectic of Enlightenment*. London: Verso Books, 2016.

Aguirre-Sacasa, Roberto, developer. *Riverdale*. Aired 2017–present. CW. www.netflix.com/watch/80133268?trackId=14277283&tctx=-97%2C-97%2C%2C%2C%2C.

Anonymous. "If I Had a Donkey." Grandma's Nursery Rhymes. Accessed January 21, 2021. www.grandmasnurseryrhymes.com/ifIhadadonkey.html.

Anonymous. "Sub-Umbra, or Sport Among the She-Noodles." *The Pearl*, July 1879.

Anonymous. *Twelve Steps and Twelve Traditions*. New York, NY: Alcoholics Anonymous World Services, Inc., 2017.

Armstrong, Jesse, Sam Bain and Andrew O'Connor, creators. *Peep Show*. Aired 2003–2015. Channel 4. www.hulu.com/series/peep-show-6c41fe11-ae9b-4c22-bf66-16b159961e28.

Ashton, John. "If I Had a Donkey Wot Wouldn't Go." Stagger Nation. Accessed January 30, 2021. www.staggernation.com/msb/if_i_had_a_donkey_wot_wouldnt_go.php#:~:text=Chorus.-,If%20I%20had%20a%20donkey%20wot%20wouldn't%20go%2C,%2C%20no%2C%20no%2C%20no!&text=His%20donkey%20wollop%20with%20all%20his%20means.

Auden, W. H. *The Platonic Blow; and, My Epitaph.* Alexandria, VA: Orchises, 1985.

Austen, Jane. *Sense and Sensibility.* London: Cassell, 1908.

Barker, Ronnie et al., writer. *The Two Ronnies.* Directed by Marcus Plantin, Marcus Mortimer, James Gilbert, Terry Hughes, Brian Penders, Peter Whitmore, and Paul Jackson, featuring Ronnie Barker and Ronnie Corbett. Aired 1971–1987. British Broadcasting Corporation (BBC), DVD.

Berlant, Lauren. "Genre Flailing." *Capacious: Journal for Emerging Affect Inquiry* 1, no. 2 (2018): 156–162. https://doi.org/10.22387 /CAP2018.16

Bersani, Leo. "Is the Rectum a Grave?" *AIDS: Cultural Analysis/ Cultural Activism* 43 (1987): 197–222.

Black, Conrad. *Donald J. Trump: A President Like No Other.* Washington, DC: Regnery Publishing, 2018.

Bob-Waksberg, Raphael, creator. *Bojack Horseman.* Aired 2014–2020. Netflix. www.netflix.com/search?q=bojack%20horseman&jbv=70 300800.

Brinkema, Eugenie. "Rough Sex." In *Porn Archives*, edited by Tim Dean, Steven Ruszczychy, and David Squires, 262–283. North Carolina: Duke University Press, 2014.

Buck, Chris and Jennifer Lee, dir. *Frozen.* 2013; Burbank, CA: Walt Disney Studios Motion Pictures, 2014. DVD.

Burton, Tim, dir. *Edward Scissorhands.* Widescreen Anniversary Edition. 1990; Los Angeles, CA: Twentieth Century Fox, 2000. DVD.

Burton, Tim, dir. *Mars Attacks!* 1996; Burbank, CA: Warner Bros, 2008. DVD.

Butler, Judith. "The Lesbian Phallus and the Morphological Imaginary." In *Bodies That Matter: On the Discursive Limits of "Sex,"* 57–91. London: Routledge, 2011.

Butler, Judith. "Melancholy Gender—Refused Identification." *Psychoanalytic Dialogues* 5, no. 2 (1995): 165–180.

Cameron, James, dir. *The Terminator.* 1984; Beverly Hills, CA: Orion Pictures, 2001. DVD.

Carter, Angela. *The Passion of New Eve.* London: Virago, 1992.

Chen, Mel Y. "Toxic Animacies, Inanimate Affections." *A Journal of Lesbian and Gay Studies* 17 (2011): 2–3. https://doi.org/10.1215/10642684-1163400.

Chesterton, G. K. *The Appreciations and Considerations of the Works of Charles Dickens*. New York: Start Classics, 2014.

Coppola, Francis Ford, dir. *Bram Stoker's Dracula*. 1992; Culver City, CA: Columbia Pictures, 2004. DVD.

Currin, John. *Jaunty and Mame*. 1997. Oil on canvas. Yale University Library. https://findit.library.yale.edu/catalog/digcoll:2285428.

Del Rey, Lana. "Venice Bitch." Released 2019. Track 3 on *Norman Fucking Rockwell!* Polydor Records/Interscope Records, digital.

Demme, Jonathan, dir. *The Silence of the Lambs*. 1991; Beverly Hills, CA: Orion Pictures, 1991. DVD.

Dickens, Charles. *Bleak House*. Hertfordshire: Wordsworth Editions Limited, 1993.

Dickens, Charles. *David Copperfield*. London: Sheldon, 1863.

Dickens, Charles. *Great Expectations*. London: Penguin Books, 1998.

Dickens, Charles. *Life and Adventures of Nicholas Nickelby*. London: Macmillan and Company, 1916.

Dickens, Charles. *Master Humphrey's Clock*. Paris: Baudry, 1841.

Dickens, Charles. *Nicholas Nickleby*. New York: Harper & Brothers, 1902.

Dickens, Charles. *Night Walks and Other Essays*. Worcestershire: Read & Co. Books, 2020.

Dickens, Charles. *The Old Curiosity Shop*. Chicago: University of Chicago, 1893.

Dickens, Charles. *Our Mutual Friend*. Philadelphia: T. B. Peterson & Brothers, 1865.

Eaton, Marcia Muelder. "Laughing at the Death of Little Nell: Sentimental Art and Sentimental People." *American Philosophical Quarterly* 26, no. 4 (1989): 269–282.

Flaubert, Gustave. *Bouvard and Pécuchet: The Last Novel of Gustave Flaubert*. Illinois: Dalkey Archive Press, 2005.

Flaubert, Gustave. *Salammbô*. New York: Doubleday, Page and Company, 1901.

Flo Rida, featuring T-Pain. "Low." Released 2008. Track 5 on *Mail on Sunday*. Atlanta Recording Corporation for the United States and WEA International Inc. for the world outside of the United States, digital.

Frangos, Steve. "The Doumakes Family: Grand Masters of the Marshmallow." *National Herald*, March 14, 2017. www.thenational herald.com/archive_history_and_science_community/arthro/the _doumakes_family_grand_masters_of_the_marshmallow-5028/.

Freud, Sigmund. *The Interpretation of Dreams: The Complete and Definitive Text*. New York: Basic Books, 2010.

Freud, Sigmund. *Jokes and Their Relation to the Unconscious* (The Standard Edition) vol. 8, *Complete Psychological Works of Sigmund Freud*. New York: W. W. Norton & Company, Ltd., 1990.

Freud, Sigmund. *Three Essays on the Theory of Sexuality: The 1905 Edition*. London: Verso, 2017.

Gaskell, Elizabeth. *North and South*. London: Penguin Books, 1995.

Giffone, Tony. "Putting 'Master Humphrey' Back Together Again." *Journal of Narrative Technique* 17, no. 1 (1987): 102–106.

Goulet, Robert. "I Won't Send Roses." Released 1990. Track 2 on *The Best of Robert Goulet*. Curb Records, digital.

Gubbins, Sarah and Joey Soloway, creators. *I Love Dick*. Aired 2016–2017. Amazon Prime Video. www.amazon.com/I-Love-Dick -Season-1/dp/B01J77H8YC.

Hansen, Victor David. "Cloaked in Intolerance." *Arkansas Democrat Gazette*, December 7, 2020. www.arkansasonline.com/news /2020/dec/07/victor-davis-hanson-cloaked-in-intolerance/?news -columnists.

Hardy, Thomas. *Jude the Obscure*. Oxford: Oxford University Press, 2002.

Harris, Thomas. *The Silence of the Lambs (Hannibal Lecter)*. New York: St. Martin's Paperbacks, 1991.

Holly, Buddy. "True Love Ways." Released 2005. Track 19 on *Gold*. UMG Recordings, digital.

Hooper, Tobe, dir. *The Texas Chain Saw Massacre*. 40th Anniversary Collector's Edition. 1974; Vortex, 2014. DVD.

Huxley, Aldous. *Complete Essays, Vol 1: 1920–1925*. Chicago: Ivan R. Dee, 2000.

Johnson, B. S. *Christie Malry's Own Double-Entry*. London: Picador, 2013.

Kail, Thomas, dir. *Hamilton*. 2020; Burbank, CA: Disney Plus, 2020. Film.

Kelley, David E., writer. *Ally McBeal*. Season 4, episode 2, "Girls' Night Out." Directed by Jeannot Szwarc, featuring Calista Flockhart and Greg Germann. Aired October 30, 2000. Fox. David E. Kelley Productions, 2000. DVD.

Lanthimos, Yorgos, dir. *The Favourite*. 2018; Los Angeles, CA: Fox Searchlight Pictures, 2019. DVD.

Lapine, James, writer. *American Playhouse*. Season 5, episode 19, *Sunday in the Park with George*. Directed by Terry Hughes, featuring Mandy Patinkin and Bernadette Peters. Aired June 16, 1986. Public Broadcasting Service (PBS), 1986. DVD.

Lawlor, Andrea. *Paul Takes the Form of a Mortal Girl*. New York: Vintage Books, 2019.

Leni, Paul, dir. *The Man Who Laughs*. 1928; Universal City, CA: Universal Pictures, 2003. DVD.

Lynch, David, dir. *Blue Velvet*. 1986; De Laurentiis Entertainment Group (DEG). DVD.

Marcus, Steven. *The Other Victorians: A Study of Sexuality and Pornography in Mid-Nineteenth-Century England*. New York: Basic Books, 1966.

Marx, Karl and Friedrich Engels. *The Communist Manifesto*. London: Penguin Books, 1967.

Morris, William. *News from Nowhere and Other Writings*. London: Penguin Books, 1993.

Mountain Goats. "Pale Green Things." Released 2005. Track 13 on *The Sunset Tree*. 4AD, digital.

Muschietti, Andy, dir. *It*. 2017; Burbank, CA: New Line Cinema. 2018. DVD.

Murphy, Ryan, writer. *Nip/Tuck*. Season 2, episode 3, "Manya Mabika." Directed by Elodie Keene, featuring Dylan Walsh and

Julian McMahon. Aired July 6, 2004. FX. Ryan Murphy Productions, 2004. DVD.

Newman, Sydney, creator. *Doctor Who*. Aired 2005–present. BBC One. www.bbc.co.uk/programmes/b006q2x0/episodes/player .

Norman, Paul, dir. *Edward Penishands*. 1991; North Hollywood, CA: Video Team. DVD.

Orwell, George. *The Art of Donald McGill*. London: Horizon, 1941.

Peachy. "Blur as Blondie for NME 1991. Damon Albarn as Debbie Harry." Pinterest. www.pinterest.com/pin/337629303302843103/.

Peters, Torrey. *Detransition, Baby: A Novel*. New York: One World, 2021.

Plett, Casey and Morgan M. Page. "No One Makes It Out Alive." *GUTS Magazine*, November 29, 2016. http://gutsmagazine.ca/no-one-makes-it-out-alive/.

Racine, Jay. *The Litigants*. Michigan: Courier Steam Printing House, 1882.

Ray, Nicholas, dir. *Rebel Without a Cause*. 1955; Burbank, CA: Warner Bros, 2005. DVD.

Reitman, Ivan, dir. *Ghostbusters*. Widescreen Edition. 1984; Culver City, CA: Columbia Pictures, 2006. DVD.

Rilo Kiley. "With Arms Outstretched." Released 2002. Track 10 on *The Execution of All Things*. Saddle Creek, digital.

Roach, Jay, dir. *Austin Powers: International Man of Mystery*. 1997; Burbank, CA: New Line Cinema, 2006. DVD.

Rossetti, Dante Gabriel. "Sonnet on the Sonnet." In *The House of Life: A Sonnet-Sequence*. Cambridge, MA: Harvard University Press, 1928, xiii.

Semple, Lorenzo, Jr., developer. *Batman*. Aired 1966–1968. ABC. 20th Century Fox Television, 2014, DVD.

Singer, Bryan, dir. *X-Men: Days of Future Past*. 2014; Los Angeles, CA: Twentieth Century Fox, 2014. DVD.

Soundtrack/Cast Album. "Somewhere That's Green." Released 2003. Track 7 on *Little Shop of Horrors—New Broadway Cast*. DRG, digital.

Stead, W. T. "The Maiden Tribute of Modern Babylon III: The Report of Our Secret Commission." *Pall Mall Gazette* (London), July 8, 1885.

Thompson, E. P. *The Making of the English Working Class*. New York: Pantheon Books, 1963.

Walkowitz, Judith R. *City of Dreadful Delight: Narratives of Sexual Danger in Late-Victorian London*. Chicago: University of Chicago Press, 1992.

Webb, Robert, writer. *Robert's Web*. Directed by Andrew Chaplin, Lucy Forbes, and Barbara Wiltshire, featuring Robert Webb. Aired 2010. Channel 4 Television Corporation, 2010.

Weir, Peter, dir. *The Truman Show*. 1998; Los Angeles, CA: Paramount Pictures, 2017. DVD.

Wikisource. "The Pearl (1879–1881)." Wikisource. Accessed January 22, 2021. https://en.wikisource.org/wiki/The_Pearl.

Wilde, Oscar. *Salome, a play*. New York: F. M. Buckles and Company, 1906.

Wilde, Oscar. "Sonnet to Liberty." In *Complete Poetry*, edited by Isobel Murray, 126. Oxford World Classics. Oxford University Press, 1997.

Wilder, Billy, dir. *Sunset Boulevard*. 1950; Los Angeles, CA: Paramount Pictures, 2002. DVD.

index

faygo, 5
fear
of being kidnapped, 193
of clowns, 17
of transition, 79–81
of writing about transition
and of transness, 135–139
femininity
defining masculinity in a
trans woman, 33–34
importance of self
presentation, 28
The Martian Girl, 52
sexual attraction to boys and
girls, 25
the teenage years, 191–192
trans women in cis women's
bodies, 151–152
Viagra use by trans women,
34–35
femmebots, 176–177, 187–188
fertility
Jude the Obscure, 22
sperm banking, 168–170
finger limes, 62–66
Flaubert, Gustave, 215–216
Frankenstein's lobster account
of transness, 80
Freud, Sigmund
decapitation and castration,
110
porn parody, 228
Friedan, Betty, 198–199
friends: effect of transition on
women friends, 172–174
Fry, Stephen, 230–231

Gacy, John Wayne, 48–50
gay people
the author's connection to
girls, 25–26
gay men and trans women,
194
her mother's view of the
author, 191–196
pre-bourgeois baroque,
235
religious and moral issues
with, 195–196
See also lesbians; queerness
gender ambivalence, 59,
209–211, 214
gender critical movement
British political affiliation,
175–176
sexual motives of trans
women, 137
genitals
complex emotional and
physical relation to, 7–8
Salome imagery, 108
shifting sensations with
estrogen, 53–55
Viagra use by trans women,
34–35
See also breasts; dicks; penises;
pussy, emerging
Ghostbusters as Juggalo reboot,
29–32
"Gillis, Mallory," 95–102,
107–108, 110–115, 128–131
Grand Canyon National Park,
152–153

INDEX

social pressures associated
with transitioning, 137–138
transporting identity as
a result of transition,
238–242
ineffability of transness, 81–82
Insane Clown Posse, 5–6, 28
Insta hashtagging, 28–30
interiority, 5, 22, 61–62
internal changes during
transition, 3–4
involuntary speech, 178–179

Japan, 141–146
"Jaunty and Mame" (Currin),
190
John Paul II, 75–76
Johnson, B.S., 23
Jude the Obscure (Hardy), 19–22
Juggalo movie reboots, 29–32
Juggalos, 5–6, 8, 28–30,
113–114

kumquats, 204

The L Word (Shepherd), 174
Labour Party (UK), 175–176
Lake Isabella, California,
154–157
Lavery, Danny, 128–131
Batman metaphor, 17–19
drunken bullshit, 146
expositions of trans life, 10–11
fight over having a dick, 60
finding the emerging pussy,
87–89

first encounter, 97–102
Insta hashtagging, 28
love and work, 131–134
the penis problem, 6–10
response to the author's
transition, 173–174
sex with clowns, 50
travels and transition,
152–159
Lawlor, Andrea, 83
le groin (snout), 20–21, 206
leaky boobs and the school run,
176
"Leda and the Swan" (Yeats),
33
legitimacy of memoirs, 22–25
lesbian phallus, 8
lesbians
the author's mother, 180
explaining bisexuality and
transness, 37, 111–112, 172
transmisogyny, 173
understanding your own body,
173–174
See also gay people; queerness
letters, 244–254
"dead names," 238–239
feminists' chores, 198–202
hate mail, 12
the introduction of clowns,
11–16
signs from the universe,
202–205
"smoking is cool," 159–164
the solitary trans woman,
113–119

281

Murdoch, Rupert, 75–76
Murphy (dog), 154–155, 157
mustache, 96–99, 101, 129–130,
    159
Myers, Mike, 188

names, 120
  choosing the name, 158–159
  dead names, 238–241,
    243–244
  mother's response to
    transition, 139–140
narrative forms: the recovery
    tale, 40–48. *See also*
    memoirs
narrator as surrogate for the
    reader, 225–227
National Review, 70–71
natural women, 68
nestling, 4
New York City: signs from the
    universe, 203–207
News from Nowhere (Morris),
    227
Nicholas Nickleby (Dickens),
    213–214
"Night Walks" (Dickens),
    224–225
"No One Makes It Out Alive"
    (Plett and Page), 68–70
non-binary transitions, 81

Oedipus complex, 172, 182–183
offal, 206
oil: the role in hormone therapy,
    60–61

The Old Curiosity Shop (Dickens),
    213–220, 222–229
oral sex, 37, 62, 132, 220
orchiectomy, 108
orgasm
  banking sperm, 169
  conceptualizing character in
    pornography, 220
  hormone therapy improving,
    66–67
  reading the news during, 78
Osaka University, 141–146
The Other Victorians (Marcus),
    220–221
Our Mutual Friend (Dickens),
    213
Oxford University, 26–27,
    89–92

Page, Morgan, 68–70
parody
  Conrad Black, 70–74
  porn parody, 228–235
paternity of the author,
    179–180
patriarchy: interpreting *Little
    Shop of Horrors*, 69
*Paul Takes the Form of a Mortal
    Girl* (Lawlor), 83
The Pearl magazine, 221
Peep Show (television program),
    207–208
penetration, sex without, 59
penis enlargers, 187, 190
penis problem, 1–2, 4–7, 53–56,
    165–166

Grace Lavery is an associate professor of English at UC Berkeley, where she specializes in Victorian literature and culture, trans feminist studies, and contemporary popular culture. She has contributed to *LARB*, *Autostraddle*, *Foreign Policy*, the *New Inquiry*, *Them*, the *Guardian*, and *Slate*, among other publications.